Migration, Diasporas and Citizenship Series

Series Editors: **Robin Cohen**, Director of the International Migration Institute and Professor of Development Studies, University of Oxford, UK and **Zig Layton-Henry**, Professor of Politics, University of Warwick, UK.

Editorial Board: **Rainer Baubock**, European University Institute, Italy; **James F. Hollifield**, Southern Methodist University, USA; **Jan Rath**, University of Amsterdam, The Netherlands

The Migration, Diasporas and Citizenship series covers three important aspects of the migration progress. Firstly, the determinants, dynamics and characteristics of international migration. Secondly, the continuing attachment of many contemporary migrants to their places of origin, signified by the word 'diaspora', and thirdly the attempt, by contrast, to belong and gain acceptance in places of settlement, signified by the word 'citizenship'. The series publishes work that shows engagement with and a lively appreciation of the wider social and political issues that are influenced by international migration.

Also published in Migration Studies by Palgrave Macmillan

Rutvica Andrijasevic
MIGRATION, AGENCY AND CITIZENSHIP IN SEX TRAFFICKING

Claudine Attias-Donfut, Joanne Cook, Jaco Hoffman and Louise Waite (*editors*)
CITIZENSHIP, BELONGING AND INTERGENERATIONAL RELATIONS IN AFRICAN MIGRATION

Grete Brochmann, Anniken Hagelund (*authors*) with – Karin Borevi, Heidi Vad Jønsson, Klaus Petersen
IMMIGRATION POLICY AND THE SCANDINAVIAN WELFARE STATE 1945–2010

Gideon Calder, Phillip Cole and Jonathan Seglow
CITIZENSHIP ACQUISITION AND NATIONAL BELONGING
Migration, Membership and the Liberal Democratic State

Enzo Colombo and Paola Rebughini (*editors*)
CHILDREN OF IMMIGRANTS IN A GLOBALIZED WORLD
A Generational Experience

Huub Dijstelbloem and Albert Meijer (*editors*)
MIGRATION AND THE NEW TECHNOLOGICAL BORDERS OF EUROPE

Thomas Faist and Andreas Ette (*editors*)
THE EUROPEANIZATION OF NATIONAL POLICIES AND POLITICS OF IMMIGRATION
Between Autonomy and the European Union

Thomas Faist and Peter Kivisto (*editors*)
DUAL CITIZENSHIP IN GLOBAL PERSPECTIVE
From Unitary to Multiple Citizenship

Katrine Fangen, Thomas Johansson and Nils Hammarén (*editors*)
YOUNG MIGRANTS
Exclusion and Belonging in Europe

Martin Geiger and Antoine Pécoud (*editors*)
THE POLITICS OF INTERNATIONAL MIGRATION MANAGEMENT

John R. Hinnells (*editor*)
RELIGIOUS RECONSTRUCTION IN THE SOUTH ASIAN DIASPORAS
From One Generation to Another

Ronit Lentin and Elena Moreo (*editors*)
MIGRANT ACTIVISM AND INTEGRATION FROM BELOW IN IRELAND

Migration, Diasporas and Citizenship
Series Standing Order ISBN 978–0–230–30078–1 (hardback)
and 978–0–230–30079–8 (paperback)
(outside North America only)

You can receive future titles in this series as they are published by placing a standing order. Please contact your bookseller or, in case of difficulty, write to us at the address below with your name and address, the title of the series and the ISBN quoted above.

Customer Services Department, Macmillan Distribution Ltd, Houndmills, Basingstoke, Hampshire RG21 6XS, England

Gender, Migration and Domestic Work

Masculinities, Male Labour and Fathering in the UK and USA

Majella Kilkey
University of Sheffield, UK

Diane Perrons
London School of Economics and Political Science, UK

Ania Plomien
London School of Economics and Political Science, UK

with

Pierrette Hondagneu-Sotelo
University of Southern California, USA

Hernan Ramirez
Florida State University, USA

First published 2013 by
PALGRAVE MACMILLAN

Palgrave Macmillan in the UK is an imprint of Macmillan Publishers Limited,
registered in England, company number 785998, of Houndmills, Basingstoke,
Hampshire RG21 6XS.

Palgrave Macmillan in the US is a division of St Martin's Press LLC,
175 Fifth Avenue, New York, NY 10010.

Palgrave Macmillan is the global academic imprint of the above companies
and has companies and representatives throughout the world.

Palgrave® and Macmillan® are registered trademarks in the United States,
the United Kingdom, Europe and other countries.

ISBN 978–0–230–29720–3

This book is printed on paper suitable for recycling and made from fully
managed and sustained forest sources. Logging, pulping and manufacturing
processes are expected to conform to the environmental regulations of the
country of origin.

A catalogue record for this book is available from the British Library.

A catalog record for this book is available from the Library of Congress.

10   9   8   7   6   5   4   3   2   1
22 21 20 19 18 17 16 15 14 13

Printed and bound in the United States of America

Contents

Preface

We completed this book in the early summer of 2012 as a number of European societies were buckling under the heavy weight of austerity programmes introduced in response to the ongoing global financial and economic crisis. While many of the consequences of such unprecedented cuts in public expenditure in Europe and the USA are yet to become apparent, one – unemployment, especially among young people – has already reached devastating levels in many countries. Arguably, therefore, to have a job is a fortunate position to be in. Such 'fortune' can be double-edged, however, as in neoliberal economies bosses and governments now add the fear of unemployment to their disciplinary armoury. Of course, this is affecting workers differently depending on where they are positioned within the employment structure and depending on what role work plays in constructing and maintaining their subjectivity.

For the professional and managerial men that form part of this book's enquiry, the disciplinary whip is one of time and commitment. The job pays handsomely, but invades ever deeper into their lives, assuming in fact, the non-existence of life beyond work. While some men enjoy the all-encompassing nature of their jobs, many also realise that it is not free of cost, and in particular puts at risk their ability to meet the competing expectation for active and involved fathering, as well as imposing penalties on their female partners who are expected to organise their own jobs to fit around those of their husbands. But as this book demonstrates, the costs extend further than their own households, as buoyed by their rising earnings (even in the midst of economic crisis) and increasing income inequalities, these households outsource the domestic work traditionally done by men. Other men (handymen and gardeners) and women (cleaners, carers and cooks) become part of the 'coping strategies' of the well-off. In the context of globalization and the uneven patterns of development that ensue, those 'other' men and women are increasingly migrant workers. Migration is 'their' means of 'coping' with the inequalities wrought by globalization, and as we show in this book, this coping strategy frequently works, in that better livelihoods are secured. But, this too is not a cost-free strategy. The status of migrants can be used as a disciplinary whip to enforce low pay, long hours and insecurity, putting at risk other dimensions of well-being, including the capacity for family life.

The well-being of families, regardless of country of origin, therefore, is increasingly constituted through transnational social relations. To be sure, these are not equal relations; because of their privileged economic and geopolitical positioning, the well-off families who outsource their domestic labour are the main beneficiaries. But migrants, their families and their countries of origin, albeit to lesser degrees, can benefit too. These private resolutions show just how resourceful people are, but they are partial, because they do not challenge the inequalities of global capitalism nor the prevailing understandings of masculinity that contribute to making these difficult choices necessary. At the time of writing it is deeply worrying, therefore, to see politicians across Europe and the USA deploy the 'anti-immigrant card' in the face of economic crisis and rising joblessness. Without doubt, this will lead to worsening conditions for migrant workers and their families. The experiences of migrant workers and middle-class families that employ them add evidence that strengthens demands for reform of economic and social policies in order to achieve more balanced and fairer lives.

Acknowledgements

The UK study reported on in this book was financed by the UK Economic and Social Research Council, grant RES-000-22-2590. Majella, Diane and Ania gratefully acknowledge their financial support. The Higher Education Funding Council for England Innovation Fund 4 and the Gender Institute at the London School of Economics and Political Science provided additional monies for a policy-oriented dissemination event in central London in March 2010 – 'Fathering and Work-Life Balance: Challenges for Policy'. This provided us with the opportunity to raise the issue of migrant men's work-life balance with UK policy makers and advocates. We are thankful to all those who contributed to and participated in this event, and especially to our research participants who attended and spoke about their experiences of working and family life in the UK. The Los Angeles study of Mexican immigrant gardeners was funded by a grant from the University of Southern California's Provost's Initiative on Immigrant Integration, and by the USC College Diversity Placement programme. As this book testifies, families – regardless of country of origin – in the UK and USA, are increasingly time-squeezed; while this hampered the collection of field data, it also highlights how generous those who did agree to participate in our studies were in giving us their precious time. We are very grateful indeed to the 126 people in the UK and USA whose stories form the basis of this book. Time was also an issue for us in completing the book, and we are grateful to Andrew James at Palgrave Macmillan for his patience, and to Robin Dunford for his help with the final editing and preparation of the manuscript.

1
Gender, Migration and Domestic Work: An Introduction

Do you need help with small jobs around your home or business? Just call The Polish Handyman – Handyman Services and we can help solve your problem.

Polish Builder (2011)

1.1 Gender, migration and domestic work

As the rich have got richer and households have become busier, demand for commoditized household services has risen, with the supply chain becoming increasingly transnational. The emergence of this international market in commoditized services is important for two reasons. First, it shows how reproduction, as well as production, has become part of the global economy. Second, it shows that individuals and households, as well as states and markets, both contribute to and are directly affected by the large-scale social processes of globalization, rising inequalities and migration that are characteristic of contemporary society. A wealth of literature has emerged on female maids and nannies, many of whom are migrants.[1] In this book we consider a parallel trend – the re-emergence of male household workers, that is, men who are paid to do traditionally masculine domestic jobs in and around the houses and gardens of generally wealthier people.[2] Many of these workers too are migrants, though the proportion of migrants in handyman work remains lower than the proportion of migrants among maids and nannies. Handyman work involves a wide range of small-scale jobs such as fixing shelves, decorating and small-scale repair on an occasional basis, while gardening can involve more regular work including lawn mowing and leaf blowing in extensive suburban gardens. This book investigates the experiences of suppliers and consumers of stereotypically masculine

1

household services at the micro level, but, through its emphasis on contemporary masculinities and the gendering of paid work, the book contributes to wider-scale debates relating to globalization, migration and social reproduction.

The book is based on empirical investigations of migrant handymen in the UK, mainly from Poland, and immigrant Mexican gardeners (*jardineros*) in the USA. First and foremost, the objective of the book is to highlight the existence of male migrant domestic services in the UK and the USA and to analyse how this phenomenon impacts on both the male workers supplying the services, and in the case of the UK, the lives of the people (henceforth, householders), who buy them. Second, in the context of the extensive literature on female domestic work, our analysis of male domestic work enables us to identify distinctly gendered understandings of domestic work and care. We show how these gendered understandings influence both the differential economic value of and emotional attachment to these different forms of work and the gendered identities of people supplying and buying these services. Third, our analysis enables us to underline the way in which gender intersects with social class, ethnicity and migrant status to influence the well-being of both the migrant workers and the householders who draw on their labour. Fourth, we demonstrate how, by outsourcing, householders can resolve or at least mitigate the 'father time-bind', that is, a difficulty in finding enough time to fulfil both new social expectations regarding hands-on, caring fatherhood and more traditional male breadwinning roles; a time-bind complicated further by a highly competitive working environment and limited state support for parents. Fifth, with respect to the two rather different groups of male domestic workers studied, we show how, despite migration restrictions, labour market discrimination and a lack of recognized qualifications, masculine domestic work can provide an opportunity for people to secure a livelihood in another country. Finally, our findings enable us to examine dynamic and varied understandings of masculinity. Because the work involves physical strength the male domestic workers are able to uphold some of the more traditional understandings of masculinity despite frequently being in subservient positions in relation to both their employers and to wider discriminatory contexts. Moreover their earnings are generally higher than they would have been had they remained in their countries of origin, and so facilitates meeting their breadwinning obligations and traditional masculine role. The case studies show the manner in which these relations are varied and highly contingent on specific circumstances, with these differences consistently linked to differential and hierarchical relations associated with the class, gender and geopolitical position of different groups of people. It is, furthermore, this hierarchical difference upon which relations between male domestic workers and householders using their services ultimately depend.

In order to differentiate between the historically distinct international patterns of movement from Poland and from Mexico at both individual and aggregate levels, we use the terms 'migrant' to refer to the Polish handymen and 'immigrant' to refer to Mexican gardeners. In the Polish case, migration is often temporary or circular, and can include multiple moves between different countries of destination. In the Mexican case, the intent to cross the border is generally long-term or permanent, and settlement in the USA is the final outcome. The original research projects were planned and carried out independently and, therefore, do not match completely, but once we became aware of each other's work we were struck by how the many similarities and differences provided a novel and stimulating way of contributing to knowledge about male migrant domestic labour.

The empirical investigations are situated within three interrelated contemporary debates: globalization, migration and social reproduction. Within these debates we focus on the overall context of rising social inequalities between and within nations. These inequalities stimulate both migration and the demand for domestic labour, impact upon migrants' motivations and experiences, and shape gendered identities with respect to paid work, domestic tasks and parenting. Through our focus on men and masculinities, we make a contribution to the literature on migrant domestic labour. In particular, our partial and retrospective comparative analysis offers exciting prospects for developing the understanding of the gendered character of paid domestic work and how it is valued, the dynamic and varied understandings of masculinity, and the manner in which gender and citizenship status intersect in ways that influence migrant well-being.

1.2   Globalization, migration and social reproduction

Globalization is associated with increasing economic integration between states and rising affluence, but also with growing inequalities within and between states; conditions which, as we shall show, stimulate both the demand for commoditized services and a supply of migrant labourers prepared to work in these sectors.

Economic liberalization with respect to trade and capital flows, growing differentiation between people's living standards, and enhanced communications, have led to increasing migration over the last three decades. This migration has continued despite the economic recession at the end of the first decade of the twenty-first century. Migration, unlike trade or capital flows, is frequently subjected to a range of restrictions which vary between nations and between different world trading blocks, such as North Atlantic Free Trade Association (NAFTA) and the European Union (EU); blocs of which the countries in our study are part.

Typically, trading blocs have preferential trading relations among member states. In NAFTA, for instance, trade and capital can flow freely between Mexico and the USA, but this freedom of movement does not extend to labour even though migratory pressures increase as a consequence of the liberal trading arrangements. For instance, while NAFTA consolidates labour intensive manufacturing in Mexico (the *maquiladoras*), the free movement of the more competitive or cheaper American industrial and agricultural goods has undermined production in Mexico, especially small-scale farm production, which has led to declining living standards among small-scale peasants and agricultural workers. In light of these decreased living standards, migration, despite being fraught with danger, is seen as a way of securing and enhancing livelihoods. By contrast, the EU, which the UK joined in 1973 and Poland in 2004, represents a deeper form of economic and political integration, with labour, capital and trade able to flow relatively freely. The UK is more affluent economically than Poland, and wages are significantly higher, providing a stimulus to migration, but in this case migration is legal. This difference in the legal status of migration in NAFTA and the EU has a profound impact on the rights and opportunities available to the migrants in our study.

Both the UK and USA have seen a large expansion of net inward migration during the last three decades, especially since the start of the twenty-first century. The USA is a major recipient country and has over a million legal and an unknown number of undocumented migrants entering the country each year, with the result that in 2009 one in every six USA workers is foreign born. In California, where one of our study areas is located, the figure is one in three. Migration to the UK is half of this level in absolute terms, but is equally significant relative to the population size. The UK also has a positive migration balance with EU migrants, especially those from new member states (ONS, 2012a).[3] The majority of migrants to the UK live in London, where they accounted for two in five of the working population in 2009.[4] With respect to OECD countries, Poland is the fourth highest supplier of migrant labour and Mexico the fifth. Their primary destinations are the UK and USA respectively (OECD,

2011a). Polish migrants have free access to the UK labour market follow-ing accession to the EU, are able to create new enterprises and have rights to family-related benefits.[5] By contrast, the USA currently has very tight migration restrictions and some of the more recent Mexican migrants in our study lack citizenship rights, exposing them to the risk of deporta-tion and to potentially exploitative working conditions. The majority of Mexicans in the study, however, came to the USA over twenty years ago and secured resident rights or citizenship in the interim.[6]

Motivations for migration vary, but on a world scale just over one-third of all migrants follow an economic gradient from poorer to richer countries and regions, and while the migrants in our studies had multiple and varied rationales for their decision to move, one consist-ent intention was to enhance their livelihoods by moving to a richer country within their world regional block. They became domestic work-ers as handymen or *jardineros*, sectors where qualification and entry restrictions are minimal and demand has been increasing.

In the last three decades, incomes and earnings have polarized in the UK and USA as a result of the top decile, consisting mainly of professional and managerial workers, moving away from the median and lower earn-ing groups (OECD, 2011b; Stiglitz, 2012). These patterns have emerged as a consequence of global economic restructuring, related changes in employment composition away from manufacturing towards the serv-ice sector, and the increasing ability of high-income groups to appropri-ate a rising share of value added as the power of organized labour has diminished (Perrons and Plomien, 2010). Correspondingly, employ-ment has become more flexible, insecure and precarious, leading to a decline in the overall share of income accruing to labour. This decline has been especially noticeable for workers at the lower end of the earn-ings profile, including less qualified migrants, many of whom struggle to provide a livelihood through paid employment. By contrast profes-sional and managerial households have seen their earnings increase absolutely and relatively to others, but they often work very long hours and experience a time squeeze, finding themselves income rich but time poor (McDowell et al., 2005). The resulting situation is one in which the time poor yet money rich households outsource social reproduction tasks to people who by comparison are currently money-poor and pre-pared to work long hours to secure their livelihoods. Increasing migra-tion, then, is intimately linked to increasing inequality.

By social reproduction we are referring to 'the array of activities and relationships involved in maintaining people both on a daily basis and inter-generationally' (Glenn, 1992: 1). These activities include the physical manual work of ensuring that people are fed, clothed, housed and cared for to the socially expected standards, the mental and emotional work associated with such endeavours, the institutional arrangements and social relations within which this work is performed, and the varying ideologies that influence these arrangements (Laslett and Brenner, 1989).[7] The existing literature in this field has focused primarily on the feminized tasks of cleaning, caring and catering, but in high-income households, maintaining housing standards has become part of the socially expected consumption norms. Typically, maintaining households draws on more masculinized domestic activities of house repair, maintenance and gardening.

While economic conditions, principally including the widening earnings inequalities between professionals and managers compared to manual service workers, influence the scale of overall demand, decisions made by specific households reflect a wide range of issues relating to the social and moral boundaries placed around commoditized domestic services. These boundaries involve ethical and emotional questions concerning the appropriate institutional arrangements – for example – what can be outsourced and what has to be done in the home to maintain social values and sense of identity. In this book we consider whether there are any parallels between outsourcing traditionally male and female work. Do men feel any sense of loss or guilt in not doing the household tasks that their fathers might have done? How does outsourcing to other men affect their sense of masculinity? Important in this regard are social and attitudinal changes with respect to ideas about more active parental care. Fathers increasingly express a desire to be involved in the nurturing of their children alongside their breadwinning activities, generating a time-bind which, in turn, has made outsourcing male domestic work socially acceptable among the middle classes and led to more complex and multifaceted understandings of masculinity.[8] This is one of a number of important social changes in the last three decades that have influenced the gender division of labour within households.

Social change in the last three decades has been profound. 'Employment' has become more feminized in the dual sense of the term: as well as becoming more flexible and insecure, conditions historically associated with female employment, the female share of the labour force has increased worldwide and among all social groups. While many low-income women have always worked in one form or another and in ways that are not always recorded in the statistics, the increase in female employment has been especially notable among highly educated mothers in high-income countries (ONS, 2011a).[9] This increase has further intensified inequalities, with associative matching between partners or homogamy among the highly educated reinforcing social polarization. In addition high-income households are more likely to stay together than low-income households (among which there is an increasing incidence of divorce and single motherhood), and are also able to invest more time in their children, reinforcing inequality in the next generation.[10]

In this context Gosta Esping-Andersen (2009: 169) argues that 'the quest for gender equality tends to produce social inequality as long as it is a middle class affair'. He argues for an expansion of the welfare state to support carework and increase social efficiency by enabling low as well as high-income women to enter the workforce. Only this expansion, Esping-Andersen (2009) argues, would complete the (gender) revolution, as he deems sufficient change in male behaviour to substitute effectively for the decline in female domestic work very unlikely. Our findings with respect to the UK are simultaneously different yet complimentary, in the sense that one of the rationales given by fathers for drawing on handymen services is to enable them to spend more time with their children, and in this regard we see some change, though not a transformation, in male behaviour and the resultant gender division of labour within employing households.[11] At the same time we also see a differentiation by social class between handyman fathers and those who employ them in terms of their opportunities for fathering. While those that employ handymen can make time for their children by outsourcing domestic tasks, both the handymen in the UK and the *jardineros* in the USA are forced to prioritize time spent breadwinning owing to their lower earnings.

Esping-Andersen (2009) is perhaps wrong, then, to say that significant change is not occurring among men, but he is right to point out that gender change remains a privilege of the middle classes; it takes wealth to employ a handyman, and it is the handyman's comparatively low income that ensures that he has to work rather than spend time with his own children. It is, therefore, these very social inequalities between men that allow fathers in middle class houses to commit more time to nurturing. This finding reflects issues raised in literature on commoditized feminized domestic work, where questions have been asked about whether this confluence of growing economic inequalities and increasing demand for domestic services and childcare, have resulted in a rearrangement of responsibilities that undermines feminist notions of justice (Tronto, 2002: 35; see also Bowman and Cole, 2009; Esping-Andersen, 2009).

Some women are enabled to pursue careers while others – less well-paid women from elsewhere – do 'their' housework and care for 'their' children. On the one hand, then, some women are empowered, but the way in which they are empowered undermines fundamental feminist concerns regarding equality, resulting in scholars raising the question of whether a feminist can employ a nanny (Tronto, 2002).

Debates on commoditized feminized work, however, tend to leave men and their domestic and caring responsibilities out of the picture. With some exceptions (Hondagneu-Sotelo and Messner, 1997) parallel questions relating to handymen and gardeners substituting for stereotypically male household work are rarely asked. This book redresses this absence through a focus on men and male migrant domestic work, while also asking questions about how different forms of work are socially and morally valued, how different forms of work are gendered, and how the outsourcing of certain forms of work influences the participants' understandings of identity and masculinity.

Analysts have pointed to the existence of male migrants doing stereotypically female domestic work in households as well as working in feminized occupations such as nursing. In these cases, the lost gender status arising from working in gender incongruent activities can be offset by the greater economic power secured through the higher earnings migration brings (Matsuno, 2007).[12] So far, however, less attention has been given to male migrants doing traditional masculinized forms of domestic work, and as a result, questions surrounding how migrants experience this work and what hiring masculinized domestic workers means for the men who are relieved from these tasks are rarely considered. What happens to the time these men save? Is it used for work, for personal leisure or is it used for caring? If it is used for caring, does their contribution enhance gender equality within their households? Does this transnational reconfiguration of domestic responsibilities expand the livelihood opportunities of migrants and, if so, what happens to their parenting aspirations and responsibilities? Are migrants able to bring their children with them, or does their absence or long working hours mean that they are confined to the breadwinning role? Building from Joan Tronto's (2002) analysis, does this migration allow middle class fathers to enhance their careers and maintain property values while simultaneously fulfilling contemporary social expectations regarding active parenting, as other men do 'their' housework? If so, does this reinforce class inequalities between men transnationally? Are migrants able to embrace new fathering, or do different understandings of fathering and masculinity emerge, with the involved father being a privilege of the middle classes in high-income countries, resulting in a transference of emotional capital (Isaksen, Devi and Hochschild, 2008)? These are the questions which this book addresses. As indicated previously the research projects were designed and carried out separately so while our questions relating to migrant domestic work, with respect to gender, masculinity and citizenship status can be addressed comparatively, those relating more specifically to the employing households, including the use of time saved, fathering and the gender division of domestic labour are only addressed in the UK project.

1.3 Masculinized domestic work

Just as markets for feminized domestic work and caring have expanded with the feminization of paid employment and ensuing time squeeze, so too have markets for masculinized domestic work, reflecting the combined effect of an absence of available (male) labour within the household, long working hours, a more active fathering role, and a preference for individual or family leisure time. In the UK, the proportion of households drawing on stereotypically masculinized services is very similar to those buying feminized services, though the frequency of purchase is lower, with the services more likely to be hired on a monthly, rather than a weekly, basis. More specifically, 6 per cent of households outsource repairs and construction and 6 per cent gardening, similar to the proportion paying for feminized tasks such as house-cleaning/tidying (6 per cent), ironing (3 per cent) and childcare (4 per cent) (Kilkey and Perrons, 2010).[13] As with feminized domestic work, migrants supply much of this labour, though male domestic work is less migrant dense. One notable difference between masculinized and feminized work in the formal and informal sector is that masculinized jobs, as in other sectors, earn a premium over feminized labour, reflecting deep seated gendered understandings of the value of different forms of work.

To explore the various dimensions of masculine domestic work, we draw on our two case studies; one from Europe focusing on Polish migrants to the UK who work as handymen and the other from North America, centred on Mexican immigrants in the USA working either as route-owning *jardineros* (gardeners) or their assistants – the *ayudantes*. In both cases the men do stereotypical masculinized domestic work; the Polish handymen do small-scale maintenance and repair jobs in and around the houses of professional workers mainly in London, while the Mexican *jardineros* mow the extensive lawns of middle class households in suburban Los Angeles on a regular contract basis.

Stereotypically masculinized forms of domestic labour, such as plumbing, electrical work, painting and decorating, are long established skilled or semi-skilled trades, but demand has increased for small-scale and arguably less skilled jobs in these areas, leading to the emergence of a range of handyman services and, in the USA more specifically, to contract gardening. The latter primarily consists of leaf blowing and lawn mowing for middle to high-income suburban households on a regular basis, while handyman work is multi-dimensional but less regular. For example, with respect to plumbing, the work would be changing taps or plugging leaks, and for electrical work, fitting lights or replacing sockets. Demand has also increased for more general tasks such as 'fixing', which might include putting up shelves or hanging mirrors, and for general household repair and maintenance work, including decorating, painting, small-scale building works and gardening. In the UK, the scale of this demand has given rise to some specialized firms: for example, 'Hire a Hubby' (2012) – 'Someone who can do all those DIY/Property Maintenance jobs that you might not have the time or skills to do?'; '0800 Handymen' (2012) – 'A man for all reasons'; Dial a Hubby (2012) – who proclaim that 'Someone's gotta do it' and 'Anything your husband can't or won't do, WE DO' and 'Rent a Hubby' (2012) 'for all those jobs that never get done'. These firms typically market themselves as taking on the small jobs that would be rejected by more specialist firms. For example, the Handy Squad (2012) aims:

> to provide a handyman service for those small jobs that other tradesmen either can't be bothered to do or for which they charge too much. Londoners can rely on our service.

The UK Automobile Association – the AA – a very well-known national emergency vehicle repair service – has recently partnered with the Handy Squad and aims to

> Make your home run as it should – smoothly. The Handy Squad loves to do any small job around the home, including putting up pictures, blinds and curtain poles, changing light bulbs, fixing doors and windows, and fitting locks, repairing your boiler, painting and decorating, tiling and grouting, radiators and pipe work, heating systems, dripping taps and burst pipes, showers and bathrooms, electrical installations and rewiring, indoor and outdoor lighting.
>
> AA (2012)

Some firms are multinational, with branches and franchises in a worldwide range of cities and regions, while others consist of individual workers or small-scale worker entrepreneurs who are more likely to advertise their handyman and gardening services through leaflets or postcards dropped door-to-door and/or in local newsagents and hardware stores. The term 'handyman' is used to denote their multitasking ability and the wide scope of services provided. In colloquial terms, their distinguishing feature is that they 'can turn their hand to anything' – 'NO job too BIG or SMALL, just give me a call'[14] – within the realm of household/garden repair and maintenance. Typically, handymen avoid work requiring certification, such as gas installation, though, exceptionally, the Handy Squad will cover these. Similarly, the *jardineros* in the USA largely confine themselves to lawn mowing and leaf blowing, though once they have established a relationship with a particular household they may be asked to do more complex tasks outside and occasionally inside the house. It is this more varied and complex work that provides higher profits.

Handymen represent themselves on the Web and in small-scale marketing often by conveying a form of muscular masculinity, through, for example, the denim covered mid body image of a man with a tool belt and power tool. Another theme is the speed of response, through images of motorbikes, promoting the ideas that the demand is legitimate and urgent and that the handyman will respond promptly, so countering common sense understandings of delay and unreliability associated with the more traditional firms and workers supplying these services. In addition, the images convey a sense of professionalism and reliability which corresponds with the householder's preferences. In this vein, 'Dial a Hubby' (2012) presents the image of a somewhat older, smiling and friendly looking man, though still with the tool belt.

The majority of the migrant handymen we interviewed worked either individually or for a small-scale entrepreneur, though only a minority were small-scale entrepreneurs who organized subcontract jobs for other handymen. Informal networks and word of mouth provided the major source of clients. By contrast the *jardineros* in our study were more likely to be small-scale worker entrepreneurs who employed a number of assistants or *ayudantes*. These different forms of employment reflect both the longer history of gardening work in the USA, with the Mexican *jardineros* building upon traditions established by Japanese gardeners in the mid-twentieth century, and the different character of the work, with lawn mowing being a more standardized and regular service compared to the more diverse and less regular handyman work.

The *jardineros* either establish their own routes – each of which consists of a number of households within a given locality, or take over routes from other *jardineros* in order to secure a viable income. Additionally, contract gardening requires private vehicles, generally trucks, to transport the large lawn mowing machines and the *ayudantes* between the widely dispersed suburban houses. Gardening therefore requires a larger minimum capital investment than that required for handyman work, where private transport helps but is by no means critical, especially in London where public transport provides fairly effective access to employing households.

In both cases, the migrant dimension is significant. Thousands of Central and Eastern Europeans registered themselves as 'handymen'/ 'gardeners'/'groundsmen' and construction workers in the UK when Poland became a member of the EU (Kilkey, 2010; Datta and Brickell, 2009). The Polish identity has also been drawn on as a marketing device, and firms have advertised as 'Polish Handyman' (2012), or similar. Effectively, they are drawing on a dual interpellation of 'Polish', simultaneously recognising and endorsing the stereotypical assumptions about the high quality and multifaceted capabilities of the idealized 'Polish plumber' held by both the buyer and supplier.[15] In reality this sector is much less migrant dense than feminized domestic work and caring, almost certainly because of the continuing associations between handyman work and the more formal masculinized trades. These formal masculinized trades are generally regarded as skilled, in contrast to feminized domestic work, and are consequently more highly paid and more attractive to the working population as a whole. By contrast the migrant density of contract gardening in the USA is high – so much so that contract gardening has become equated with Mexican workers in the public imagination.

Migrants find both sectors attractive partly because of the comparative ease of entry. Typically *jardineros* begin work as *ayudantes*, assistants who join a *jardinero*'s team using their networks of relatives and friends to do so. Handymen too, often acquire work in a similar way, but subsequently obtain work through their clients' recommendations or by advertising their services on the Internet on sites such as Gumtree (2012).[16] In both cases, and similarly to feminized domestic work, the labour intensive character limits productivity and profitability, especially in the case of the contract gardeners, where the work is standardized and the market highly competitive. This means that profits generally depend on long hours of work and a high degree of self and family exploitation and/or the exploitation of the *ayudantes*, conditions that make the sector less attractive to those with alternative employment opportunities. Even so workers in this sector generally earn more than in stereotypical feminized domestic work. Given the character of the work and the material competencies required, this may reflect deep seated social norms regarding appropriate pay on the basis of gendered identities. In this respect, the handymen benefit from the association between their work and the comparatively high prices charged by specialist firms in these masculinized trades, though the more bespoke character of the work means that it is likely to be less regular than that of the *jardineros*. In both cases, however, earnings are rarely predictable.

What becomes apparent is that domestic work carried out by men is more highly valued than that carried out by women, supporting the comment made over three decades ago by Anne Phillips and Barbara Taylor (1980), who claimed that the value of work is determined more by the sex of the worker than by what is done. The higher earnings available in male domestic work facilitate a form of worker entrepreneurship, less frequently found among female domestic workers. This provides some opportunities for earning high incomes, though it was less clear, especially in the handyman sector, whether this high level of earnings can be sustained. In both cases a minority of the migrants we interviewed reported earning in the top decile, and those who do are able to secure some degree of social mobility for their children, if not for themselves.

Circumstances vary considerably, however, within and between the two groups of migrants, especially regarding citizenship status, a factor which impacts profoundly on the opportunities subsequently available to them. In both cases the focus on male migrant domestic workers enables us to distinguish more clearly between aspects of migrant's wellbeing linked with domestic work, those that are more closely connected to how domestic work is gendered, and those that relate more directly to migrants' citizenship status.

1.4   Gender dimensions of migrant domestic labour

Feminist analyses have given considerable attention to migrants carrying out domestic work. This scholarship has typically focused on feminized work and the international division of domestic labour which describes a form of transnational mothering that is socially and racially hierarchical and corresponds to patterns of uneven development (Parreñas, 2001; Hondagneu-Sotelo, 2001). This body of work on the relationship between gender, migration and social reproduction provides a rich resource for analysing male migrant domestic work and is discussed in more detail in Chapter 2. These forms of work reflect and respond to wider economic and social processes, including uneven development, widening social divisions, and the feminization of employment. While individual motivations are always specific, migrants are frequently responding to the imbalance between their aspirations for an economically and socially rich life and the opportunities presently available to them. Similarly, the households drawing on the migrants' services are reacting to their growing material affluence and increasing time poverty, more specifically their ability to fulfil their widening aspirations for careers, their roles as active parents and their desire to fulfil middle class expectations with respect to home maintenance and décor. To set the context for our research, Chapter 2 reviews this literature and establishes, first, that domestic work tends to be constructed almost exclusively as female work and its commoditization is a response to women's difficulties in reconciling work and family life, and second, that to the extent that recent research has started to acknowledge the presence of migrant men within the domestic sector labour market, the focus, with some exceptions (Cox, 2010, 2012; Palenga-Möllenbeck, 2012[17]), has been on men doing feminized forms of domestic work. Chapter 2 highlights how ideas from this extensive body of literature have been drawn upon to inform our study of the outsourcing of male domestic work to migrant men.

While female migrant domestic workers have become a heavily researched group, less has been written about the research process in this field. Chapter 3 responds by introducing the two cases studies and provides a reflexive account of the methodology, primarily from the perspective of the authors who organized and carried out the majority of the interviews. The chapter highlights some of the epistemological issues involved as well as the more practical challenges the authors experienced in carrying out the research, in particular how the micro level research experiences are influenced by the researchers and respondents' gender, class, ethnic, migrant and professional status. Securing trust was especially important given that some of the Mexican *jardineros* lacked citizenship, and in both cases some of the work was informal and off the record. Likewise, managing tensions between personal risk and successful completion of research also involved making difficult decisions in the field, especially in the case of cross gender interviews. Trusting interviewees, even if this meant stepping away from risk guidelines, allowed access to a wider range of participants and secured a more textured and complex picture of their lives.

Chapters 4 to 6 form the heart of our analysis, and draw on 126 in-depth interviews. A total of 79 in-depth interviews were carried out in the UK between 2009 and 2010 with four groups: men and women (interviewed separately) in households with dependent children which buy in handyman type domestic services, migrant handymen, non-migrant handymen, and agencies that employ or service handymen. In the USA 47 in-depth interviews were carried out in 2007 with Mexican immigrant men working as gardeners, *jardineros* – either as self-employed owners of independent gardening routes or as waged employees – the *ayudantes*.

Chapter 4 focuses on migrant handymen in the UK, people largely from the accession countries, predominantly Poland. In addition, though it displays findings from a small number of interviews with non-Polish and non-migrant handymen, agencies operating in the sector, and households with dependent children that buy-in handyman labour. These interviews were performed for comparative purposes, helping us highlight the specific effects being a migrant has on handyman work. Particular emphasis is placed on migration patterns and labour market insertion, work and working relations and the migrants' views about their relative well-being in the UK and Poland. The data were gathered at a point when the UK officially entered an economic recession, so we were able to ask the workers about their perceptions of the crisis, how it affected their work, and whether it influenced their ideas about whether to make their stay more permanent. Attention is also given to the relations with the clients, both the women and men, as this contributes to perceptions about how this work is gendered. Finally consideration is given to their lives outside of work, whether they have any time for leisure, what expectations they have for the future and, for the fathers among our sample, the extent to which they are able to realize their aspirations to be a nurturer as well as a provider. Comparing our findings with those from the extensive literature on feminized domestic labour allows us to consider gendered understandings of domestic work, which are discussed further in Chapter 7.

Chapter 5 focuses on the interviews with households that outsource male domestic work. The study selected households with dependent children and a resident father, as these households are among the most likely in the UK to outsource male domestic tasks. We provide an analysis of the households' rationale for outsourcing male domestic labour, how outsourcing is managed by the households, and how the fathers used the time saved as a consequence. We show that by supplying household services, migrant handymen enable labour-using households to alleviate time pressures and reduce, if not resolve, conflicts in time priorities. These conflicts arise from tensions between economic expectations regarding working hours and work commitment and social expectations regarding contemporary ideas of active parenting and house maintenance. In this respect, outsourcing male domestic work provides a private resolution to the father time-bind by resolving conflicting tensions between 'competing work-life scenarios' – the 'free competitive disembodied worker' presumed within economic policy, and the embodied worker expected to be a hands-on nurturing father in contemporary social thought (Hobson and Fahlén, 2009: 214). This private solution is required because, in the UK, these competing expectations are only partially supported by company and social policies (Lewis and Plomien, 2009).

As with the outsourcing of feminized domestic care, which saw one set of women empowered as a consequence of drawing on female domestic labourers, this father time-bind is in part resolved for labour-using households by extending class divisions across national boundaries, while leaving gender divisions within households changed but not transformed. In addition, while outsourcing provides work for the migrant handymen and so enables them to fulfil their breadwinning role, the long working hours necessary to build up and sustain their incomes limits their opportunities to embrace new fathering, despite their aspirations to do so. This situation is similar for the *jardineros* in the USA. In both cases teenage children were drawn on to help their fathers at weekends and school holidays which arguably represents a different way of establishing intimacy.

In Chapter 6, the spotlight turns to Mexican gardeners in Los Angeles, drawing primarily on 47 interviews with the immigrants. Similarly to Chapter 4, it shows how migration was an individual response to a common contextual condition; the uneven level of development between Mexico and the USA, and the resultant prospects for higher earnings. The contract labour system (Bracero Program) that operated between 1942 and 1964 established a tradition of migration from Mexico to the USA. Although the programme ended, migration, sometimes unauthorized, continues owing to the sustained high level of labour demand in the USA, especially in agriculture and a range of service occupations. The immigrants in our study come from predominantly agricultural backgrounds but work in private residential gardening in suburban Los Angeles; a migrant niche established in the 1940s by Japanese immigrant men. From the 1970s and 1980s onwards, Mexicans moved into this sector, which expanded rapidly as more households outsourced gardening as a consequence of rising incomes, desire to maintain real estate values and neighbourhood standards and, similarly to UK households, desire to relieve time pressures.

In discussing the work and lives of the migrant domestic workers, Chapters 4 and 6 underline how individual identity characteristics relating to gender, social class and ethnicity together with migrant status intersect and influence occupational opportunities and individual well-being. Two issues are particularly significant. The first relates to the way in which these characteristics are understood especially by the autochthonous population, and how they frame migrants as being particularly appropriate for the work they do. The second relates to the agency of and differentiation among the migrants themselves. Especially significant in the case of the *jardineros* is migrant status. As Chapter 6 explains most migrants begin as low paid wage employees, as *ayudantes* or assistants, to worker entrepreneurs (or route owners) who own the trucks, tools and negotiate contracts for lawn mowing for groups of households on a regular basis. Becoming a route owner secures the possibility of a much higher income, but to do so the *ayudantes* have to acquire gardening skills, accumulate sufficient capital to buy a truck and equipment and, critically, secure a driving licence. Driving licences are only available to documented migrants. Polish handymen are a much more recent phenomenon, but a similar differentiation is emerging between those who negotiate the work with the households and those who only perform the work. As Polish migrants have citizenship rights and capital requirements can be much lower, the differentiating factor in this case is largely English language ability. A further difference between the two groups of migrants is that the Mexicans are racial minorities in the US while Poles in the UK are part of the racial majority. By exploring the experiences of the *jardineros* and migrant handymen and their relations with clients, the case studies contribute both towards general debates regarding intersectionality between gender, migration, race, ethnicity, work and identity and towards a more specific analysis of the interplay between exploitation and resistance as well as agency in the lives of migrants.

Chapter 7 brings the book to a close, by drawing on both of the case studies to highlight the contribution of our analysis towards understandings of gender, identity and work. Particular attention is paid to the gender differentiated values attached to domestic work and to dynamic and varied understandings of masculinity, understandings that are reflected in decisions regarding work. We examine how and why different forms of work are constructed as masculine or feminine, what implications this has for their economic valuation and social status and how the work environment itself permits and constrains different expressions of masculinity. Finally, we contrast our findings with feminized domestic work by reference to the literature reviewed in Chapter 2. We conclude the book by showing how our findings contribute to discussions of gender identity and social reproduction in a global context.

1.5 Conclusion

Gender, Migration and Domestic Work explores the relationships between gender, migration and social reproduction through the lens of male domestic work, paying attention both to the ethnic and class dimensions of this relationship and to the manner in which these identity characteristics intersect with legal status or citizenship. By providing a detailed analysis of male migrants carrying out stereotypically masculinized forms of domestic work in the homes and gardens of European and US citizens, the book enriches the growing literature on migrant domestic work and global care chains through the focus on men in three rather different ways. Most obviously, the book fills an empirical gap, significant because the scale of male domestic work parallels feminized domestic work but nonetheless remains largely unacknowledged in the literature. Second, by situating our findings within the extensive literature on feminized care and domestic work we highlight some of the specifically gendered dimensions of domestic work. Third, the book addresses (im)migrant men's lives beyond the world of paid work, examining in particular their experiences of fathering. Such a focus adds another dimension to the migration literature, since while there is a large body of work on transnational mothering, less has been written about (im)migrants' social reproductive worlds within their country of destination, and even less about how migrant men perform their fathering roles, whether in their country of destination or transnationally.[18] A further contribution derives from the comparative dimension, which, although partial, nonetheless helps highlight the influence of citizenship, ethnicity and the characteristics of work on migrants' capacity to fulfil their migration strategies and aspirations.

In addition, the evidence and analysis presented has significance for a wider range of debates including: feminist theory, through the focus on relations between gender, work and identity and relations between agency, coercion and structure; feminist political economy, through its consideration of how people in different social positions manage their daily work and lives in the context of continuing uneven development between and widening social divisions within states; social policy, through providing some awareness of how fathers manage their work life balance transnationally, and how household divisions of tasks may be changing but gender divisions of labour within the home and in the workplace have yet to be transformed; and finally, contemporary policy debates on migration, employment and citizenship.

Overall, the book contributes to analysing how wide-scale economic and social change impacts on the daily lives of people in different ways across the globe, especially in relation to increasing inequalities within and between different countries which stimulate both migration and the demand for commoditized domestic services. This impact is differentiated according to both prevailing migration and social policies in states and the specific social positioning of people. Some of these changes result in new gender divisions of labour such that women play a greater role in the labour market and men a greater role in childcare. At the same time, our analysis also shows that these changes are quite limited, and that more traditional gender expectations continue to shape patterns of work and identity. Despite some change, gender stereotypes continue to frame understandings about the appropriate tasks for women and men both inside and outside the home and by so doing sustain and reinforce uneven gender relations.

2
Globalization, Migration and Domestic Work: Gendering the Debate

2.1 Introduction

Our concern in this book is with the commoditization of male domestic work. We situate this process within the wider phenomenon of households' outsourcing of social reproductive labour, an increase in which, alongside other aspects of personal and intimate life, is a marker of late capitalist service economies. In doing so, this book builds on the rich body of feminist scholarship that has examined the economic, social and cultural dynamics and consequences of the contemporary commoditization of 'female' areas of social reproductive labour, namely cleaning, cooking and care-giving – areas which in terms of time commitment account for the bulk of domestic work undertaken in households.[1]

Commoditized domestic work is not new: feminist social historians have shown how the leisure and philanthropic pursuits of middle and upper class women in Europe and the USA depended well into the twentieth century on the domestic services of the working classes (Chaplin, 1978; Davidoff, 1995). Even working class women in relatively well-paid jobs in the past relied on paid domestic help to alleviate the pressures of their 'double day' (Anderson and Bowman, 1953 on the USA; Barrett and McIntosh, 1982 and Glucksmann, 1989 on England). Historically in Europe and the USA, men also worked in domestic services.[2] Men not only did the same jobs as women, but they did other, masculinized, jobs too. These included indoor male-servant occupations such as butler, footman and clerk of the kitchen, and outdoor service related to both horse-work (coachmen, grooms and postillions) and garden and estate work (gardeners, park, lodge and gatekeepers and gamekeepers) (Ebery and Preston, 1976; Meldrum, 2000). Historically, domestic work was also inextricably bound up with migration, with the supply of domestic workers depending on both internal (rural-urban) and international migration flows (Moya, 2007: 567–70).

In the UK and USA, domestic service declined from the 1920s partly as a consequence of alternative, more attractive employment opportunities, including work in the new factories producing domestic technologies, such as vacuum cleaners, washing machines and refrigerators that made the employment of domestic workers less necessary (Glucksmann, 1990; Miller, 1991). And, in the early 1980s it was predicted that as the cost of purchasing domestic technologies decreased relative to incomes, we would become a self-servicing society (Gershuny, 1985). Evidence derived from empirical studies in that period seemed to support this prediction. In the UK, Pahl's (1984) Isle of Sheppey investigation of which tasks households do and the source of the labour for them pointed to an increasing rate of self-provisioning – 'the production of goods and services outside the market by household members for their own use and enjoyment' (Pahl and Wallace, 1985: 219). From the 1990s onwards, however, academic commentary has highlighted a counter-tendency towards domestic outsourcing – 'the process of replacing unpaid household production with market substitutes' (Bittman, Matheson and Meagher, 1999: 249).

As we shall see further on, in the feminist scholarship on the contemporary outsourcing of social reproductive labour, the relationship between migration and domestic work remains a central focus. While there is a small body of recent research on migrant men working as domestic cleaners and caregivers, men's domestic labour has all but disappeared from view in the contemporary literature. One reason is because the migrant domestic work literature treats the domestic sphere as synonymous with women's work. The result has been that while feminized areas of domestic and care work have been widely researched, stereotypically male areas such as household and garden maintenance and repair have been largely ignored. In this chapter, we establish how bringing men and their domestic labour (back) into the analysis contributes to the thematic and conceptual frames of the contemporary feminist scholarship. To do so, we review that body of work through the lens of men and male domestic labour. The chapter is organized into two main parts. In section 2.2, we examine the ways in which the increasing demand for commoditized female domestic and care services in advanced capitalist societies has been explained by the feminist scholarship, and identify the implications for those explanations of analysing the source of demand for commoditized male domestic services. In section 2.3, we turn to the supply-side. We review how the feminist scholarship has explored the contemporary relationship between migration and commoditized female domestic and care work, and examine the ways in which it can contribute to understandings of the relationship between migration and the commoditization of male domestic work.

2.2   Accounting for the commoditization of domestic work: Gendering the debate

2.2.1   Explaining the rise in demand for commoditized female domestic services

The increase in demand for commoditized domestic services such as care, cooking and cleaning, is widely linked to the ways in which globalization processes are impacting on advanced capitalist societies. The shift towards a service economy has been associated with the feminization of the labour market, and an attendant increase in women's, and especially mothers', employment rates and hours of paid work (Harkness, 2008; Jacobs and Gerson, 2004).[3] As a result, in the UK and USA, as well as elsewhere, the combined paid working time of couples has increased (Harkness, 2008; Jacobs and Gerson, 2004). Those changes have challenged the sexual division of labour assumed by the male breadwinner family model, and the ensuing de-specialization of roles, at least as it relates to women, has created time dilemmas for households around the fulfilment of paid and domestic work responsibilities (Jacobs and Gerson, 2004). As Creighton (1999) notes, the male breadwinner family model also rested on a 'time compact' between workers, employers and the state on the appropriate distribution and scheduling of time between the family and the workplace. This too has been modified through the de-standardization of working practices, in part facilitated by the rise in ICTs, which has also contributed to the intensification of paid work, as well as to its increasing spatial and temporal flexibility (Wajcman, 2008). Both the increase in couple's paid working hours and the flexibilization of working practices are widely seen as creating a 'time-bind' (Hochschild, 1997) in households. Socio-demographic changes further exacerbate the problem. Late capitalist societies are ageing societies, and as motherhood is delayed for many women, in part due to greater commitment to their professional lives, it is increasingly common for dual-earning households to be 'sandwiched' between care responsibilities for children as well as elders (Hammer and Neal, 2008).

    The redistribution of domestic and care work from women to men would be one way of addressing the time dilemmas experienced by households, but this has not occurred to a sufficient degree (Miranda, 2011).

Examining the distribution within UK households of time spent on cooking, cleaning and laundry (but not care), Harkness (2008: 239) finds 'no evidence of a rise in the number of hours of unpaid work carried out by men to compensate for the greater engagement of their partners in the labour market'. Comparable data from time use diaries for a set of seven countries including the UK and USA, and controlling for employment and family status, show that between 1960 and 1997 men's contribution to the core domestic work of cooking and cleaning increased by 20 minutes per day, while women's declined by one hour, suggesting some movement towards greater gender equality in this respect, though in absolute terms a wide gender gap remains (Sullivan, 2004). Across a set of nations comprising all OECD countries and three emerging economies, the gender gap in the distribution of domestic work is estimated to average 148 minutes per day, ranging from a low of 57 minutes in Denmark to a high of 300 minutes in India. In the UK and USA it is 123 and 104 minutes, respectively – below the average but considerably above Denmark and other Nordic countries (Miranda, 2011). In the context of such persistent inequalities in the distribution of domestic work, it is suggested that households' use of commoditized domestic services has been adopted by women as a strategy to ease their time-bind (Hochschild, 2000).

Intransigence in the face of women's increased labour market participation is not only apparent in men; it has also characterized, at least until very recently, the response of many governments to transformations in the male breadwinner family model. In the USA, while there is a strong expectation that all adults, including mothers, will be in paid work, the issue of how families manage paid work and care is seen as a private matter for individuals and employers, and there has been very little in the way of public provision for care responsibilities (Lewis, 2009). The situation in Europe, which exhibits a variety of 'care regimes' (Bettio and Plantenga, 2004), is more mixed. The Nordic countries, and especially Sweden, with their longstanding commitment to gender equality, have a comparatively well-developed work-family balance (WFB) policy package comprising time, service and cash provisions (Lewis, 2009). Other countries, albeit to different degrees, lag behind. A deeply rooted familialism in Southern European countries, although more so in Italy, Spain and Greece than in Portugal (Wall and Nunes, 2010), for example, has constrained the development of public care provision, and left the reconciliation of paid work and unpaid care and domestic work very much in the hands of families (Bettio, Simonazzi and Villa, 2006; Lewis, 2009). In the UK, the influence of liberalism resulted in a non-interventionist orthodoxy with regard to how families manage paid work and care, which prevailed until the late 1990s. Since then, as is the case in many other EU member states, the issue of WFB has gained political and policy prominence (Daly, 2010, 2011; Grimshaw and Rubery, 2012). The particular configuration of drivers varies from country to country, but almost universally a desire to increase women's employment – a goal linked to concerns to heighten economic competitiveness – has been central.[4] In this context, the work/ family balance measures advocated by the EU reflect only 'a weak version of the Scandinavian gender equality model' (Duncan, 2002: 305), neither equipping governments to directly fill the care gap created by women's increased hours of paid work, nor laying the foundations for a redistribution of domestic and care work between women and men (see also Daly, 2011). The quality of recent policy developments in the UK around the reconciliation of work and family life has been further constrained because, as Duncan (2002: 305; see also Grimshaw and Rubery, 2012) argues, the UK more than any other EU country has been simultaneously straddling another horse, namely, the 'US/Atlantacist/liberal' model which emphasizes free market competition and individualism. One result is that social policies in the UK and USA have not challenged time-greedy employers, whose expectations for flexibility and long working hours, especially from male employees, intensifies the household time-bind.

While in failing to respond adequately to the household time-bind welfare states are indirectly implicated in the rising demand for commoditized domestic services, there are also ways in which they are more directly responsible. Specifically, across North America and Western Europe, neoliberal policy agendas are requiring welfare states to be restructured in line with market principles. One result is that governments themselves increasingly outsource their social and personal care provision through a range of privatization and marketization strategies (Misra, Woodring and Merz, 2006). A policy instrument recently favoured by governments, including those in Austria, Italy, the Netherlands and the UK, for elder and disabled care, is direct payments for care, whereby states deliver financial support directly to those in need of care, who in turn pay someone to provide the care and/or domestic support (Ungerson and Yeandle, 2007).[5] Some governments, including Finland, France, Spain and the UK, have extended this principle to childcare (Daly, 2011; Lister et al., 2007; Williams and Gavanas, 2008), and even domestic work more generally (Windebank, 2007), through the introduction of cash payments, tax credits or tax incentives to meet the costs of services.[6] The result is the growth in private, both commercial and not-for-profit, provision of services (Yeates, 2010).

Significant numbers of households, though, purchase domestic and care services without state subsidies, and as Lutz and Palenga-Möllenbeck (2010) have found in Germany, even those receiving 'payments for care' of one type or another are likely to have to top up fees from their own resources. The ability of households to do so is partially associated with rising earnings inequality among women and between households (McDowell et al., 2005; Nyberg, 1999, cited in Platzer, 2006). While income inequality has increased throughout OECD countries over the past two decades (OECD, 2011b), its rise has been particularly sharp in the 'global cities' (Sassen, 2001) of neoliberal regimes, such as London and Los Angeles. These cities, furthermore, are characterized by a polarization of occupational structures (Kaplanis, 2007; Waldinger and Lichter, 2003; Wills et al., 2010), as growth at the top end of the labour market associated with the concentration of the central corporate functions of global capital fuels growth at the bottom, especially in the low-wage service economy, including domestic services (Sassen, 2001). This is apparent in the UK, where domestic sector workers are overly concentrated in London and the South East of England, and where their degree of over-concentration in the capital and its commuter-belt has been increasing over time (Kilkey, 2008). Surplus income among the wealthy has been invested in property in cities such as London and Los Angeles, where in the context of neoliberal economic and social policies, it has also come to be regarded as a 'pensions pot'.[7] Home has become a status symbol, and affluence is displayed through bigger and bigger houses and more elaborate decoration and ornamentation. Homes as both investments and symbols of wealth, therefore, require more care, cleaning and maintenance, and in the feminist scholarship on domestic outsourcing this has been identified as a further source of demand for cleaners in particular (Cox, 2006).

2.2.2 Gendering the debate

In the previous account of the contemporary drivers of demand for paid domestic work, men are largely missing. Any allusion to their role relates to their intransigence in the face of the changing norms and practices vis-à-vis home and paid work of their female partners as they respond to the underlying socio-economic shifts wrought by globalization processes. This construction of men's part, accurate as it probably is in relation to heterosexual couples and the domestic division of 'women's' household tasks, obscures important ways in which middle class men play a more direct and agentic role in driving demand for commoditized domestic services. There has been some recognition (Cox, 2006) that single men, either living alone or communally, are more likely than single women to employ cleaners, implicating men very directly in the commoditization of domestic work. The evidence of the commoditization of stereotypically male areas of domestic labour, however, suggests another dimension to men's role. Further examination of this commoditization entails a more explicit acknowledgement of the role gender plays in the processes of globalization, its effects on individuals, and on the ways in which individuals in turn respond. Building on the literature on demand for commoditized female domestic and care work, we need to ask, therefore, what it is that is changing, materially and normatively, in the worlds of middle class men that leads to the outsourcing of their domestic work. To address that question, we examine the implications of shifts in middle class men's configuration of work and home lives for their gendered identities and practices. We also consider what role, if any, state policies play in contributing to men's norms and behaviours relating to paid work and family. Moreover, we ask what the consequences of rising income inequalities are for men and their domestic work: what role, for example, do commoditized male domestic services play in enhancing and maintaining the status and monetary value of 'the home' for the middle classes? Finally, what do men do with the time saved from outsourcing their domestic work, and what implications are there for gender equality within and between households?

2.3 Migration and the supply of domestic workers: Gendering the debate

2.3.1 The international division in female reproductive labour

The literature on the contemporary commoditization of female domestic work commonly describes domestic sector employment as an 'immigrant niche' (Schrover, van der Leun and Quispel, 2007). In this section, we review the feminist scholarship on the link between migration and the supply of workers for commoditized female domestic labour, addressing how this relationship is seen to operate at the scale of the global economy, at the institutional and policy level, and the level of individual migrant domestic workers and their customers/employers. We then turn to assess what a focus on commoditized male domestic labour implies for that scholarship.

In her pioneering study, *The Servants of Globalization* (2001), Rhacel Parreñas analyses the tendency for commoditized female domestic work to become migrants' work through the lens of an 'international division of reproductive labour'. Her concept situates the contemporary development of an international market for maids, nannies and carers within global processes of economic restructuring and resulting patterns of uneven global economic development, which in turn impact on patterns of international migration, including its feminization, and the supply of migrant labour. The result, she argues, is in 'core' migrant-receiving countries, the transfer of middle class households' social reproductive labour, generally done by women in those households, to migrant women from 'peripheral' countries. Parreñas' concept expands Evelyn Nakano Glenn's (1992) notion of 'the racial division of reproductive labour' to capture the transnational character of the relational net of inequalities in paid domestic and care work. It also develops Sassen's (1984) gendered analysis of the 'international division of labour' by demonstrating that households, as well as states and markets, are embedded in globalization processes, and that social reproductive work, as well as productive labour, is part of the global economy.

Parreñas developed the concept of an international division in reproductive labour through an analysis of global female domestic work migration from the Philippines to Los Angeles and Rome. As others have noted (Sarti, 2008; Williams, 2010), the global dynamics captured in the international division of reproductive labour are played out at a regional as well as at a global level, and can help explain more localized movements of domestic and care workers, such as those from Mexico to the USA (Hondagneu-Sotelo, 2001) and from Central and Eastern Europe to Western Europe (Perrons, Plomien and Kilkey, 2010); the flows that form the focus of this book's enquiry. The spatial dimensions to the international division of reproductive labour have been further analysed by Sassen (2010a) who observes that, as with the demand for commoditized domestic services, the tendency for domestic work to become migrants' work is especially sharp in global cities, where the growing volume of low-wage service jobs are increasingly filled by migrants, resulting in what Wills et al. (2010) term a 'migrant division of labour'. Specifically, Sassen argues that migrants constitute 'strategic infrastructure maintenance workers' for advanced sectors in richer countries where households 'have to function like clockwork because the professionals have to function like clockwork' (Sassen, 2010a: 11).

Others, including Williams (Williams, 2005; Williams and Gavanas, 2008), Lutz (2008; 2011) and Misra, Woodring and Merz (2006), have suggested that the relationship between migration and domestic work also operates at the level of state policies; as Misra, Woodring and Merz (2006: 321) argue, 'classes and groups are displaced by processes of uneven global capitalist development, and institutional arrangements then emerge to serve the reproduction of global capital'. This observation has led to a particular focus in the literature on the role that migration policies play in configuring the scale, characteristics and experiences of migrant female domestic workers.

Thus, for example, a focus on migration regimes has helped explain why domestic work has become a migrant niche. As 'rich' countries attempt to reassert the link between migration and economic and labour market imperatives, entry conditions are ever more tightly managed, and except in the case of global elites tend to be linked to particular 'skill' gaps (Castles, 2006; Wills et al., 2010). One consequence is the production and criminalization of a rising number of irregular migrants (Gutiérrez-Rodríguez, 2010). In this context, employment in the private sphere, with its greater capacity to avoid state surveillance, as well as the provision of accommodation in the case of live-in domestic service, has been found to be an important survival strategy among migrants (Anderson, 2007; Cox and Watt, 2002; Pfau-Effinger, 2009). There are cross-national variations, however, in the extent to which domestic and care work has become 'migrant work'; variations which are also in part explained through analysis of migration policies. Thus, for example, estimates suggest that Spain and Italy have higher concentrations of migrants employed in domestic and care work than Portugal; a situation arising in part because while the former two countries have accorded such work a special status in their migration policies, through entry quotas for domestic workers (Italy) and regularization programmes for undocumented migrants (Italy and Spain), Portugal has not introduced any special measures (Kilkey, Lutz and Palenga-Möllenbeck, 2010).

A focus on the intersection between domestic and care work and migration policies can also help explain the working conditions that migrant domestic/care workers experience. Migrant domestic and care workers are often irregular migrants, and that status, along with other factors such as the private and highly personalized nature of the work, can make them vulnerable to exploitative employment practices (Anderson, 2000; Lutz, 2011). It is important, however, not to over-homogenize migrant domestic and care workers. The attempt to 'manage' migration has resulted in the increasing differentiation of migrants by legal status, and this can cut across nationality and occupational group (Vertovec, 2007). Moreover, migration regimes intersect in ever sharper ways with welfare and labour market policies (Bolderson, 2011; Bommes and Geddes, 2000; Wills et al., 2010), and in some contexts at least, the immigration/welfare/labour market nexus is one that is also increasingly stratified (Bolderson, 2011). The result is growing diversity among migrant workers, including those doing domestic/care work, in their entry, residency, employment and social rights, which in turn contributes to differentiating their working conditions (Wills et al., 2010).

While the increasing density of migrants in the domestic and care work sectors can be understood at a structural and institutional level, individual level dynamics are also relevant; these relate to both employers/customers and migrants themselves. Turning to the former first, in their study of labour market segmentation in Los Angeles, Waldinger and Lichter (2003: 121) advocate 'bringing the bosses back in'. They suggest that employers hold categorical (both in terms of gender and race) assumptions about the most appropriate worker for the job, which in the context of a racialized society means that 'entire ethnic groups are ranked according to sets of socially meaningful but arbitrary traits' (Waldinger and Lichter, 2003: 8). This results in a 'hiring queue' (ibid.), which plays a critical role in the 'sorting' (Ellis and Wright, 1999) of workers into different sectors and strata of the labour market; in other words, in the construction of migrant niches. This notion of employer stereotyping has been taken up in the literature on migrant domestic/care work, with evidence that householders often prefer migrants, and moreover, may differentiate among migrants, preferring some nationalities and religions over others (Anderson, 2007; Cox, 2007; Hochschild, 2003; Williams, 2010).[8]

Interestingly, Waldinger and Lichter (2003: 16) distinguished between the operation of employer preferences in the public world of paid work and the private world of home life. As they put it, '[t]he employer is not looking for friends, just hired hands', and they applied their concept of a 'hiring queue' to paid work in the public sphere only. Situations in which the 'home becomes a workplace' (Lutz, 2008: 50), however, unsettle such distinctions, precisely because it is waged labour performed in a highly personalized and intimate space. The sense of personal intimacy means that employers and workers alike often construct the employment relation as a family tie (Gregson and Lowe, 1994). This 'personalism', however, occurs in the context of status differences between the employer and employee, such that in practice the relationship is highly asymmetrical (Glenn, 1986), and is in reality a 'false kinship' (Gregson and Lowe, 1994). The historical separation of 'home' from 'work' or 'public' from 'private' renders the meanings attached to the space of 'home' are distinct from those of a public workplace. 'Home' has been constructed as the sanctuary from the outside world; the place where we can truly be ourselves. And, in a consumer society, what we fill our homes with is a presentation of self. As Lutz (2008: 50) suggests, those allowed into our homes, including domestic/care workers, are 'expected to share, respect and honour the emotions that the members of the household associate with their belongings, their items and the order of things. In other words … they have to accept the 'habitus' of the household'. As a result, householders may deem some people more appropriate for their home than others. Preferences are not random, however. Instead, there are general patterns. But, as Williams (2010: 386) notes, the patterning of preferences varies from country to country, and this, she suggests, 'points to a complex interrelationship between the gendered gradations of care work with colonial histories, past and contemporary religious antagonisms, and essentialist stereotypes based on gender, nationality and ethnicity'.

Racial and religious stereotyping can work the other way round, however, as revealed by Búriková and Miller's (2010) recent study of Slovak au pairs working in London, who expressed a preference for some types of employers over others. Moreover, it has been suggested that migrant domestic workers utilize the stereotypes employers hold about them to strengthen their own position within the occupation. Sarti (2005), for example, draws attention to the tendency observed in a number of studies for Filipina domestic workers to refer to themselves as the 'Mercedes Benz' of domestic workers. Such evidence, it is suggested, points to the agency of migrant domestic/care workers, challenging a tendency in much of the literature to construct them solely as victims (Búriková and Miller, 2010). The agency of migrant domestic and care workers has also been highlighted in relation to their reasons for migration (Búriková and Miller, 2010; Parreñas, 2001), as well as in relation to the social networks through which migration and employment may be facilitated (Búriková and Miller, 2010; McGregor, 2007). The agency-victim debate, however, remains a complex one in relation to migrant female domestic workers in large part because such work can be associated with significant downward occupational and class mobility (Parreñas, 2001).

Laura Agustín (2003: 391) reminds us that '[T]o pay attention only to the jobs migrants do is to essentialize them as workers and deny the diversity of their hopes and experiences'. Agustín's argument is one that is implicitly acknowledged in much of the migrant domestic and care work literature, a significant theme within which has been the implications of migration for migrants' family and care responsibilities. In particular, the concept of 'global care chains' – 'a series of personal links between people across the globe based on the paid or unpaid work of caring' (Hochschild, 2000: 131) – together with the large body of work on the transnational mothering experiences of migrant domestic and care workers (Hondagneu-Sotelo and Avila, 1997; Hochschild, 2000; Madianou and Miller, 2011; Parreñas, 2001; Zontini, 2004), takes a broader perspective and recognises how this migration generates complex interdependencies between the work and lives of people across the globe.[9] The transnational mothering literature captures the complexity of the agency/victim debate in relation to migrant domestic and care workers, highlighting simultaneously both the social and emotional costs associated with mother-child separation for the children left behind, their parents and wider communities and the agency of mothers, who reconfigure traditional definitions of motherhood to include their new roles and practices as breadwinners.

2.3.2 Gendering the debate: Migrant men doing women's domestic labour

In the literature reviewed previously, migrant domestic workers are assumed, often implicitly, to be female. Based on observations of the entry of migrant men into traditionally female (at least as constructed in Western cultures – see, for example, Bartolomei, 2010; Qayum and Ray, 2010) areas of domestic and care work in a number of European societies, recent research has recognised the significance of male domestic work, both past and present (Bartolomei, 2010; Manalansan, 2006; Näre, 2010; Sarti, 2010; Scrinzi, 2010). Thus, for example, the historian Raffaella Sarti (2010), in acknowledgement of the fact that, historically, domestic service was a highly masculinized sphere in European societies, argues that there has been a slight re-masculinisation of domestic service in a number of countries. She points to Italy, for example, where national social insurance data indicate that between 1991 and 1996 the proportion of the *declared* domestic sector workforce that was male increased from 6 to 17 per cent. While there has been a decline in men's representation since then, by 2005 it was still over the 10 per cent mark. Significantly, Sarti finds that it is *migrant* men rather than *Italian* men who are mainly responsible for this trend, with men composing only about 3 per cent of Italian domestic workers in the period 1991 to 2005, but constituting between 15 and 30 per cent, depending on the year, of foreign domestic workers.

The apparent increase in migrant men working as carers and cleaners in private households in some parts of Europe, as with migrant women, can be linked to contemporary globalization processes. Domestic work, rejected by European men in past centuries in the face of the better opportunities afforded by industrialization, becomes 'attractive' to migrant men in the context of uneven development and widening income inequalities within and between the global North and South. As Sarti (2008) suggests, migration policies are also implicated, although the precise nature of the relationship is context specific. Where domestic work has been designated as a legal route of entry to the country and/or it has benefited from post-migration amnesties, as we saw before has been the case in Italy and Spain for example, the attractiveness of domestic work increases, and it becomes susceptible to redefinition in gender (as well as class and ethnic) terms, coming to be regarded as acceptable work for migrant men. As also noted earlier, while elsewhere domestic work may not provide a route of valid entry or regularization, its tendency to operate in the 'grey economy' opens it up as a source of employment to irregular migrants too, and this is likely to be the case for males as well as females. Moya (2007) suggests that the processes underpinning migrant niching within domestic and care work also contribute to a re-masculinization. This is the case in two senses. In the first place, the endogenous and informal mechanisms of information, assistance and selection associated with immigrant niche formation means that ethnic group membership, rather than or alongside of gender, is the key determinant for working in the domestic sector. Secondly, the transformation of domestic work into an immigrant niche also facilitates entrepreneurialism within the sector, and '[I]n so far as house-cleaning becomes a family business ... husbands and adolescent sons tend to participate' (Moya, 2007: 574). Research has also located the rise in male domestic workers performing feminized domestic labour in the ageing of European societies. Bartolemei (2000) finds in Italy a demand for male domestics to work especially in eldercare, and, in particular, in male eldercare. Likewise, in England Cangiano et al. (2009: 67) find that men make up almost one-third of 'recent migrants' working in the elder social care sector; this compares with 13 per cent among UK-born workers. While this demand is important, so too is the demand from dual-working households with dependent children – the focus of our research.

2.3.3   Gendering the debate: Migrant men doing men's domestic labour

Highlighting the involvement of migrant men in commoditized female-typed domestic and care work contributes to gendering analyses of the relationship between globalization, migration and social reproduction, analyses which hitherto had focused solely on women's positions within this relationship. Specifically, investigation of male domestic workers who do traditionally female jobs has potential to contribute to understandings of masculinities and, in particular, how these masculinities are inflected by ethnicity, nationality, race and location, and how they may or may not be redrawn in the context of globalization and migration. The focus on migrant men doing typically male domestic work and the householders who employ them, however, contributes to understanding the complexity and relationalities of contemporary masculinities, and the gender dynamics of households.

Fully gendering the relationship between globalization, migration and domestic work requires that we examine whether and how the contemporary commoditization of masculinized domestic labour can be understood as signifying the emergence of a new international division of *male* domestic labour, paralleling what Parreñas (2001) has observed for female domestic work. That question focuses attention on relations between men, and on how men are differently and unequally positioned, economically and geopolitically, in the processes of globalization. It also focuses enquiry on the institutional, policy and individual level dynamics underpinning the tendency for commoditized male domestic work, like its female counterpart, to become migrants' work. What role do migration policies play, for example, in constituting handyman work in the UK and gardening work in the USA as respectively a Polish and a Mexican migrant niche? Do migration policies lead to differentiation and stratification within those sectors, and with what consequences for workers' economic and social well-being? What role do classed, gendered and racialized processes play in constituting Polish and Mexican men as appropriate for this work, and how does this vary between men's indoor work and outdoor work on the one hand, and between female and male domestic work on the other hand? Do householders, for example, care differently about which male bodies they permit to enter the domesticated and feminized sphere of the home than they do those who remain outside? Do they care differently about who is allowed contact with their food, dishes and children and those who work with their gardens, shelves and plumbing? What is the patterning of exploitation and agency in migrant male domestic work? Specifically, do Polish handymen and Mexican gardeners experience downward occupational and class mobility, and how and why might this differ from what has been observed for migrant female domestic workers? How and why is migrant male domestic work differently valued, in both normative and material ways, from migrant female domestic work? Finally, what are the implications of migration and the jobs that they do for the family lives of Polish handymen and Mexican gardeners, and how does the configuration of work and family in their lives compare with that of the men whose domestic labour they are now doing?

2.4   Conclusion

The feminist scholarship on the contemporary outsourcing of feminized domestic work has contributed important insights into the ways in which the rising demand for commoditized domestic and care services in late capitalist societies is intimately linked to globalization processes. It has also demonstrated how the very same processes, through their differential and unequal impact across the globe and accompanied by institutional arid individual level dynamics, have led to a new contemporary 'international division of reproductive labour' (Parreñas, 2001), such that in many countries, commoditized domestic and care work has increasingly become migrants' work. Through the focus on domestic work, the research has revealed how contemporary globalization and migration processes are gendered. Those insights, though, have been developed exclusively in relation to the commoditization of traditionally female areas of domestic responsibility – caring, cleaning and cooking in particular – and their transfer to migrant women and to some extent to migrant men. In this chapter, we have reviewed the key themes and concepts in that literature, and highlighted how the empirical studies at the centre of this book will build on the existing scholarship through a focus on commoditized male domestic work in order to more fully gender the relationship between globalization, migration and social reproduction. It is to a discussion of the methodology of those studies that we now turn.

3
Researching Men in the Relationship between Gender, Migration and Domestic Work

3.1 Introduction

In this book, we bring together two separate but interrelated studies about the relationship between gender, migration and domestic work in the UK and the USA. A transnational comparative approach was not built into our respective research designs. Although we were aware of each others' work, each project was conceived, planned and executed independently of the other. In the latter stages of research and analysis we realized that our transatlantic conversations generate additional insights both with respect to the substantive areas of men's migration, work and care discussed throughout the book, and with regard to the research process – an issue taken up in this chapter. A close retrospective comparison of the two studies – grounded in different social, economic, and geopolitical contexts yet operating within similar neo-liberal settings – offers a broader analytical outlook than each on its own. As a result, we carry out the discussion at two levels: at one, we reflexively engage with themes that emerged within and were distinct to each study; at the other, we pay attention to patterns of similarity and difference gleaned from the two cases.

While migrant domestic workers have become a heavily researched group, less has been written about the research process itself. Yet, the challenges and dilemmas we have faced in researching migrant, predominantly Polish, handymen and middle class labour-using households in the UK and Mexican immigrant gardeners in the USA raise a number of methodological and epistemological issues, of which we select a few. These examples, which emerged through recruitment and interview encounters, centre on the problems of time as a scarce resource, attaining the desired sample composition and size, establishing and maintaining rapport, and overcoming unequal power relations within the research process. Our reflections permit us to critically examine the micro level research experiences and practices and assess how they are mediated through our and our respondents' gender, class, ethnic, migration or professional status. We thus show how agentic decisions taken in the field are underpinned by positionality and by structural relations of power. The specific configurations of these links have a range of implications for both the particular piece of research and the extent to which it meets its objectives and the role it plays in the construction of knowledge, and for the professional and personal lives of research participants (researchers and researched alike) with respect to the ways in which they are constrained, advanced or otherwise affected.

Both studies contribute to the process of gendering the understanding of the relationship between globalization, migration and domestic work. The qualitative research, on which this chapter is primarily based, investigated the micro enactments of – and responses to – processes occurring at macro or global scales. The UK study examined situations in which households buy in the labour of migrant handymen to undertake stereotypically male domestic tasks and illuminates men's positions on both sides of this relationship. The main objectives were to obtain new information on the determinants and characteristics of employment of migrant handymen in the UK, on how the use of their labour affects employing households' work, family and leisure practices, and on the work and family biographies of migrant handymen themselves. The focus was on men as care-providers, on men's paid and unpaid work in households, and on fathers, fatherhood and fathering practices. The two-part study adopted a mixed-methods approach analysing complementary data sources combining quantitative and qualitative methods. The first part comprised of secondary data analysis, which produced a picture of the scope, scale and character of household outsourcing of typically male domestic tasks and of migration to the UK (see Kilkey and Perrons, 2010). In the second stage, results from the quantitative study informed the design of the qualitative enquiry carried out between October 2008 and October 2009 mostly in and around London. A total of 79 in-depth interviews were conducted with four groups: both partners[1] in households with dependent children which buy-in handyman-type domestic services, migrant handymen, non-migrant handymen, and agencies that employ or service handymen.[2]

The USA study was designed to examine the experiences of Mexican immigrant men working in a gendered occupational niche, suburban maintenance gardening. Like the migrant handymen in the UK, these gardeners (or *jardineros*) undertake stereotypically male domestic tasks, such as mowing lawns, pruning trees, and generally looking after the upkeep of the exterior landscape of their clients' homes. The main objective was to describe the structure of the occupation, the significance of gendered migrant networks within it, and the extent to which self-employment in gardening has allowed some Mexican immigrant men to both provide for their families and experience upward socioeconomic mobility. The primary focus was on men's dual roles as manual labourers and small entrepreneurs, but this focus also shed light on the difficulties the men face in balancing their work and family lives. Though male immigrant labourers have been prevalent in this sector for many years, with Mexican workers establishing a strong position by the late 1970s, scant research had been devoted to this phenomenon. The study was conducted throughout Los Angeles.

Between June and September 2007, a total of 47 in-depth interviews were carried out with Mexican immigrant men who earn their livelihoods and support their families by performing maintenance gardening work on the properties of mostly white, American-born homeowners. This included two types of gardeners: waged employees (referred to by their Spanish-speaking employers as *ayudantes* or helpers), and self-employed, financially solvent owners of independent gardening routes.

Each study was collaborative, with all authors either co-sharing or assuming the lead responsibility for aspects of research, analysis and writing. Because in this chapter we draw on the conceptual notion of positionality, it is relevant to note that it has been co-authored by Ania (who conducted 58 of 79 interviews in the UK) and Hernán (who conducted all 47 interviews in the USA); but it benefits from contributions of the other team members – Majella, Diane and Pierrette. During research and analysis of the UK study, Ania had completed her Ph.D. and was combining two temporary part-time research and teaching contracts at the London School of Economics. She is Polish-born and speaks Polish fluently. During research and analysis of the USA study, Hernan was a Ph.D. candidate in sociology at the University of Southern California. He is USA-born of Mexican parentage and speaks fluent Spanish. Incidentally, we both have first hand experience with gendered processes of migration and domestic work in the contemporary globalized era – Ania has worked for several years as live-in nanny in Canada, while Hernan spent many weekends and summer holidays working with his gardener-father in Los Angeles. At the time of writing of this chapter, we are both in full-time career track academic posts.

In what follows, we take each study in turn, briefly describing research designs and processes of data collection and analysis, providing sketches of the participants, before discussing some of the epistemological and methodological issues that emerged during recruitment and encounters. The UK case is discussed more extensively as it was wider in scope and permits some comparative reflections. In this chapter we highlight the role of positionality and argue that the ways in which we – the researchers – managed it in the field is an important feature of the research process in its own right. But, we also draw attention to some of the challenges involved in linking micro level studies to broader gendered processes of globalization, migration, and social reproduction. The role of the institutional contexts shaping research practice in contemporary neoliberal university settings is further elaborated upon elsewhere (Plomien, 2013).

3.2   Research designs: Methods, data and participants

The research design for the second, qualitative part of the UK study was guided by a quantitative analysis which contributed to the estimation and description of the migrant handyman phenomenon (see Kilkey and Perrons, 2010; and Chapter 4). In accordance with ethical guidelines[3] we developed in-depth semi-structured interviews and conducted them face-to-face.[4] All individual interviews comprised of mostly open-ended questions about personal and family biography and about attitudes and practices around fatherhood, fathering and gender equality. Both partners in households were also interviewed about the use of handyman labour and outsourcing more broadly, and about attitudes and practices around typically male domestic work. Handymen were also asked about their trajectory into the occupation, work and working conditions, attitudes and practices around dealing with clients, and, in the case of migrant handymen, about motivations and experiences of migration. Interviews with agencies focused on sector-wide perspectives on supply and demand issues and on migration and migrant labour.

Interviews were carried out in either English or Polish, were digitally recorded, and all but two were transcribed *verbatim*.[5] The Polish-language interviews were translated fully into English. On average, individual interviews lasted approximately 1 hour and 15 minutes. Transcripts were analysed using grounded theory (Glaser and Strauss, 1997; Strauss and Corbin, 1994). Each project team member independently identified concepts and themes for half of all the transcripts for each group, which were then compared and discussed collectively.

Remaining transcripts were analysed in depth by just one person, but new concepts and themes as well as meanings and interpretations were discussed among the team and continued into the writing stages.

Engaging participants for the research, as described in the following section, proved more difficult than anticipated, particularly among households. A total of 90 interviews were planned, but in the end 79 were conducted. First, we interviewed 25 migrant handymen, of which two were asylum seekers without full entitlement to live and/or work in the UK. The remaining were from EU8[6] countries and were targeted as they had come to dominate migration flows to the UK in the period relating to the project. In our sample, 21 were Polish, while the others were nationals of Iran (2), Estonia and Hungary. Given our interest in the role of migration and working conditions in opportunities to fulfil social reproductive responsibilities, we sought to recruit men in a variety of family situations, and about half were fathers. Although the primary focus was on men working as handymen, one participant was female – part of a Polish husband and wife handyman team. As analysed in Chapter 4, and similarly to Mexican gardeners interviewed by Hernan, the migrant handymen in our study were socio-economically differentiated. A sizeable proportion (five out of 25) reported income in the top decile, while the majority's earnings were closer to the male median (£13.08 per hour in 2009, based on ONS, 2009). A number earned £7 to £8 per hour in line with the London living wage of £7.60 in 2009 (based on GLA, 2009), with those from outside EU8 countries earning significantly less.

Second, we interviewed five non-migrant handymen, all of whom were fathers. Their employment status and earnings were similarly differentiated; as in both groups of handymen we found self-employed entrepreneurs as well as employees, and income varied between £10 and £20 per hour. While the small sample size demands caution in drawing definitive conclusions, it appears that the British handymen charged a somewhat higher rate for similar services than their migrant counterparts. Both groups of handymen were compensated for their time with a £20 cash payment.

Our third research group comprises of companies in the handyman sector. We carried out four interviews with spokespersons of this diverse category: one was a British male owner of a handyman franchise business; the second was a migrant female co-owner of a web portal through which EU8-handymen advertised their services; the third was a migrant female entrepreneur providing a range of business services to self-employed EU8-migrants, including handymen; and the final was a Polish female office employee of a British-owned residential letting agency which employed handymen.

The final group comprised of households with dependent children and a resident father that repeatedly use the labour of handymen. We carried out interviews in 24 households, seeking to speak separately with fathers and mothers. We interviewed 45 individuals: 21 co-residing partnered couples, in two household fathers refused to participate (stating time pressures and lack of interest as reasons) and one case involved a non-partnered gay father. Dual-income earners comprised the majority, with men employed full time and women either full or part time. In some instances women were on maternity leave, while several had withdrawn from the labour market to raise children. Our householders tended to be higher income earners – a large proportion of the combined net monthly income of both partners fell in the range of £5000 to £6000, with half in excess of £7000, both groups corresponding to the top quintile of disposable household income (based on ONS, 2011b). At the lower end of the scale the range started at £2000 (only one case in our study) and at the top extended to over £16,000 (this was certain in two cases and plausible in further four instances as our income scale ended at £10,000 or more per parent and exact figure was not obtained above this level).

The USA study employed a qualitative approach centred on in-depth interviews conducted face-to-face. Despite a plethora of literature on Mexican labourers in the USA, very little has been written about Mexican gardeners. A qualitative approach enabled the collection of rich data on this enduring, yet understudied, gendered occupational niche. In addition to demographic profile data on age, marital status, income, place of origin, legal status, and number of years living in the USA, we constructed a semi-structured interview guide with primarily open-ended questions about gardeners' migration and employment histories, occupational experiences (e.g. job entry, duties, wages, income and expenses, relations with clients and co-workers), and other themes related to working conditions, such as workplace safety and injuries. Standard Institutional Review Board (IRB)[7] protocols were followed and participants received a small gift (a box of chocolates) as a token of appreciation.

The interviews lasted between one and a half and two hours, were recorded using a digital audio recorder, and were transcribed verbatim. We read through each transcript and coded it into themes for analysis, translating into English only those portions of the interviews that we considered to be germane to our central themes. The extended case method (Burawoy, 1998) guided our analysis in light of existing theories of immigrant entrepreneurship, gender, and the informal sector, while grounded theory (Strauss and Corbin, 1994) directed us in coding, organizing and analysing the data.

We set out to conduct 50 interviews during the summer of 2007. Ultimately, after some last-minute cancellations by gardeners with exceedingly busy work schedules, our sample consisted of 47 interviewees. This included men who worked for other gardeners as paid employees (nine), self-employed 'route-owner' gardeners (36), and a few state-licensed landscaping contractors who also maintained gardening routes on the side. The small number of paid employees in our sample was a result of our effort to focus on the route-owner gardeners, a focus necessitated by the dearth of qualitative data on self-employed Mexican immigrants in the US. We consciously restricted our sample to Mexicans because they now prevail in this occupation, and the majority of the studies' participants (40 out of 47) were from the Mexican state of Zacatecas. We may have oversampled Zacatecanos, or it may be that their social networks allowed them to get a toehold into gardening in Los Angeles. Numerically, there are more people from the states of Jalisco and Michoacan in Los Angeles, but Zacatecanos in the US disproportionately reside in Los Angeles (Quiñones, 2002).

The majority of the men were married (40 out of 47) with children and were their families' sole or primary breadwinner. The men's ages ranged from 20 to 63, most were legal permanent residents or naturalized US citizens (36 out of 47), although many had once been undocumented immigrant workers. Most had migrated to the USA for the first time in their teens or early twenties, and had spent the vast majority of their lives working as gardeners. The paid employees were younger, undocumented, and lived in rented apartments, while the route owners were older, legal permanent residents or naturalized citizens who lived in their own homes.

Like most Mexican immigrant workers in the USA, the majority of men in our study had primary school education or less – only thirteen had gone further than ninth grade. Most had grown up on *ranchos* in the Mexican countryside. Although precise information on income was difficult to obtain, it was clear that its range was vast. Paid employees made $20,000 to $25,000 a year, while many route owners cited incomes of $60,000 to $100,000. While the employees' wages were in line with the mean annual earnings of Mexican-born male wage workers aged 25 to 64 in the USA ($24,270), the route owners' earnings were considerably higher than those typically found among self-employed Mexican-born men in the USA ($33,667) (Valdez, 2008a: 173). The highest earning respondent, a landscaper with an eighth-grade education, claimed a gross annual income of $800,000 and his posh residence supported his account. The gardeners in our study were thus quite differentiated with respect to their socio-economic status.

3.3   Positionality in research recruitment and encounters

The issue of the positionality of the researchers relative to the researched has been subject of a considerable number of reflections (e.g. Arendell, 1997; Broom et al., 2009; Henry, 2003; Lee, 1997; Mazzei and O'Brien, 2009; Schwalbe and Wolkomir, 2001; Walby, 2010). In both our studies the relevant and intersecting dimensions of positionality were multiple and shifting, and included gender, class, age, ethnicity, occupation and migration status. Moreover, we experienced a dual positioning. Interacting with handymen, labour-using households, undocumented *ayudantes* and well-established owners of lucrative gardening routes, we felt that we variously belonged to higher or lower socio-economic groups, embodied a greater or lesser degree of expert knowledge, elicited various expressions of respect, and commanded different degrees of control, power and authority over the research encounter. Additionally, positionality emerged as relevant beyond the researcher-researched dyad. Our professional situations in terms of employment status and degree of experience – in our cases holding a temporary part-time research contract or being a Ph.D. candidate – had bearings on the research processes and outcomes, as well as potentially affecting our non-working lives and our longer-term career trajectories. In the following sections we bring these issues to light by reflecting on the way in which we engaged participants for our studies in the recruitment process and by discussing some experiences we had in our encounters with them.

3.3.1   Ania's account of recruitment for the UK study

Finding and engaging participants for the UK project required a wide range of strategies, which varied according to the study's stage as well as the target group. Both scientific rigour and pragmatism guided the process, and several interrelated methodological difficulties arose along the way. The main problem was that recruitment took much more time and effort than anticipated. A related challenge was the composition and size of the sample. While, by definition, representativeness in a limited scale qualitative study, such as this one, cannot be ensured, a key goal was to contribute to discussions about the relationship between gender, migration and domestic work in the UK and more broadly. It was important, then, that the participants matched our specific criteria and reflected the socio-economic groups and processes we aimed to say something about.

In engaging handymen, we started by snowballing from all three researchers' personal and professional networks and referrals. In addition, we used migrant organizations, adverts in print media and websites which offer or seek handyman services, and focused on venues patronized by migrants. In some cases interviews took place soon after establishing contact, in others, scheduling (and rescheduling) required much more time and effort, and many pre-arranged interviews never materialized. For handymen, most of whom were self-employed, work could be unpredictable and irregular and interviews were often postponed at short notice. Some could not be rearranged. The onset of the recession in the UK was an unexpected backdrop, as our target population diminished in size and became more transient – some potential interviewees had returned to their country of origin in the period between identification and contact; others had changed jobs; and a number had stopped communication altogether.

Towards reaching the quota for this group, a sample composition concern arose. The worry was the potential impact of my being Polish on skewing the sample towards Poles. Although having a Polish researcher on the project was not built into the design of the study, my nationality and language skills did facilitate recruitment. Often, communicating in the native language of participants' was the only option and references to shared experiences of migration or cultural contexts helped to establish rapport and trust. But, has the 'migrant handyman phenomenon' inadvertently been transformed into 'Polish migrant handyman phenomenon'? This is unlikely for two reasons. First, many steps were taken to minimize the bias by aiming recruitment strategies at a wide range of individuals, organizations and venues. In several instances I approached migrant handymen from other countries, but participation was refused on the grounds of lack of time or interest, misinterpreting the request, or insufficient compensation. Similarly, efforts to reach participants through non-Polish migrant organizations proved 'unproductive' – in one instance even after making arrangements for location, time, and translation, the limited capacity of the agency to follow through yielded no interviews. The second argument against the charge that the Polish-density of the sample was solely the result of my nationality is based on the earlier quantitative analysis (Kilkey and Perrons, 2010), which had revealed that a substantial proportion of migrant handymen in the UK are indeed Polish. As such, our qualitative findings add meaningful dimensions to the broader themes associated with the migrant handyman phenomenon.

In both groups of handymen there was an attempt to speak with matched providers and purchasers of services. This succeeded only in one instance involving a household and in two involving a lettings agency. Several householders offered to facilitate an introduction to their handymen, but failed either because they were no longer contactable or because the task proved too demanding for the busy parents in our study. Generally, the handymen interviewed were not keen to assist in contacting their employers, although in some instances they agreed to relay my request. A typical response was like this one from Daniel: 'I talked to people but somehow it is hard to convince families to agree ... this is a very difficult task, they'd rather avoid such initiatives ... I am sorry I cannot help in this matter.'

In one case I came close to an employee-employer match. Filip, a migrant handyman from Poland and father of a five-year-old boy, agreed to put me in touch with his boss. Filip works for a small company and provides handyman services for the owner in both business and household settings. In the latter, the handyman's tasks include driving his employer's children to sports training sessions or assembling their Christmas toys – activities that require time flexibility and sacrifice of his own fathering aspirations (see Chapter 5). I was keen to talk to Filip's employers particularly because their outsourcing of typically male domestic tasks appears to go beyond household and garden maintenance to include direct fathering activities. It was thus an analytically interesting case which parallels with research on global care chains with respect to migrant women and mothering. To my disappointment, after several phone conversations and email exchanges, Filip indirectly declined the request by stating: 'I tried to mention this to the boss, but he changed the subject so I don't think it would be easy for me to convince him. If anything happens I'll get back to you.' I did not hear from Filip on this issue again and during a project meeting we decided to abandon the pursuit. What we anticipated to be an interesting and useful interview reminded us of the tensions and ethical dilemmas between, on the one hand, instrumentality in meeting our research objectives, and, on the other, the limits imposed by participants' willingness and ability to collaborate.

Similarly, difficulties emerged in the process of recruiting householders. Here too a range of strategies were applied, including through schools, nurseries, parks, playgrounds, employers' intranet and newsletters, university alumni networks, community websites, parent/father/mother Internet forums, researchers' personal and professional networks and snowballing. The goal was to obtain 60 separate interviews with mothers and fathers from 30 households, but as fieldwork was taking much longer than anticipated, the team decided to stop at 24 incomplete households yielding 45 interviews. Who we did and did not manage to speak with has implications for our findings. One instance of a 'failure' in obtaining an interview is particularly telling, expressed by a member of our personal network and a friend of potential participants:

> She wouldn't have minded doing it, but she is convinced her husband would refuse ... he has a very senior job in a large multinational and works very long hours. One of the reasons they employ extra help is because he simply does not have the time to do those tasks himself, and he likes to have at least a bit of time to relax with his family. So ... he is highly unlikely to find the time to talk to you I'm afraid! ... She has noticed how her five year old son is very interested in what the male employees are doing ... he likes to help the gardener who finds him little jobs to do. He obviously identifies with these people and sees them as some kind of role model.
>
> Email communication, Anonymous

In this excerpt, at least three points are evident in relation to methodological and epistemological issues we encountered in recruitment. The first is the recurring problem of time scarcity. While there was much interest in the project, converting interest into participation was challenging. As the quote indicates, time pressures were acute and securing interviews from busy people proved to be more difficult than anticipated. The second point concerns sample composition. In the majority of cases mothers were the initial recruits to the research, and fathers' participation was negotiated subsequently. Usually we proceeded with interviews once we had agreed meetings with both partners. This, however, was not always possible. In those instances where there was a slight chance, even if uncertain, of speaking to both partners, we tended to pursue it – with various outcomes. For example, although the following email contact I had with Mary, a mother of two, did not hold much promise: 'sorry to be difficult happy to take part myself but George is so busy I can't bear asking him.' I still scheduled an interview with Mary who replied: 'next week around 6.30 pm at my house then, with me if that's still helpful – maybe George will be in too.' In the end I was able to speak with both parents during the same evening. On other occasions we were not as fortunate, and three of our parents are not matched with a counterpart. The third point emerging from the unsuccessful recruitment email cited earlier is another indication that outsourcing of stereotypically male tasks may go beyond domestic maintenance jobs to include activities involving children, that is, tasks akin to fathering. We do not have sufficient data to explore this dimension in our analysis, but this theme points to direction for future research.

A different aspect of the composition of the households we talked to was an assumption of heteronormativity. As our guiding motivation was to examine the way in which fathers negotiate the conflicting demands of paid employment and increasing expectation of active fathering, with a particular focus on how these demands are articulated within gender relations, we focused on households with a resident father and dependent children. All but one of our households were composed of a mother, father and dependent child(ren). A colleague facilitated an introduction to Hugh, a handyman-labour using father, and when I emailed him about our study, he replied:

'I'm very happy to take part – but I'm now not sure if I do satisfy the criteria: my kids are with me one or two nights a week only. I have though had a handyman round.' The discussion among the team, whether to pursue this interview or not, reflects our preoccupation with the study's focus:

I'd go for it – looks like a shared-parenting situation, and could throw up issues around time and household maintenance for such men, who perhaps have to do more 'fathering'; would also be interesting to see what else he outsources. Would we want to interview his former partner though?

Email communication

I interviewed Hugh and was able to talk to him about the relationship between migration, outsourcing of male domestic labour, and fathering; however, these linkages and their situatedness within gender relations were complicated by Hugh's parenting situation involving two gay (now separated) men and two lesbian women – a situation not built into our research design. This suggests yet another potential avenue for research, though reaching the 0.04 per cent of UK families with dependent children composed of same sex cohabiting couples (ONS, 2012b) may be difficult.

A final recruitment story highlights the need for researchers to be flexible, responsive, and in this instance even opportunistic in allowing for possible divergence from the research design by following contacts that potentially did not fit our criteria:

> With my income there is not much chance of outsourcing any-thing ... but if you need me as a 'control' case against the life led by all my mates who never seem to have lifted a hammer or mowed a lawn in their life.
>
> Email from James, HH

Here, we were motivated to talk to James by virtue of the possibility of contacting his friends who use handyman services, by an opportunity to visit an area in London in which many Polish migrants live, and indeed, because of the opportunities it afforded for understanding why some middle class families with dependent children do not hire handymen. I thus devised new questions for a mother and father in a non-outsourcing situation. To my surprise, this was a household with three young children that did outsource male domestic tasks on which James was both knowledgeable and reflexive, and, ironically, snowball-ing did not lead to any further interviews.

To round out discussion of the difficulties associated with securing participation in the study I recall here an email written to the other members of the team after considerable recruitment effort:

> Today I went to Hampstead to distribute leaflets – I was semi-successful with 5 schools: they will post them on notice boards, dis-tribute to parents, and ask the Head teacher to see if this is OK – this was about 60 leaflets. One school will do a holiday club and I will send them electronic copies for parents. Others either did not want to agree to any of this, or already broke for summer holidays. I also went to parks and asked people on the streets ('hunting' for those with children) – given out 15 leaflets to moms, three to nannies, and a further few for people to give to co-workers or neighbours. I came across an English painter and gave him leaflets for handy-men; asked two guys walking with a drill to take and pass leaflets to friends – they had an accent but I am not sure from where. I also approached a couple of gardeners, but they were English and said they could not help out. I hope something will come out of this. Next week my family is in London (with my two nieces age five and seven) and I will take leaflets with me on our kid-friendly adventures.
>
> Email communication

This recruitment fieldtrip was one of several conducted in affluent residential areas in London. Not one yielded an interview. And, as I happily recall, I did not end up recruiting while swinging off monkey bars in parks or visiting dinosaurs in the museum with my nieces. But, save for two themes – non-heterosexual parenting and male domestic labour spilling over into fathering – additional interviews no longer offered new information. We achieved a volume of interviews which took us to the point of theoretical saturation (Glaser and Strauss, 1967) with a reasonable degree of validity – an outcome that allows for linking micro and macro level processes. Still, to reach the number of interviews we have required great time flexibility. It seems ironic that a project generating data about time pressures of contemporary UK households and the migrant workers who help relieve them depended on researchers working unsocial hours (evenings and weekends) with reduced 'time sovereignty' (Reisch, 2001) – a theme we discuss in the following section on encounters. First though, we turn to recruitment of migrant Mexican gardeners.

3.3.2   Hernan's account of recruitment for the USA study

The USA study relied on the snowball sampling technique, common in research where economic informality and diverse immigrant legal statuses prevail (Hondagneu-Sotelo, 2001; Menjívar, 2000; Zlolniski, 2006). The initial participants were found through several different snowballs, beginning with family members, personal acquaintances, and university colleagues with ties to Mexican hometown associations. The fact that I was a Spanish-speaking son of a Mexican immigrant gardening route-owner with over 30 years of experience proved to be very helpful. A few of the initial interviewees were acquaintances of my father who readily agreed to participate. Others were members of a Zacatecan hometown association referred to me by graduate students with family connections to Mexican immigrant gardeners. From the initial contacts a purposive sample was built. Snowballing subsequently continued, with interview participants asked to name someone who worked in maintenance gardening and may be interested in participating in our study at the conclusion of each interview.

After gathering the men's contact information, I would telephone them, briefly describe the study and ask if they would be interested in participating or if they would like to take some time to consider. Cognizant of the men's heavy workloads and irregular schedules, I would express readiness to work around the gardeners' schedules and to meet with them at a time and location of their choosing. Overall, I was pleased by the men's willingness to participate, both during the initial weeks of research and as the snowball sample grew in size. A few of the gardeners I contacted refused to participate altogether, citing their busy work schedules. Nevertheless, many of my interviewees were able to refer me to relatives and friends who worked as *jardineros* and who were also interested in participating.

It is certainly possible that the men felt more inclined to participate because I described my personal connection to and general familiarity with the maintenance gardening occupation during these initial phone calls. Specifically, I would mention the fact that my own father was a *jardinero*, and that I had spent many weekends and summer vacations going to work with him when I was growing up. Instead of simply identifying myself as an academic, I was thus able to use my intimate familiarity with the *jardineros'* everyday milieu as a 'selling point'. I also tried an alternative recruitment strategy by distributing a subject recruitment form at a local lawnmower repair shop that was frequented by Mexican immigrant gardeners. This strategy yielded no interviewees; a reminder not only of the power of social capital and trust among gardeners who are friends and family, but of the importance of personal contact and *franqueza* (or 'candid, frank speech') among *ranchero* immigrant men (Farr, 2006).

The recruitment of Latino immigrants into research projects may be fraught with challenges such as language barriers and unique cultural experiences (Domenech-Rodríguez et al., 2006). In this respect, my ethnic background, bilingualism, and first-hand knowledge of gardening and of Mexican culture were clearly advantageous, both during the recruitment phase and during the research encounter. Researchers have noted that some Latino immigrants perceive university researchers as having ties with the government, and this perception may prevent them from engagement (Ojeda et al., 2011: 189). Unfamiliarity with the research process or fears that information they provide for a study will be reported to 'immigration' may contribute to Latino immigrants' consideration of participating in research (ibid.). Following standard protocol, I included a Spanish-language information sheet that fully disclosed the nature and purpose of the study, how the data would be used, and the rights of research participants. I would carefully explain the information contained on these informed consent sheets before each interview. However, when visiting with the *ayudantes* – the paid employees who were likely to fall within the vulnerable population of 'illegal aliens' – I would go a step further by reassuring them that I was in no way affiliated with *la migra* and that the information they would provide would remain anonymous and not be shared with authorities who could deport them.

Although I was able to recruit participants relatively quickly, it was often difficult to arrange interviews due to their busy and somewhat unpredictable work schedules. This was exacerbated by the fact that the interviews were taking place during the summer months, which can be some of the busiest for the gardeners. As discussed further in Chapter 6, the nature of the job is such that gardeners routinely work six, or even seven, days a week under the hot Southern Californian sun. In many cases, only rainy days offer gardeners respite. Alas, rainy days are few and far between in Los Angeles, and are virtually unheard of during the summer months. Consequently, it was often difficult for them to predict when they would have time to sit for an interview. Some men would tentatively pick a date and time for the interview but would call back at the last minute and apologetically ask to reschedule, citing an unforeseen change in their work obligations. A few initially agreed to participate but ended up cancelling their interviews, citing their busy work schedules. These experiences, though frustrating in the context of the research process, offered me tremendous insight not only into the sheer amount of hours the men worked but also into the challenges they faced in balancing their work and family lives – a theme I continue in section 3.3.4 on research encounters.

3.3.3   Ania's reflections on encounters in the UK study

In the UK study, interview venues included community centres, cafes, pubs, researchers' and participants' workplaces and homes. To secure participation I always stressed readiness to meet at a time and place convenient for the respondent, but tended to suggest meeting handymen in public and labour-using households in their homes. My differing approach resulted on the one hand, from negotiating the tension between concern for personal safety as a female researcher conducting interviews alone and often at night (interviews frequently ran later than 10.30 pm) in unfamiliar parts of London and its suburbs, and on the other hand, the commitment to reach the sample target by minimising the cost of participation for interviewees. The rationale for interviewing handymen in public places was also based on the fact that I knew very little about them prior to the interview. I was less apprehensive when meeting people who hire their services because the information gained about them, such as presence of dependent children, known fixed address, or referrals, put me over the subjective threshold of feeling unsafe.

I also took other considerations into account. The general knowledge that many recent migrants live in temporary or shared accommodation was one, and the fact that our budget allocated £10 per interview in expenses made it possible to meet in cafés or pubs and buy the participant a drink, was another. I recall only one instance where I lost contact with a handyman after specifically requesting meeting in public. Household interviews could not be easily arranged outside the home – this occurred only in a handful of cases. The time required was greater, as we asked to speak to both partners individually and a minimum two hour slot was, in practice, more like a three or even four hour commitment on their part. Furthermore, as the majority of householders in our study were in employment, we tended to meet after work or on weekends which meant that interviews had to be fitted around busy family life routines involving meals, bath time, or putting children to bed. Juggling time and childcare (being there) was a recurring backdrop to my visits. In one instance I was conducting an interview while a mother was cooking supper, tidying up, and upon realising she ran out of nappies we continued the conversation in her car and in a nearby convenience store with the digital recorder fixed to her belt. For many of our participants meeting outside of the home was thus not a feasible option.

This is not to say that my tactics always worked as planned, or when they did they were not in themselves disconcerting. For instance, one afternoon I met Jakub, a Polish handyman, in a shopping mall café on the outskirts of London. This was to be followed by an evening interview with another participant in a pub a few miles away. I had used public transportation throughout the research, and as usual, gave myself what I thought was sufficient time to conduct the first interview and move locations to arrive at the second. However, Jakub turned up very late and the interview took longer than average to get started and then to carry out. The delay entailed a risk of loosing my second interview. Jakub offered to give me a lift in his van, which happened to be on his route home. Given the added difficulty of London transport engineering works taking place and slower replacement buses operating instead, with conflicting sentiments I accepted his offer and made it to the second interview safe and on time.

Recalling this incident at a team meeting my colleagues expressed concern, asking why I had not taken a taxi, and advising me not to accept rides from strangers. I agreed (and still do) with their stance, but following through on that agreement proved tricky. Several weeks later I scheduled an interview with another Polish handyman, Daniel, and agreed to meet him at a suburban train station on a Sunday, his day off, in a neighbourhood where he lives and works. I followed my usual strategy of researching the unfamiliar area on the Internet and planned to conduct the interview in a nearby café. As always, I gave myself an extra half hour before the interview to check the surroundings and potential venues. Upon arrival, this being a Sunday and the station serving commuters to London, I found the café closed and no other suitable setting in sight – only parklands, tree-lined streets, and residential properties. When Daniel arrived in his van he suggested driving to a supermarket café – the only place open within a few mile radius – to which I agreed. A final example of diverting from my usual practice is an interview with Wiktor. We coordinated to meet at the underground station near his home on a weekday afternoon. Upon arrival before the meeting, I inspected the area to find only a couple of public venues, which were loud, squalid, smelt of alcohol and therefore not ideal for an interview. When we met, Wiktor proposed that we talk at his home, which turned out to be next to the pub I had resigned myself to just a few minutes earlier. We considered the pub, but Wiktor pointed out the noise and I thought about his willingness to talk candidly in a place in which he seemed to be a regular. We decided to proceed to his house.

As I cringe recounting these actions, I must stress that I did not approach them in a cavalier manner. One problem with keeping the promise to my colleagues (and myself) is that making decisions on the spot is not the same as analysing the process in retrospect. Another is that of cultural affinity and trust – by refusing a ride or an invitation to the handyman's home I was not only risking not being able to conduct these interviews, but also was displaying mistrust to Polish migrant men who gave up their time to participate in our research. This point is particularly significant as I had accepted station pick-ups and drop-offs from the women and men in our households and had visited their homes with much less anxiety. So, my politics of gender and my politics of class did not align here so neatly. Finally, as a researcher on 'someone else's' project, my sense of autonomy to make decisions that may jeopardize the timely completion of the study was also a factor. What these instances of not following the protocol show is how difficult it can be to interpret specific micro level interpersonal situations through the lens of general macro level relations based on unequal, gendered distribution of power. That said, safety concerns over (female) researchers should not be minimized and being caught in a predicament between 'overreaction' and 'lack of precaution' (see Lee, 1997) requires more assertive individual solutions as well as stronger institutional level support.[8]

Methodological discussions of the role of gender in qualitative research highlight the ways in which gender identity is displayed and accomplished (West and Zimmerman, 1987), especially when women interview men. Research participants portray themselves as masculine by being 'competent, assertive, controlling, and rational' (Arendell, 1997: 347); by emphasizing heterosexuality, power, and knowledge (Pini, 2005); or by taking control of the interview process in a manner that can affect the perceived or real safety of female interviewers (Lee, 1997). Gender identity work is also performed by researchers who either minimize or mobilize its various aspects (see Lee, 1997; Pini, 2005). But, meanings emanating from interview encounters cannot be fully anticipated as the identities of researchers and respondents emerge from the encounter itself (Walby, 2010), and theorising power as resting either with one or the other is not possible (Grenz, 2005). The field work experiences with Jakub, Daniel, and Wiktor serve to illustrate how the dynamics of power, control, and vulnerability shift throughout the research encounter and are not consistently paired with or determined by macro level social positions or micro level characteristics.

Consider the interview with Jakub, who within a few minutes of our meeting made several racist and sexist 'jokes' which I found intolerable and, on personal level, wanted to challenge. Professionally, though, I sought to facilitate an open discussion and re-directed the conversation towards more neutral topics instead. His offensive and assertive remarks were followed by a confident account of his professional past:

> I did lots of things ... for people who hold prominent positions, famous TV stars and others ... at the end of the 90s I was set up well: I had my own house, business. Everything prospered beautifully. I earned so much money in Poland that I can only dream about earning so much money here. That much money is hardly possible to earn over here ... I had good money. I was Mr Businessman.
>
> Jakub, HM

At one point, Jakub called me 'Miss Single', which I found provocative, given that I had not disclosed my marital status, and somewhat nervously laughed it off. On first reading, Jakub's success contrasted with my temporary, part-time research position, as well as his vocal, confident manner of expression as opposed to my listening, passive, neutralising response – could be interpreted as enactments of stereotypically masculine and feminine behaviour and uneven power relations. But, Jakub's story and our interaction were more complex. As a new migrant to the UK (since 2007) and following a one-year unskilled job contract, his personal and occupational experiences turned out to be more precarious:

> I tried to work for different companies ... unfortunately I was made to understand that I'm too old ... that there are younger and quicker. Of course, there are younger and quicker. I'm 49 years old ... I nearly had, maybe not a nervous break down, but I didn't feel well. I put on a brave front ... and, honestly, I need to say that the woman I'm with now gave me a lot of support ... I could feel safe that we'll have enough money for bread ... it lasted for months. I had some jobs from time to time. I earned about £1000 a month.
>
> Jakub, HM

This insecurity stands out against my opportunities as an early career scholar based at a prestigious academic institution and receiving expressions of respect for my academic achievements from many of the handymen I interviewed. Additionally, my listening mode and facilitation of Jakub's narrative was not in the context of conversation between two private individuals. Instead, I was acting and making decisions primarily as researcher. As such, I was destabilising the stereotypical gender roles and power relations (see Grenz, 2005). Our interaction, and with it the experience of power, shifted from that of two strangers engaging in a brief ice-breaker conversation (if based on diametrically opposite politics), to a script defining the researcher-researched role, to a chivalrous gesture of compatriot 'gentleman' giving a ride to 'damsel in distress', and finally to the post-interview stage which placed me in position of potential betrayal. Betrayal can manifest itself in a number of ways, for example in biased analysis or dishonest presentation. It can also be more direct and personal. Several weeks after the interview with Jakub I received a phone call from a woman who introduced herself as his partner and expressed concern over his honesty. She asked me to confirm his participation in the interview to verify his account of his whereabouts. Because of the commitment to anonymity I was unable do so; but, I could validate that, indeed, an interview took place at given time and location, which perhaps provided substantiation to his account.

My interactions with Wiktor and Daniel were similarly contradictory, and what could be interpreted as loosing control over the research process had differential impact on my perception of safety, comfort, and interview quality. For example, interviewing Wiktor at his home was unsettling and I could not form a congruent picture of his situation. He lived in rented accommodation in a small terraced house. Entering immediately from the area's high street, in what should have been the front (sitting) room I noticed a large unmade bed, there were nails and a broken lock scattered on the floor, and when I was asked to sit in the intermediate room (just before the kitchen located at the back of the house) space had to be cleared from a small settee covered with clothes, food and boxes with prescription medicines. It was difficult to decide where to place the recorder, and I had to shift it throughout the interview as Wiktor was moving about the room. At the beginning Wiktor introduced me to his British wife, which made me feel more secure to have someone, another woman, sitting in the garden; but, when she asked me to translate something to him from a letter written in English into Polish, I found it confusing – she did not speak Polish and his English turned out to be poor, which did not seem to add up. Other pieces of information complicated the picture further. Wiktor talked about making 50 litres of wine a month, about his daughter in Poland being raised by his ex-mother in law, and about involvement of Polish child services via the consulate in London to obtain outstanding child support payments. In my field notes I wrote:

> I was very conscious around 'fathering questions' – tried to achieve balance between sensitivity and probing. I was careful not to make the participant feel 'guilty' about these issues. I also felt uncomfortable in the interview – the kind of topics discussed, showing me letters from the consulate or welfare offices, not getting straight answers to questions, asking me to help with Construction Industry Scheme[9] offices, all that talk about him establishing a Foundation (not sure what that is all about), comments that people with children have it better in the UK because of the benefits they receive seen as extra income – all this affected the quality of my questions, I wanted to finish this interview quickly and leave as soon as possible.
>
> Field notes

Wiktor was not necessarily asserting power and control over the situation, and in soliciting my assistance in interpreting documents or contacting various offices he deferred to me as better educated and able to navigate the intricacies of the English welfare and business systems. But, I did not feel sufficiently in command of the situation and had this interview been conducted in a more neutral setting, it would probably have solicited different, potentially better information.

In contrast, the encounter with Daniel and the informal chat in his van before and after the interview led to a richer picture than following the script alone. With a sense of pride, he drove me around a gated community and pointed to a number of large family houses with well-kept gardens belonging to his clients, he talked about his aspirations of reaching this level of affluence himself at some point, and he was generally more relaxed and forthcoming than on tape. Our informal conversation also allowed me to note discrepancies:

> In the interview Daniel was quite certain that it is men who are in charge of managing handyman work and that he mostly deals with men, but when we talked in the car about clients, he would always refer to them as 'she' – it was obvious he often deals with women.
>
> Field notes

In this case, then, relinquishing command over some aspects of the research process had quite a different impact on my perception of safety, level of comfort, and the quality of the interview. The perception of risk and safety is not the only challenge in qualitative research, as accounts on same-gender interviews in the USA study reveal.

3.3.4   Hernan's reflections on encounters in the USA study

I used ice-breaking strategies at the start of my encounters with immigrant Mexican gardeners. I would repeat that my father was a *jardinero* and show a copy of a 2007 USC College Newsletter that featured a picture of my father and I on the cover. A few of the men even said that they recognized my father, having seen him around the nurseries and lawnmower shops frequented by gardeners. Another visual aide was a copy of *Green Makers* (Hirahara, 2000) containing photographs of Japanese American gardeners from the 1920s through the 1990s. I would show the photographs to the men, who would find them fascinating, and explain that I would like to someday write a book about Mexican immigrant gardeners.

Even though most of the older men in my sample spoke English fairly well, their preferred language was Spanish and it was easy for me to converse with them in a relaxed manner. I could understand their colloquialisms, jokes and random asides that might have gone over the head of someone who was not familiar with *ranchero* Mexican culture. Moreover, as the son of a *jardinero*, I was able to establish rapport with the men relatively quickly. For one thing, I was familiar with their argot. For example, when investigating their income, I would ask the men

'*Cuanto trae de ruta ahorita?*' or 'How much of a route do you have right now?' which is the typical way that *jardineros* refer to the value of their gardening routes. I was also able to show that I could relate to what they were telling me, either by referring to my personal experiences or to those of my father. For example, when men would describe coming home with wet feet and sore knees after the end of a long workday, I would say, 'Yes, I know what you mean. My dad comes home like that all the time.'

Then again, I was not a Mexican immigrant but rather a US-born and raised Mexican-American, or a *pocho*. Though some of the *jardineros* would actually compliment me on my Spanish, saying that they could not tell whether I had been raised in the USA or in Mexico, I would often find myself taking a bit longer to think of a probing question in English and then ask it in Spanish. Also, despite my familiarity with the world of suburban maintenance gardening, I had to be careful not to take things for granted. I had to check my preconceptions at the door and listen carefully to what their work lives were like, because I realized that not everyone had gone through the same experiences that my dad had. For instance, I knew very little about what things were like for undocumented gardening route-owners. Listening to them describe how they drove especially carefully in order to avoid being pulled over by the police and having their trucks impounded was eye-opening.

Interviews with the Mexican immigrant gardeners took place in their homes, which included modest bungalows in working class neighbourhoods such as Inglewood and South Los Angeles, hot, cramped apartments in central Los Angeles, and sprawling, ranch-style homes in the San Fernando Valley. Often, Latino immigrants indicate preference for being interviewed in their home or in locations they are familiar with in their community (Skaff et al., 2002). This was very beneficial to our project because it allowed me to get a sense of the socio-economic differentiation between the least experienced *ayudantes* and the most prosperous gardening route-owners. While the former lived in sparse apartments, which they typically shared with other single, undocumented men, the latter lived in well-tended single-family residences, usually with a family vehicle and one or more work trucks in the driveway. Moreover, it offered me a glimpse into the men's family lives, as they were greeted by their wives or children or prepared for family outings.

The self-employed men were generally very proud of their accomplishments as independent gardeners, and their homes served as physical manifestations of their realization of the so-called 'American Dream'. Upon arriving at each *jardinero's* place of residence, I would take note of the outward appearance of their homes, and of the number of pick-up trucks and family vehicles in their driveways. A few of the men gave me informal tours of their homes, highlighting special features such as custom-designed backyard barbecues or decorative hardscaping and small fountains which they had installed. One *jardinero* had just moved into his ranch-style home in the San Fernando Valley when I visited him, and was relying on the skills he learned as an employee at a large landscaping company to design and install his own sprinkler (irrigation) system. As I looked around the men's yards, I was often reminded of my own father and the improvements he had made to our family home, many of which involved the use of surplus plant material from large landscaping jobs on wealthier clients' properties. Then again, the *jardineros'* own gardens were not always well maintained. Some of the men's homes were surrounded by lush vegetation and colourful flower-beds, but most were rather sparse and not particularly attractive. In the words of one *jardinero*, this could be explained by the Spanish proverb, *'En casa de herrero, cuchillo de palo,'* which conveys the same message as the English saying, 'the shoemaker's children always go barefoot'.

Importantly, interviewing the men in their homes provided me with a glimpse not only of the material trappings of their success as small entrepreneurs, but of the symbols of their children's success in the USA: living room walls lined with high school or college graduation portraits; framed diplomas, prominently displayed; and all manner of special achievement awards, from sports trophies to first-place ribbons in arts competitions. The men would often point out their children's academic accomplishments during the course of our interviews, both figuratively and literally, as they would point to their graduation portraits and describe their current occupations. They symbolized an important part of the men's personal narratives, as they described having migrated to the USA and having worked hard at a dirty, tedious job, to see their children do well and have an opportunity to thrive.

This is in sharp contrast to Ania's experiences as a female researcher, and while we think that gender is salient in qualitative research, we also suggest that gender alone does not shape it (see also Riessman's 1991 account of woman-to-woman interviews in Anglo-Hispanic encounters). Instead gender matters in interaction with other features of positionality and the wider context. In my case, being male, having personal connections, some first-hand experience of *jardinero* way of life, shared Mexican culture and heritage, or even driving to interviews, all combined to shore up my confidence in visiting the men in their homes. Safety concerns did not come up as an issue, although I sometimes had to visit respondents in 'run-down' and unfamiliar neighbourhoods, particularly the young, undocumented workers. I simply remained alert and went about my business.

On time and intrusion, however, our encounters resonate more strongly. While I sometimes worried about staying too late in the evenings in the men's homes, it had more to do with not wanting to be rude, inconsiderate or to interfere with their daily routines than it did with my safety. Because gardeners work long hours and six days a week, the interviews took place during the evenings and on Sundays. During the summer months, with extended daylight hours, many of the men did not return home until 6.00 or 7.00 pm. At the time of the interviews, they were tired and some were still dressed in their work clothes. Gardeners' jobs keep them so busy that the time they are able to spend with their families is often very limited. This is especially true among younger, less well-established gardening route-owners, whose clients may expect to see them personally tending their gardens instead of sending helpers to do the work. The autonomy and personal schedule flexibility that comes with being self-employed is one of the route owners' favourite aspects of the job. Nevertheless, men who are able to take a midday break or to cut their workday short in order to attend a child's school-sponsored recital or sporting event tend to be located at the upper end of the socio-economic spectrum.

Regardless of the men's age or level of experience, I often found myself worrying that I was intruding upon their precious family time. Because Sundays were often their only full days off work, many chose to schedule their interviews on those days. But because they were used to spending their Sundays with their families, it was important for me to monitor the duration of the interviews and avoid digressions. During a recruitment phone call, one gardener specifically mentioned that he could meet for an interview on a Sunday, but only after having breakfast and going to Mass with his family. Another agreed to be interviewed on a Sunday morning, but during the interview it became apparent that his children were anxiously waiting for him to finish so that they could go on a family outing. At one point, his young son interrupted the interview, tugging on his father's sleeve, and the gardener reassured him, '*Sí, mijo. Ahorita voy*' ('Yes, son. I'm coming'). My transcripts and research memos provide a record of my reactions to such events. In this case, I noted:

I've skipped over some questions in the interview, because I can sense that his children have been waiting for him to finish. Their patience seems to be wearing thin, based on his son's interruptions

and the expression on his daughter's face. I can see her through a
sliding glass door, sitting in the family room, none too pleased with
her father's Sunday morning visitor.

Field notes on Victor

Similarly, during the middle of another Sunday interview, a gardener's
son-in-law and young grandson unexpectedly stopped by for a visit.
Before long, the boy was also pulling on his grandfather's sleeve. No
stranger to dealing with children, the veteran gardener diplomatically
replied:

'Can I have a minute? I need a minute. I'll talk to you in a little bit.
Okay, three minutes. Give me three minutes'. The child whines.
'Hey, I'm busy right now. I need four more minutes, okay? Okay,
thank you'.

Teodoro

After another interruption by his restless grandson, and after having
generously answered questions and discussed his work experiences for
more than two and a half hours, the *jardinero* jokingly asked, '*A ver.
Qué más?*' ('Let's see. What else?'). Fortunately, the interview had come
to a close by that point. Nevertheless, this experience underscored the
importance of asking probing questions judiciously and monitoring
the pace of the interview in order to collect the required data without
taking more time than necessary from the men. This particular *jardinero*
was outgoing and had shared stories about his early days as a travelling
musician, which, though fascinating, strayed from the main themes
of the interview. Because I was a graduate student and was relatively
inexperienced as an interviewer, this came as an important lesson.
But, on reflection, concern for the participants' time is not only a kind
and thoughtful gesture; analysed critically and with reference to the
structural constraints of our encounters, my motives to be 'judicious'
and 'collect the necessary data' also conjure themes of efficiency, productivity, and instrumentality. My decisions on how to deal with scarce
time resources (mine and the participants') are potentially in tension
with research ethics' notions of reciprocity, collaboration, and non-
exploitation – in this case, allowing *jardineros* to tell their stories in a
manner that is satisfactory to them despite these falling outside the
remit of our project.

Time is thus a key and recurrent theme. Interviews that were conducted during the week often took place immediately after the men

had returned home from work, exhausted and dirty. The length of gardeners' workdays can be unpredictable, as can the traffic conditions they face during their long commutes back home from the city's more affluent suburbs. As the son of a working class, self-employed *jardinero*, I knew full well what it was like to have my father return home much later than anticipated, tired, hungry, and eager to rest. Consequently, I knew that a willingness to wait patiently for the men was essential, even if things fell behind schedule. For instance, one gardener said he was eager to participate in the study, but was forced to postpone his interview due to his busy work schedule. Ultimately, the interview was rescheduled for 6.30 pm on a Monday night, at the gardener's home in the working class neighbourhood of South Los Angeles. However, the interview did not start until 8.00 pm. As I noted:

[Jesus] called me on my cell phone around 7.30 pm, apologized, and explained why he was running late: he still had to finish cleaning a client's yard and then he had to go drop off his helper in Inglewood. ... He got home rather late – just before 8 o'clock – straight from work, in his beat-up Ford pickup truck, along with his son, who appeared to be around 13 or 14 years old. He was in his dirty, sweat-stained work clothes. His wife and teenage daughter were there to greet him with a kiss.

Elsewhere in my notes, I reflected upon this experience:

I remember being really disappointed when Jesus postponed the interview. But then I told myself 'Wait a minute. Stop and think about how hard this man works'. I felt a little embarrassed about having gotten upset about this. I'm over here scheduling interviews over the phone, and he's working his butt off, getting home at sundown, and still taking the time to grant me an interview. These feelings were all confirmed when I actually got to meet Jesus and interview him in his home. He was very friendly and informative.

Field notes on Jesus

Dealing with the issue of time takes on another dimension in research with Mexican immigrants and requires particular cultural competency with respect to *plática*, an informal post-interview, which if not engaged in can be regarded as awkward or even rude (Ojeda et al., 2011). My familiarity with Mexican customs meant that after completing the interview and shutting off my audio recorder, I would often 'stick around' and engage in *plática*, which would sometimes be the source of additional relevant information regarding the men, their work, or their families that I would proceed to record in my field notes. This parallels some of Ania's off the record encounters, albeit without the layer of anxiety associated with risk and safety.

3.4   Conclusion

In this chapter, we outlined some methodological and epistemological aspects of the two studies which contribute to the process of gendering the understanding of the relationship between globalization, migration and domestic work. Through reflecting on research conducted with migrant handymen and households with dependent children who buy their services in the UK and with immigrant Mexican gardeners in the USA, we drew attention to a number of challenges. Among them, we highlighted the role of positionality and the ways in which we managed it in the research field, with particular reference to recruitment and encounters.

With respect to recruitment, what can we conclude about the reasons why, in contrast to the USA study, it was so difficult to engage participants for the UK project? Two possible explanations might be given. First, our study, though by no means the first qualitative research on gender, migration, and domestic work, differs from previous studies, which focus on stereotypically female domestic work through interviews with female migrant workers. It differs by focusing on outsourcing stereotypically *male* domestic tasks and by seeking interviews with *men* – both with handyman service providers and users. Are such male services, providers and users so uncommon as to make the research trivial and participants difficult to find? This seems an unlikely explanation as the quantitative analysis in the first part of our study has shown that: (a) when care is excluded, equal proportions of households report outsourcing stereotypically male and female domestic jobs; and (b) significant proportion of the domestic sector workforce in the UK is male. Indeed, this was reflected in the fact that obtaining interviews with handymen in the UK, while challenging, was ultimately successful. But it was speaking to both mothers *and* fathers in households with dependent children that proved more difficult. Here we meet the second possible explanation for our difficulty in the UK. The households' busy work and family lives provided a major obstacle as participation in qualitative research, invariably entails disruption to working or personal lives (Clark, 2010). But, is lack of time a sufficient reason? If it were, similar difficulties would be expected in interviewing the *jardineros* and handymen, but they were, for the most part, very generous with their time and willingness to help. Furthermore, busy lives are an issue for both mothers and fathers in the demographic group our study focused on, yet mothers tended to be the initial recruit and often the route to negotiating fathers' participation. The reasons why potential respondents, particularly fathers, chose not to engage are difficult to gauge. And while, as we argue in Chapter 5, the new father time-bind is a key issue for our male, middle class, professional householders, we note that time, like other resources, is used with some discretion, and people make decisions from their respective positions within the hierarchy of power and privilege. Lack of (individual or collective) motivation to participate in a study on male domestic work among middle class professional men, and how it is underpinned by their higher status position vis-à-vis the researcher, domestic workers, and their partners, is a plausible explanation.

In terms of encounters, our reflections confirm that qualitative research is an interactional process with variable risk to benefit ratio and changing statuses and power dynamics. The risk is especially evident in cross-gender interviews, and there are more and less problematic ways of managing it. But our experiences also point to tensions – what is sometimes interpreted as risky can lead to opportunities integral to the success of the project, be it by gaining access to a wider range of participants or obtaining a more textured and complex picture of their views, practices, and lives. As we have experienced, real and perceived differences in power and status between interviewers and interviewees, and the dilemmas emanating from them, are neither one-sided nor straightforward. Addressing the tensions between personal risk and successful completion of research certainly requires individual level awareness and strategies, and some judgment calls taken in the research field cannot be abrogated to project reviewers (peer and institutional) or to supervisors (Iphoen, 2011). However, these tensions and dilemmas must be seen in the wider research framework and socio-economic context in which particular configurations of positionality acquire specific enabling or constraining meanings, and as such demand greater institutional level awareness and support.

While we have described a number of challenges, vulnerabilities, and the sometimes messy, unpredictable nature of qualitative research, we did not reflect here on the full range of issues to have emerged. We did not discuss the many positive, rewarding experiences of collaborative research, of which the ultimate highlight is the novel input of both projects to ongoing debates. In both cases, research designs and methodological decisions enabled us to investigate micro level enactments and subjectivities with reference to macro level processes. As such, our analysis and findings make valuable and original empirical, theoretical and methodological contributions to the understanding of the relationship between globalization, migration and domestic work by (a) focusing on the roles of men in this relationship; (b) drawing on the perspectives gained from households buying-in domestic services stereotypically associated with male tasks (in the UK case); and (c) with respect to insights gained from retrospective comparative reflections on the qualitative research process focused on men.

4
Migrants and Male Domestic Work in the UK: The Rise of the 'Polish Handyman'

> You must not give up. You have to buckle in. You come here with a goal, earn a little, save, see some places. Of course it's hard. I came here and it was hard for me at the beginning, I didn't have a job or a place to stay but I've survived, I've managed.
>
> Bartek, HM

4.1 Introduction

In the first decade of the twenty-first century Polish migrant handymen in the UK and Mexican immigrant gardeners in the USA propelled the trends of globalization, migration and the outsourcing of social reproduction. In this regard, they reflect profound multi-level changes in social, economic and political spheres. Their micro level, individual and interpersonal decisions to move from comparatively less economically developed countries and regions to more affluent areas are motivated by a desire to attain a better life. This desire, centred on but not exclusive to work and employment, is the more poignant at a time when the notion of the good life is given considerable attention in the context of the financial and economic crisis originating in the finance centres in the UK and the USA, and against the background of growing inequalities in these and other countries.

In this chapter on migrants and male domestic work in contemporary UK we focus our analysis on the narratives and experiences of 21 Polish migrants (20 men and one woman) working as handymen, but we draw for comparisons on interviews conducted with all four groups of participants, and thus include the non-Polish and non-migrant handymen, agencies operating in the sector, and female and male partners in households with dependent children that buy in handy-man labour. Our micro level inquiry focuses on individual and family level decisions, projects and practices, but placed within the wider aggregate and geopolitical context, it reveals the complexities and nuances inherent in macro level processes of change. With particular reference to the EU enlargement of 2004, does the European politi-cal and economic integration project, orchestrated by policy makers converging in Brussels and securing overwhelming support from the acceding societies, achieve integration among the citizens to whom it applies? Does it expand opportunities and facilitate the hopes of the Polish handymen, who take advantage of these new possibilities? We consider the extent to which our participants are able to fulfil their work, family, and leisure aspirations relative to their well-being in Poland, and relative to other socio-economic groups in the UK, in particular non-migrant handymen and the middle class professional families who buy in their labour.

In the following sections, we first establish the broad background with respect to the timing and magnitude of Polish migration to the UK and the changing migration and labour market policies, especially after the enlargement of the EU in 2004. We then place the handyman occupation within the context of domestic work and analyse the proc-ess of migrant niching. Thereafter, we consider the extent to which the objectives of the relatively privileged Polish migrants (and EU8 nation-als more generally) have been fulfilled with respect to their personal and professional lives. This analysis is considered in light of the economic crisis and its potential impact on working conditions and decisions to leave or remain in the UK.

We thus analyse how individuals experience and manage their work-ing and personal lives within an evolving regulatory framework and socio-economic climate. We find that while, in the main, the migrant handymen participating in our study feel that their circumstances have improved by working and living in the UK, the various dimensions of well-being are not attained without risk or without cost and, generally, do not reach the level enjoyed by the middle class professional house-holders that buy in their labour. Therefore, this micro level response to uneven development within Europe (see Perrons, Plomien and Kilkey, 2010) is an imperfect path towards the good life – crossing the border between Poland and the UK allows for bridging some of the socio-economic distance between the two countries, but substantial inequali-ties between and within them persist unchallenged. This fact, combined with the preference of many of our interviewees for not having to migrate in the first place, demonstrate that the European integration project remains incomplete.

4.2 The Polish handyman phenomenon

4.2.1 Polish recent migration to the UK: Migration and labour market policy regimes

International migration features strongly in Poland's history. From the mid-nineteenth century onwards it reached a mass scale and comprised of labour seeking or family reunification decisions, political asylum cases and forced repatriations or resettlements of whole communities. The evolving push and pull forces influenced both the scale and the type of migration such that by the late 1980s, millions of Poles moved temporarily to work or trade abroad. By 1989 more than two million had migrated indefinitely – in both instances involving either documented or irregular arrangements at the point of exit and/or settlement (Stola, 2010). After the 1989 fall of socialism, overall migration from Poland diminished (Kaczmarczyk and Okólski, 2008), as the newly relaxed exit system was not matched by equally liberal entrance regulations elsewhere and the precise destination, scale and character of migration flows corresponded to a series of bilateral visa and migrant-worker agreements. For example, arrangements with Germany were the most significant in facilitating documented migration (Kicinger, 2009). In the late 1990s the magnitude of migration increased again and Poland was considered one of the key European migrant-sending countries even prior to the enlargement of the EU in 2004 (Kaczmarczyk and Okólski, 2008). Decades of mass migratory waves, while fluctuating in intensity and character, have nevertheless acquired an almost taken for granted cultural or institutional quality and, more practically, set off a chain process of transnational connections sustaining subsequent moves.

Accordingly, migration from Poland to the UK has a long tradition with the first substantial Polish community establishing itself in the UK in the aftermath of the Second World War, numbering more than 160,000 by 1951 (Burrell, 2009; Fihel and Kaczmarczyk, 2009: 31) and attracting about 1 per cent of Polish migrants from the late 1960s onwards (Stola, 2010). Following the accession of Poland to the EU on 1 May 2004, however, its magnitude increased rapidly and by the end of 2006 the UK replaced Germany as the major country of destination for Polish citizens. As summarized in Table 4.1, drawing on a number of databases GUS (2011) estimated that by the end of 2007[1] some 690,000 Polish migrants lived in the UK compared to 490,000 in Germany. After the peak in 2007 the total estimated number of Poles living abroad declined, corresponding with the onset of the global economic crisis and the start of our UK fieldwork (a theme we return to later). The specific patterns, extent, and timing of decreases and subsequent rebounds have been uneven (see Table 4.1), and to a large degree reflect the differential labour market opportunities in various countries.

On the whole, the 2004 enlargement of the EU was a significant event for Polish migration patterns. It was managed differentially by the existing Member States. Only Ireland, Sweden and the UK permitted nationals of the eight Central East European (CEE) countries joining the Union a relatively open access to their labour markets from the first day of accession. Other governments implemented various transition arrangements for a maximum duration of seven years. Poland became the single most dominant source of inward migration from the EU8, though the majority of migrants to the UK continue to come from outside of the EU (ONS, 2012a). The UK's transition measures were comparatively minor, comprising of the Workers Registration Scheme (WRS) and restricted access to social benefits. The WRS was an administrative database running from 1 May 2004 and expiring after the seven-year transition period on 30 April 2011, and required nationals from the EU8 to register with the Home Office to work in the UK. This condition applied to new employees and granted them access to a restricted range

Table 4.1   Estimated number of migrants from Poland (in thousands) living temporarily* abroad, 2002–2010 in select European countries

Category	2002**	2004	2005	2006	2007	2008	2009	2010
Total	786	1,000	1,450	1,950	2,270	2,210	1,870	1,990
EU	451	750	1,170	1,550	1,860	1,820	1,570	1,615
France	21	30	44	49	55	56	47	55
Germany	294	385	430	450	490	490	415	455
Ireland	2	15	76	120	200	180	140	125
Italy	39	59	70	85	87	88	85	92
Netherlands	10	23	43	55	98	108	84	108
Spain	14	26	37	44	80	83	84	50
Sweden	6	11	17	25	27	29	31	37
UK	24	150	340	580	690	650	555	560

Source: GUS (2011: 3).
*Temporary stay defined as more than two months up to 2006 and more than three months from 2007 onwards. GUS estimates that in 80 per cent of the cases this is at least 12 months.
**2002 data based on the Polish census.

of social benefits. Those who have worked legally and continually in registered employment for 12 months or more without interruption[2] were entitled to full free labour movement rights and social benefits. The self-employed were not required to register with WRS, but had to register with HM Revenue and Customs and arrange for tax and National Insurance contributions.

The collective migration biography of our interviewees working as handymen reflects these broader trends and underscores the significance of eliminating or lowering formal obstacles to free movement of labour within Europe. Of the 21 Polish migrants working as handymen, the majority (15) had arrived in the UK (although not necessarily for the first time) post-accession. Based on our interviewees' experiences, migration regimes matter in enabling and constraining their movement. The legal framework constitutes an important factor in deciding on a country of destination, as in the case of Fryderyk who arrived in the UK in 2004 and whose wife and child joined him within two months:

I planned to go to Holland because my ex-boss got a big contract so when still in Poland I started to ... refresh my Dutch ... but the Dutch parliament didn't allow Polish people to work legally there. I could open a business, but my wife couldn't work legally so she would have, I don't know, quite a bad job cleaning or something like that, and she didn't want to do this because she is a teacher.

Fryderyk, HM

Despite the fact that Fryderyk had worked in the Netherlands for five years in the 1990s and had accumulated social and human capital, such as contacts, language skills, and most importantly possessed a firm offer of employment, labour market opportunities for his wife were an additional consideration and weighed in the decision to migrate to the UK instead. At the time of the interview Fryderyk worked as a handyman and his wife as a primary school teacher in London.

Migration and labour market regulations thus play a significant role in the ability of migrant workers to execute their plans. For several of our participants numerous pre-accession attempts to enter the UK were unsuccessful. Jan's experiences are not unusual in this respect. Jan's brother-in-law had arrived in the UK in the 1990s, followed by Jan's brother, who had entered the country with his wife during an organized tour but the couple had not returned with the group to Poland. They had settled in London and eventually arranged for a job for Jan, whose first brief two-week working episode was interrupted by a birth of his daughter back in Poland. This happened in the year before Poland joined the EU, so when Jan attempted to return from a short visit with his family to his informal job in the UK, he was turned back from the border:

> When I was here for the first time I had this coach ticket and I stayed. When I tried coming for the second and third time I did not have the ticket and they thought I came to work illegally. And I spent the whole day at the airport. They took thirty photographs and there was a lot of paperwork as if I was a crook, and they took me back to Poland. Well, actually the third time I came here not only did I stay for the whole day but also for the whole night and only in the morning did they send me back … When we were in the [European] Union … then I could, legally, I could work … My wife came after three months with my daughter.
>
> Jan, HM

The changed legal framework also made a significant difference for Adam. He migrated to the UK in 2000 (shortly after being deported from Germany). In 2003, however, he was refused entry and deported upon returning to the UK from a trip to Poland visiting his partner and children, something he had done successfully four or five times previously:

> And you know, suddenly I had to stay in Poland. I already had everything here [London], a flat, furniture, bike, friends … Suddenly I lost everything, there was no chance … I was thinking all the time about Great Britain … Then, the borders were open. We joined the Union. It's freedom finally.
>
> Adam, HM

Marta, Adam's life and work partner (the only handy*woman* in our study), migrated to the UK in 2004, and their children followed a year later. Thus, our findings support the argument that international mobility of Poles is highly responsive to migration policies (Stola, 2010), especially when migration involves partners and children. The cases of Jan and Adam reflect a number of our interviews, and the patterns reported in Table 4.1 confirm that EU enlargement and the ensuing relative ease of access to the UK labour market was a key geo-political event.

At the same time, however, substantial numbers of migrants managed to bypass formal regulations, and liberal accession rules were by no means a necessary or a sufficient condition for all migration flows.

Sweden, for example, also permitted EU8 citizens a relative ease of labour market entry, but, as detailed in Table 4.1, was a far less popular destination for Polish workers. The relatively small number of migrants there has been linked to limited job opportunities, linguistic distance, or undeveloped migrant networks (Doyle, Hughes and Wadensjö, 2006). On the other hand, Germany upheld its existing labour market restrictions, yet the size of the Polish labour force there increased at a rapid pace. The Association Agreement (1991) signed between Poland and the European Communities[3] providing for the right to take up and pursue economic activities in a self-employed capacity turned out to be a crucial formal mechanism allowing for certain types of documented labour migration throughout the 1990s in a number of countries. Self-employment became an effective mechanism for labour market entry for Poles in the UK (Drinkwater, Eade and Garapich, 2009; Düvell, 2004) and in Germany, where new migrants were more likely to be self-employed than in waged employment (Brenke, Yuksel and Zimmermann, 2009).[4] Polish nationals thus used the loopholes of the generally 'closed door' migration policy regimes in place before (UK) as well as after (Germany) the 2004 accession.

Of the 21 Polish participants in our study, ten (including Fryderyk and Jan quoted previously) had prior labour-migration experiences involving agricultural and construction work in countries such as Germany, Sweden and the Netherlands during the 1990s, work in the agricultural and hospitality sectors of Italy and Greece in more recent times, and work of various kinds in the UK. There were six men in our sample whose current stay in the UK pre-dated 2004. These men either took advantage of the self-employment route or arrived on a tourist visa, but with the intention of staying longer than six months and finding work. Take Dawid, who came in 1998 following in his brother's footsteps, and found a job relatively quickly:

> I was looking for a job as gardener, and my friends told me that a building company had a vacancy ... I worked as a labourer ... and continued working there for a few years ... At that time we were not in the European Union, but the company employed Poles, Russians. I don't know how they organized this, but they paid taxes on our work ... it wasn't 100 per cent illegal ...There is another thing; before Poland joined the EU I applied for a working visa ... I needed it, I wanted to be here legally, I didn't want to have any problems with coming and leaving. It was easier when you had the visa ... much easier.
>
> Dawid, HM

In other instances, both crossing the border and securing formal employment were much more of a challenge, as in the case of this man who migrated to the UK in 2001 and was one of only three people allowed to enter from a group of more than 20:

> [T]he worst was entering England ... it was a holiday tour ... I staked everything on one card and started to argue with them on the border thinking to myself they would either soften and let me in or throw me out. I told the immigration officer, through an interpreter, that I wouldn't answer his stupid questions and to put me in touch with the Polish Embassy because the border officers here in Britain had broken international law on non-visa border movement. I dug my heels in and every time he asked me a question I requested to talk to a senior officer. He ran out of the interview room. He was furious. In five minutes he brought my passport with a six-month visa to enter ... and I entered.
>
> Wojtek, HM

Wojtek's confrontation with border staff, in contrast to Jan's or Adam's difficulties recalled earlier, did not prevent him from entering the UK. Once in the country, he found employment and accommodation in London the day he began searching – in his words 'there wasn't any problem at all and there was a lot of work' and a work permit was irrelevant as 'nothing was required from anybody but willingness to work'. Indeed, irregularity was a common feature of these migrants' situations, and by some accounts Poles constituted the third largest group among those being identified by UK authorities for 'illegal' entry in 1996 (Hansard, 1996, cited in Düvell 2004). For Wojtek, and many like him, Poland's political pre-accession status was not a deterrent to realizing his labour market migration project. This agentic behaviour is in line with the argument that international migration should not be seen through the paradox of opposing forces of states and governments closing and market forces opening borders, but should instead be understood at the point of their intersection, where 'different migrants operate within different legal and market opportunity structures' (Garapich, 2008a: 739). Nevertheless, in another sense, the pre-2004 attempts to live and work in the UK carried much risk and, when not regularized, limited these migrants ability to contribute to and benefit from various social provisions. This potentially diminished their capacity to attain the good life they set out to do.

4.2.2 The rise of the Polish handyman: Migrant niche formation?

The recent dynamic developments in international migration form a relevant backdrop to the rise in the outsourcing of traditionally male domestic work in the UK, introduced in Chapter 1 and analysed in Chapter 5. The male domestic work sector has assumed a migrant dimension, although UK-born workers continue to dominate (about 13 per cent of foreign-born and 41 per cent of UK-born domestic workers perform handyman-type jobs). Analysis of WRS data up to March 2008 indicates that nearly one per cent of EU8 workers registering with WRS have done so as handymen, gardeners and groundsmen, with Polish nationals, at 71 per cent, comprising the vast majority of the handyman category (Kilkey and Perrons, 2010). However, our interviews with migrants working as handymen suggest that this figure is likely to be an underestimate. All but two of our participants were self-employed and thus not required to register, and others had switched to handyman work after initially registering for other jobs. In addition, many of our interviewees had multiple jobs. Handyman work in the domestic sector was often done in evenings and weekends on top of other jobs, many of which were located in the construction and building sector more generally; a sector which accounted for an estimated five per cent of WRS registrations in the same period (Kilkey, 2010). In summary, although we cannot claim that handyman work has become an exclusive migrant niche of a similar degree as gardening in the Los Angeles area, analysed in Chapter 6, migrant men's presence in this type jobs in the UK is increasing, especially in the London area[5] where, as we noted in Chapter 2, both the domestic sector and its migrant density are greater than elsewhere in the country. Furthermore, the concept of a migrant niche also has a qualitative dimension, with certain ethnic groups linked to occupations that are seen as typical to them (Schrover, van der Leun and Quispel, 2007). A strong connection between EU8 workers and handyman and construction sectors has entered the popular imagination (Garapich, 2008b), with the Polish plumber and builder becoming particularly pervasive stereotypes, not only in the UK but also more widely in Europe. This popular imaginary has not gone unnoticed by the handymen themselves. As Fryderyk notes: 'It is the only thing that I hear over and over again. I heard that in Germany, in Holland ... that, simply, I am Polish so probably I can do this.'

In accounting for the patterns of labour market insertion of recent arrivals to the UK, actor-oriented and structural approaches have been highlighted either as separate or interacting explanatory frameworks (examples include Anderson et al., 2006; Datta and Brickell, 2009; Dyer, McDowell and Batnitzky, 2010; Garapich, 2008b; McDowell, Batnitzky and Dyer, 2007). In our study too, the development of handyman services as something of a Polish migrant niche rests on more than a simple demand and supply scenario. In Chapter 5, we outline the main reasons householders give for outsourcing typically male domestic tasks to handymen, and in Chapter 7 we indicate the complex ways in which understandings of class, ethnicity, and masculinity interplay to frame migrants as especially appropriate for handyman and gardening work. Here, in analysing the subjectivities and perceptions of handyman service buyers and sellers and in tracing the underlying mechanisms that converge in creating a particular opportunity structure for our migrant participants, we highlight the relevance of both agency and structure in the possible formation of a migrant niche. At the same time we acknowledge that, in light of our emphasis on the Polish handyman sector and limited data from 'control' groups of mainstream or other migrant workers, our research design is limited in its ability to be conclusive about migrant niching. In addition, our findings can only be provisional given the relatively recent and potentially evolving nature of this phenomenon.

What are the specific themes that construct the Polish as particularly suited to handyman jobs within the UK domestic space? In our study, the labour-using households listed a range of personal, technical and social qualities as important. These included a strong work ethic, reliability, flexibility, a high level of skill, high standards of work, competitive pricing, trust, sociability, and respect for the clients' home space. In many cases, these characteristics were linked to ethnicity as Polish people, and CEE nationals more generally, were identified as embodying them. Of the 24 interviewed households, nine had used Polish handymen and a further two were interested in doing so. Clients' preferences were often based on specific recommendations and past experiences, but sometimes also on vague, reified or romanticized notion of what being Polish or Eastern European represents:

> [Our] neighbours had … selectively chosen people either on the basis of price or a notion of, kind of, Eastern European attention to detail … mythological ideas about still having apprenticeships … skills guilds and so on, and so forth … I think ours ultimately came down to the kind of recommendation of friends on the basis of such and such was nice, good, reliable, flexible.
>
> James, HH

Although some research suggests that the coding of EU8 migrants as 'white' (McDowell, 2009a) and 'culturally proximate' (Garapich, 2008a) may give them an advantage in the UK labour market over 'non-white' or 'culturally distant' migrant workers, such racialization was not an explicit theme in our interviews.[6] Explicit and common were shared understandings of attributes such as skill. Harold (HH) talked about a 'street knowledge' which suggested 'that Polish people come here, they're hard working'. These understandings also feature strongly in the press – in a number of UK newspapers migrants from Poland are often portrayed in a favourable light,[7] especially in relation to industriousness, reliability, job quality, or willingness to accept modest wages (Fomina and Frelak, 2008). These generalized views reinforce a positive stereotype of the Polish handyman which can influence clients' expectations and motivate the demand for particular migrant workers:

When I was looking for a plumber I was pretty disappointed because I wanted ... I initially looked for a Polish plumber because I heard, you know, they're extremely well trained and reasonably priced ... And there's a website called 'Polish plumbers' (2012) ... and it didn't work.

Hugh, HH

In the majority of our household interviewees' assessments, these expectations were met or exceeded. Martha (HH) enthusiastically affirmed that the Polish handyman she and her husband frequently hired for jobs around the house 'was a godsend, he was an angel [laughs] he did fabulous work at all times, never let us down ... always fulfilled his contract, really good'.

Such positive perceptions of clients linking high quality services and value for money with Polish migrants were widely shared and actively endorsed by the Polish handymen and by the agency representatives in our study. This handyman uncritically essentialized such associations, depicting them as natural and inherent in the Polish identity:

Every nation has some sort of defining features. We, Poles ... are above all valued for our speed, professionalism and price ... we have a hard-working nature; we are valued for our work ... we like to get the work done well, quickly, and cheaply ... which explains why people are happier with Poles than others ... which makes us unique.

Piotr, HM

As in Piotr's case, for the most part, handymen considered themselves and their compatriots as having a wide and sought after combination of attributes, including being highly competent and skilled, reliable, fast, thorough, hard-working, neat and tidy, flexible, competitive, able and willing to carry out a wide range of jobs, and adept at customer service and interpersonal traits by virtue of their polite and personable natures. Indeed, the embodiment of a number of these qualities in a single individual is what makes the Polish handyman desirable. But, as shown in Chapter 7, most handymen reflected that their skills were acquired through more and less formal training, work and life experiences, rather than being innate.

The reputation of Polish handymen, generally shared by household-ers and migrant handymen, was also understood in a relational manner, through opposition to stereotypical notions of British handymen. Not only were the Polish seen as good, skilled and reliable, but the British were judged as less capable, as having an inferior work ethic and a poorer serv-ice culture. Similar claims to 'superiority' were found in research on Polish builders in London (Datta and Brickell, 2009). Trust was the most frequent catchall theme identified by our householders, expressively articulated by Jeff,[8] who did not trust the British 'cowboys' to do a job well and to enter the private sphere of the home, but had full faith in Polish workers. As such, positive and negative associations are frequently at play – Polish handymen acquire and validate their image both in their own right and because of their perceived comparative advantage over the British.

Just as in the case of the Filipina cleaners discussed in Chapter 2, these positive connotations of Polish identity with high-quality handyman work acquired something of a brand property. In several instances they were used for marketing purposes where Internet advertisements of the handymen participating in our study (and many of those who refused participation) often included a reference to their Polish nationality. Patryk (HM) noticed that 'when an ad says "Handyman" or "Professional handyman" there are fewer visitors than when it says "Polish profes-sional handyman"' and went on to recall a rumour that 'Romanians, Albanians and Bulgarians … claim in front of the English to be Polish'. Websites providing a platform for handymen or builders to advertise their services also utilize the Polish brand, as in the case of Marzena, our agency interviewee who runs a web portal intended as 'the first port of call for English customers who are looking for Polish builders'.

Many of the aforementioned subjectivities, expressions and tactics resonate with the process of 'interpellation' (McDowell, Batnitzky and Dyer, 2007),[9] as migrant workers simultaneously recognize and endorse shared stereotypical assumptions about their qualities. The fact that they are stereotypes is reflected in the way in which some clients and handymen pointed to differentiation among Polish as well as British workers. This householder speaks from experience:

[B]etween the two Polish ones there has been a considerable difference. So the first Polish ones were younger and a bit less dependable ... but they were certainly higher skilled, but ... I didn't feel I was getting as good value. And the Polish man we're currently using is a bit older ... I feel like I'm less likely to get fleeced.

Nancy, HH

Similar nuances emerge through the observations of Joanna, an agency representative, who reflecting on several years of working with about 25 Polish builders and handymen, noted that some were 'really good and hard-working' whereas others were unskilled and inexperienced in these trades. Joanna's view was that after the enlargement of the EU many more people arrived to the UK as students or as individuals who did not have any background in the building and construction industry, but they would nonetheless use the Polish brand to enter the sector. According to Joanna, these opportunists 'don't know what they are doing ... I spoke with them ... and they are not builders and they have never done any building work in Poland'. A few of the handymen shared this more heterogeneous assessment:

Three or four years ago ... only skilled workers came to England, good, skilled workers. Now everybody comes over. I don't believe that a guy who is 22 years old has experience ... They come to England and it seems to them that if they can do a few things they can be handymen ... We should differentiate between 'a handyman' and 'a professional handyman'. A handyman is somebody who can carry out repairs at theirs or at a neighbour's house. And then, there is somebody who does this for a living. Not a 'cowboy' but a tradesman, a multi-tradesman.

Patryk, HM

Furthermore, Patryk (and a number of others) stresses that 'the way you work as a handyman should be learnt over here' because of the specificity of working in the UK. Handling particular materials, operating certain technologies, or managing the business environment and dealing with British clients requires the acquisition of new human, social, and cultural capital and therefore cannot be considered a 'natural' trait. The more complex views expressed by Nancy, Joanna, or Patryk thus challenge the 'wholesale' deployment of stereotypes. However, they do not controvert this common association of Polish migrants with handyman, plumber, or builder occupations. Indeed, Patryk himself observed that he receives more attention by advertising his services as 'Polish professional handyman', rather than 'professional handyman' alone.

While the perceptions and subjectivities of buyers and suppliers of handyman labour are important dimensions in accounting for migrant niche formation, they, like the perceptions of migrant female domestic work discussed in Chapter 2, operate within a given structural framework of state regulatory migration, labour market regime, and the broader economy. This wider environment influences a range of relevant mechanisms and processes bridging, at the macro level, the political and the economic through migration flows, operation of migrant networks, and ease of entry into particular employment sectors or pay differentials among them. These macro level processes form the backdrop for micro level actions, which in turn play a role in forming and shaping the macro level processes. In other words, the wider political-economic context, the social capital of ethnic communities and on-the-ground activities (of migrants and non-migrants alike) intersect, evolve and must be considered in a broad and relational perspective (Garapich, 2008a; Jones and Ram, 2007).

In section 4.2.1, we described the role migration and labour market regulations played in the recent increase of volume of migrants moving from Poland to the UK. A key outcome of this process is the numerical visibility of Polish nationals in the construction and handyman sectors, an outcome also noted by our interviewees: 'Because there are many of them that's why they are successful ... Two million of Poles came over and 10,000 Czechs. Who should be handymen? (Krzysztof, HM).

The large numbers of Polish migrants filled existing gaps in particular areas of the labour market, a relationship that, as we saw in Chapter 2, is noted about recent migrants more generally in sectors such as agriculture, hospitality, health, childcare, social care, and construction. In many cases, the specific labour market insertion relied on personal or social networks. In some high-growth areas of the economy, like domestic and commercial construction and maintenance, the supply of labour could barely keep up with the demand, particularly prior to the onset of the recession in 2008:

We had a property boom here in the UK, like two years ago, everyone was selling, everyone wanted a conversion ... so there was lots of demand for Polish builders ... we had lots of projects at the time ...

and the Polish builder would phone me saying 'Oh God, do you know anyone? Because I, you know, I'm running out of people. I need more people' and then 'I don't really mind how just get me some people to work for me'.

Joanna, A

Reflecting on the pre-2008 period, handymen noted that they were booked for several months in advance, often had a number of jobs, big and small, lined up and their phones would 'ring 100 times a day' (Dawid, HM). In such a booming economy, our entrepreneurial interviewees who owned small businesses tended to hire co-nationals, often starting with family and friends,[10] before developing professional networks which expanded further. The Polish handymen, then, reflected more general findings regarding entrepreneurial reliance on social networks (Granovetter, 1985):

[H]e knows a Polish plumber whom he gives the jobs that he can't do himself or needs a certificate to do them. He uses the same people ... he knows that this guy is a fantastic plasterer ... That guy would recommend somebody else who can do tiling very well.

Marzena, A; referring to her husband's business

Such networks did not necessarily require a strong or long-standing connection as a number of the newcomers to London arrived in the city without knowing anyone, without having a pre-arranged job placement, and frequently without any English language knowledge. Nevertheless, all of them found jobs and accommodation almost immediately after arrival. A common scenario would start with arriving by bus to London's Victoria Station:

A: I saw a Pole and asked him what to do, where to go. He took me to a Polish shop, gave me a Polish newspaper and said: 'Listen, here you have this, this, and that ...'

Q: So where did you stay on your first night?

A: At the guy's that I met at the station ... He helped me ... I just started talking to him at Victoria, because when you don't speak the language, it's your first day, and everything's overwhelming, it's what you do.

Q: And you say you found a job after a week, how did that happen?

A: At the flat I lived with other Poles ... I introduced myself and
     asked if they knew anything about getting a job and they said
     'wait, we'll make a few phone calls'.

                                        Interview with Bartek, HM

Bartek's experience, along with similar examples in our study, supports
the 'strength of weak ties' thesis (Granovetter, 1973) in labour market
insertion among recent migrants from Poland. It also reveals the manner
in which knowledge of the English language (see also Chapter 7) adds
a further layer with respect to the role of migrant networks for work
placement. English language skills were not seen by our interviewees
as necessary for co-nationals working side by side, collaborating on
larger renovation jobs involving complex manual skills, or in sharing
information about specific jobs and clients. In contrast, the ability to
speak English was considered crucial in obtaining and negotiating jobs
with British householders and in tasks related to the management of
the business environment, such as bookkeeping or sourcing materials.
Therefore, the level of English language knowledge does not act as a
barrier to the handyman sector, although it plays a role in the specific
modus operandi within it (see section 4.3). For entry into other areas of
the labour market, as our interviewees noted, insufficient language skills
were much more of an obstacle.

A related structural feature of the UK economy is the comparative
ease of entry into the building and construction sector. Indeed, it is so
regardless of whether migrant networks are involved. A typical career
trajectory among the handymen in our study was to first work as a general labourer or as a specialized and skilled worker in a larger company.
Handyman type-roles would then be taken on subsequently or, at times,
in parallel. Such progression occurs especially as English language skills
improve and contacts develop – in particular among our participants
working individually and managing their own small businesses. This
ease of sector entry stands in contrast to several other industries into
which a small number of our participants could not move, despite having the relevant credentials and a desire to do so. Franek, for instance,
is an experienced IT specialist who would rather work in IT than as a
handyman, while Ewa was only offered administrative posts despite
having a degree in Mathematics, Computer Science and Economics. In
light of her limited labour market opportunities, she eventually decided
to open her own business advice firm (see further on).

Another attractive aspect of the handyman sector for the migrant men
in our study was the relatively high earnings. Many of our participants

noted that their hourly or daily rates were much better than restaurant, office, or bank-teller positions would pay. The links between the construction sector and handyman activities seem to be a factor in pay levels being much higher than in other domestic or service work. However, with respect to pay, many remain in an inferior position to those who buy their labour (see Chapter 7).

The high visibility and concentration of Polish migrants in the construction and building industry, including handyman services, is not just a function of new, post-2004 migration flows. Our participants who moved to the UK before the accession followed family members or friends who were already established in this line of work. The view that 'at the time when I came over [1998], some 80 per cent of Polish men, guys, worked in the building sector and 20 per cent somewhere else' (Dawid, HM) was commonly held. So, migrant networks relying on informal contacts in both initial migration to the UK and in subsequent labour market insertion have a considerable history and reach. Alongside these personal connections, what Michal Garapich (2008a) terms the 'migration industry' is also of key importance. The migration industry emerged as a result of and in response to the recent Polish migration to the UK before and after 2004. It consists of business consultancies, travel offices, recruitment agencies, communications and media groups, and other ventures that specifically target migrant populations. It operates commercially, but also fulfils civil society, political, and marketing functions and helps to sustain social and economic relations among Polish migrants. Of the four agencies in our study, two in particular fit this description: a web portal designed for Polish builders, plumbers, handymen to advertise to English customers, and a London-based accounting, financial and business advice firm servicing almost exclusively Polish self-employed migrants, including those working in the domestic construction and maintenance sectors.

The business advice firm, set up by Ewa in 2003, initially specialized in providing assistance in business visa applications which allowed migrants to legalize their status and granted them the right to work in the formal economy via the self-employment route (see section 4.2.1). When Poland joined the EU, the firm's main focus switched to new business registrations, and this covered both new arrivals and those who were in the UK before May 2004 but had not registered their commercial activities:

They were in the shadow and nobody knew anything about them, they earned money illegally. They started to register because they wanted to be here legally so their working years would count in their pension ... During the first year, until May 2005, there was a wave of new registrations.

Ewa, A

Self-employment provisions were thus an important mechanism facilitating large numbers of migrants to establish themselves in the UK – Home Office (2003) statistics suggest that of the 24,800 business permits granted in 2003 alone, as many as 9410 (a 156 per cent increase) were given to nationals from Poland.[11] The handyman sector, like the construction and building industries in general, easily lend themselves to self-employment, either in addition to or in combination with informal working. Such informality and irregularity surrounding self-employment had been tolerated by businesses and authorities alike for many years. A number of our participants who had entered the UK before 2004 had taken advantage of this toleration, laying the groundwork for a smooth transition toward the Polish handyman niche that emerged once migrants came in larger numbers after accession to the EU. Here we see another example of how a range of factors intersects in generating the Polish handyman phenomenon. The initial labour market regulatory framework allowing for self-employment provided a basis for the subsequent 'boom in the Polish migrants industry' (Garapich, 2008a: 741) after accession to the EU. But this alone would not have caused the rise in the Polish handymen. Also crucial are features of the UK economy and its segments, notably, the demand for handyman-type labour (elaborated upon in Chapter 5) generated by inequalities and the time-squeeze produced by long working hours among the wealthy, particularly in London. Furthermore, individuals and their skills, themselves a product of life in a less wealthy country, where they would not hire people in for handyman tasks but learned the skills themselves, subjectivities, combined with the perceptions and actions of people, householders and handymen alike, help to constitute the Polish handyman identity. This, in turn generates demand for Polish handyman services, further fuelling migration. It is, then, the interaction of wider structural processes and micro level perceptions, actions and decisions which form the environment in which the Polish handymen operate.

4.3   Polish migrant handymen and well-being: A better life?

The migration and labour market policy regulations described in section 4.2.1 mark EU8 migrants as privileged within the UK's highly differentiated migration regime. In comparison to non-EU nationals and to citizens of Bulgaria and Romania,[12] this advantageous position is based on a unique set of conditions for the configuration of migration, work and family. Nowhere does it come into a sharper relief than in relation to the situation of the asylum-seeker handymen participating in our study, whose migrant status denied them recourse to social, political and economic citizenship rights.[13] As labour market access and the resulting job opportunities were seen as a key ingredient for well-being among all of the Polish handymen (and handywoman) we interviewed, asylum seekers' exclusion from these possibilities severely limited their welfare. Engagement in the formal labour market became nearly impossible when the official regulations had become tighter:

> [M]any times I tried ... bread factory, chocolate factory, pizza factory, flour factory ... after three months they said 'bring your passport', no passport, out, very easy, believe me, I've got now around maybe fifteen, sixteen different payslips ... now everything change, law is change. They said, you have to show them first passport, if you not a passport they no give you any more job in the factory ... Especial after ... [East] European comes ... without passport is quite hard.
>
> Said, HM

But the two asylum-seekers did not passively submit to their situation. While obtaining a regular job was not an option, working as handymen and directly selling their work to households or subcontracting their labour to a handyman entrepreneur enabled some income generating activities, albeit subject to substantial exploitation, with reported pay well below the national minimum wage.

Polish migrants, with the possibility of self-employment before the accession, were thus relatively better off even before Poland joined the EU. Post-2004, when a business visa was no longer required, the process of registering is reported by Polish handymen as surprisingly straightforward and quick. This process allows for the regularization of employment and more complete integration into the British economy and society. It also serves as a further reminder of how the UK regulatory migration regime constructs different categories of migrants within a hierarchy (Wills et al., 2009).

Why do Polish handymen migrate to the UK? As Bartek's (HM) motives, quoted in the opening of this chapter, point out, they want to 'earn a little, save, see some places'. The rationales are quite varied, but largely constitute responses to new opportunities to secure the economic means to attain a range of (non-economic) goals. The opportunity to earn a higher income than in Poland was therefore a commonly stated reason, but it was rarely the only one. And, as Bartek's remarks further illustrate, previous migration episodes encouraged a sense of interest and adventure, with Bartek saying that part of the reason he migrated was 'to see the world, you know, I went to Sweden and it was fun, different country, different people, different language and different culture'. So, while limited levels of wealth limit the pursuit of international travel in purely leisure-terms, migration to the UK allows some migrants to real- ize ambitions to travel. Indeed, some migrants offered reasons similar to those given by tourists when choosing their destination when explain- ing why they chose to migrate to London. Olek, for instance, specifically decided that:

> London was my destination. I like football, concerts and all that is here. I chose this place because there are lots of shops here with records. I'm going to the music shops afterwards ... so, yes, football, music and work too.
>
> Olek, HM

These deliberate decisions, along with those based on 'ups and downs in my life, in my relationship' (Patryk, HM), those that show a desire 'to become independent, to prove, to show my parents that I can stand on my own feet' (Antoni, HM), and those that are based on a 'feeling of stagnation, a feeling of going nowhere' while in Poland (Mateusz, HM) together serve to demonstrate how structures (patterns of development and migration legislation) and agency (specific desires and projects of people) interact. Indeed, it was not only individual desires that played a role, with family building projects featuring among the motivations for particular moves:

Q: What was the reason? Why did you want to move?
A: Opportunities, simply.
Q: What kind of opportunities?
A: My wife worked for the whole year and then she could start uni- versity. She started university ... here ... she finished university.
Q: Could you not achieve the same in Poland?
A: No, we wanted to have another child and in Poland we couldn't afford it. In Poland it would be impossible to study and to have another child.

> Interview with Fryderyk, HM

In most cases then, the economic gradient was accompanied by a range of other, professional as well as personal triggers, underscoring the strong work-life connection for attaining well-being. To what extent have the Polish handymen managed to realize their goals through migrating to the UK? For the majority the start presented a significant challenge. Setting aside issues of language and culture, while important in their own right and related to well-being, establishing a decent standard of living in a material sense was crucial. It often was attained at significant personal cost:

Q: How would you describe the very first days or weeks over here?
A: Massive stress. ... The first half of a year was very hard. I had to deny myself many things. ... My wife worked too. She is well educated and she worked in a hotel as a cleaner. She worked there, sweat and blood. Sometimes she came back from work 'more dead than alive'. I also did my best. And we managed.

Interview with Patryk, HM

And the outcomes, while generally positive, were quite varied. There were a number of related factors at play among the Polish handymen we interviewed, which positioned them differently based on employment status and income. Only two of our participants were employees with standard employment contracts, entailing work related benefits such as annual holiday entitlement, steady and regular working hours, and a set remuneration at about £8 to £10 per hour. Such income from the main job could easily be supplemented, as many handyman services can be provided on the side:

[E]very builder, handyman, plumber, electrician, we're talking here about the whole construction industry, has private work ... probably that's where the biggest money comes from ... sometimes it can be better just from a few small jobs during the week.

Piotr, HM

Piotr indicated that for the extra jobs he charged around £30 to £40 per hour – a significant amount in comparison to his regular wages. Such additional earnings make a big difference to the household budget, but as they require work in the evenings and on the weekends (on top of the core working hours) they come at a cost of leisure and family time. Piotr, a father of a young baby, experienced this as a real dilemma, as he had to make a choice between time and money, both of which his young family

needed. Due to pay differentials, his options were much more constrained than those of the professional fathers we discuss in Chapter 5,
who were able to circumvent this difficult choice by hiring out domestic
tasks to relatively disadvantaged handymen like Piotr to make time to
spend with their children despite their frequently long working hours.
In contrast, Piotr fared much better than our asylum-seeker father, who
did not have any income generating opportunities, nor any possibilities
for hands on fathering, as his only son had remained in Iran.

All other Polish handymen in our study were self-employed. Among
these there were several working models. The first group was formed of
those that were formally self-employed, but sub-contracted their services to other English or Polish small business owners. They occupied
the lowest rungs of this hierarchy. Typically, they did not possess strong
English language skills, tools, a driver's licence or a vehicle, and as a
result, generally reported wages in the range of £8–10 per hour, occasionally dropping to £5–6, often when they were first starting out. Low
pay and exploitation were mentioned on several occasions:

> I had worked for those companies as self-employed ... Most of these
> companies, it's sort of exploitation. I got money, I earned £40–50 a
> day, but I had to start exactly at 8.00 am and finished at 6.00 pm. No
> more, no less, and hard work.
>
> Olek, HM

Several of the sub-contracting Polish handymen had aspirations to
make progress on pay and autonomy over the work process issues, but
personal and professional development featured too. Dawid, for example, complained that the company where he had worked for five years
failed to recognize that his skills and expertise expanded since starting
as a 'simple labourer', and did not pay him a sufficiently high wage.
He estimated that at £70 per day he was paid about half of what non-
migrant workers were paid, encouraging him to ask for a raise. When it
was not granted, Dawid, thinking he deserved more, decided to quit. He
also embarked on a more promising strategy and enrolled in college:

> Only recently, in September last year, I went to school, to a college
> Carpentry and Joinery course ... It was difficult to find a job and have
> Mondays off. I went to college every Monday and had to be off from
> work all day. And not everyone liked it. I mean companies or pri-
> vate people ... didn't like me having Mondays off. That was another
> reason for giving up the school. I didn't have enough money to study

and not to work, and, as I said, everything that we did, practical work or the theory, I already knew.

Dawid, HM

This example of difficulties in fitting work responsibilities with formal training illustrates how individual level experience of low pay and little or no control over working time and work schedule constrain human capital development and, as a consequence, limit the realization of personal growth and a higher level of security. With respect to the broader context it shows that flexibility – a distinctive feature of the UK labour market – can be difficult to negotiate when required by workers rather than employers. It thus problematizes the EU-wide policy goal of flexicurity (Lewis and Plomien, 2009), which aims to combine flexibility and security in a win-win situation for workers and employers alike. Ironically, the problem of realizing flexicurity encountered by Dawid made it impossible for him to engage in vocational training, one of the EU's four pillars of flexicurity being lifelong learning.

The second working model, which would often develop from the first, comprised of handymen who were self-employed, operated independently and worked alone (except for the wife-husband partnership cited later). Such evolution signified a rise in income, since handymen were able to eliminate the intermediary level between themselves and the client and charge £10 or more per hour or a daily rate of £90–120, depending on the type of a job involved. Marta and Adam operate such a model and regard it to be a considerable achievement:

A: After two years of hard work together, and sacrifices, huge sacrifices, we both invested in driving licences, in cars, in tools ... a lot of money. At first, my wife argued with me. She couldn't understand, but in the end it worked out. She understood. We got money.

M: We have tools that are worth a lot of money.

A: Oh, not a lot.

M: No, but £4000 is not little.

A: We started from nothing and we have something now so it's kind of success. But it's hard work from morning till night. At the cost of the children, oh yes, yes.

Adam and Marta, HM and HW

This second category displays considerable improvement from the first in terms of working and living conditions. While Marta worked cleaning houses, Adam had previously worked in a number of irregular positions: carer in a social home; mowing lawns, and as a handyman in a hotel. But, as they mention, difficulties remain despite their progression to this second category, and they miss spending time with their four children when they are at work.

The final model comprised of self-employed handymen running slightly larger operations. These handymen would take on bigger maintenance contracts with landlords or lettings agencies and larger renovation projects in private households. To complete these tasks, they worked with other Polish handymen, but in a hierarchical manner where the small entrepreneur would obtain the job contract and deal with the client, before sub-contracting all or part of the work to others at a profit. In both the second and third models, upward social mobility (at least with respect to initial labour market position in the UK) required a number of skills, especially English language, but it was possible to attain without much initial capital:

At the beginning, it's good to think about it now, I can say I made the business running on a bike and had everything attached to my bike with a tape, a mower in one hand. Some people were laughing, some felt sorry for me [laugh]. But after a year I managed to buy a car and ... everything started working out ... I have so much work that I employ a plumber, carpenter, decorator, bricklayer ... I have those people employed permanently.

Tomek, HM

These examples highlight that, as in the case of the Mexican *jardineros* in the USA described in Chapter 6, occupational mobility is possible for Polish handymen, and while most had experienced exploitation and unfair treatment, many were able to overcome them. Furthermore, all of our respondents noted that the standard of living that their UK wages afford them is higher than it was in Poland, even though some had experienced downward occupational mobility. Their earnings allow for satisfying their and their families' basic needs, pursuing hobbies, or travelling back to Poland and elsewhere. Nevertheless, while these successful handymen who participated in our study attained significant progress, their achievements are still relatively modest and incomplete:

Many of the migrant handymen and builders I met complain about the way they're treated at work. They often felt like 'second class' employees, they earn less than their colleagues, work longer hours, and have difficulties in getting things done for them. I know a handyman who worked without a contract for months and his taxes and national insurance contributions were not paid even though he was promised.

Joanna, A

Furthermore, Fryderyk lives with his wife and two children, but sub-lets a room to a lodger to help make ends meet; Filip does not have the time to play football with mates, like he used to back in his home town in Poland, or to play with his seven-year-old son; Marta and Adam leave for work at 7:00 or 8:00 o'clock in the morning and when they get back 12 hours later they are so tired they don't have the energy to play with their children; and while a handful of our respondents had a flat back in Poland, not a single one, not even those who planned to stay in the UK indefinitely, owned a property. A number of them were acutely aware of their position within the unequal British society, as was expressively put by Daniel (HM): 'You see, when I look at those houses then I can see my position. So I, in relation to them, I am a "zero".'

This sense of unease at their relative status may be related to the down-ward occupational mobility experienced by some Polish handymen. While they earn more in England than they did before in Poland, some held more traditionally middle class jobs in Poland and some were better qualified and educated than British handymen (e.g. Filip, with a mas-ter's degree in management and marketing worked in a car sales office; Daniel was Polish-German language translator; and Patryk held a mas-ter's degree in political science and a diploma from a two-year Building College). In addition, some of their cultural interests and identities were closer to those of the householders who would employ them than those of British handymen, as reflected in Olek's earlier comment on moving to London because he enjoyed concerts. Indeed, this sense of class and cultural proximity, as we shall consider in Chapter 7, possibly generated a trust among the householders who made them more comfortable in allowing them into their homes and might have provided one reason why Polish handymen services were often preferred by householders.

The kind of inequality that Daniel, and others, perceived in their everyday life has been linked (Krugman, 2012; Seguino, 2010; Stiglitz, 2012) to the global financial and economic crisis that started in the UK in the late 2007, persisted during our fieldwork in 2008–9, and is still unresolved at the time of finalizing this book in mid-2012. Has the economic contraction and the resulting loss in aggregate wealth had any discernible impact among our participants? All of the handymen, Polish and British, were aware of the economic recession and thought it had significant implications for the related construction, building, and handyman sectors. Reflecting on the impact of the crisis at an individual level, however, their perceptions and experiences were differentiated. All of the British handymen stated that they were not personally affected by it, although a couple anticipated a possible negative outcome in the future. Among the Polish participants the situation was more mixed, as many had either direct experience of it or knew of others who had. With such a small number of cases, of course, interpretation demands caution. Nonetheless, even with our limited qualitative data, we were able to observe that there are certain dimensions in which migration status intersects with the wider economic environment and matters in ways that result in greater insecurity for the individuals involved.

The Polish handymen generally noticed that there was much less demand for their work; those whose phones rang '100 times a day' were no longer in a position to pick and choose jobs that were most lucrative or most pleasant to carry out. For Wojtek, who before the crisis used to set up a few big jobs to return to from a holiday in Poland, the 100 phone calls a day situation was completely reversed:

> I used to come back, call one or the other place and start organising jobs one by one. Unfortunately, I came back, called them: 'We are very sorry but we can't because we are not sure whether my husband will keep his job'. This week I have made about 100 phone calls ... to ask for a job. It is very hard.
>
> Wojtek, HM

The shortage of work available had implications for the working and business strategies our handymen developed. Lowering what many considered already competitive prices was a common response, entailing, in some cases, as much as a 30 per cent drop in income. Downsizing of operations among the entrepreneurs in our sample was another tactic. In a number of instances handymen were no longer employing or sub-contracting work to others, and in one case, Adam and Marta decided to keep the income 'within the family' and occasionally relied on their teenage son to substitute for hired labourers.

A key dimension of the lower demand for handyman labour was the current or anticipated continuity of work and work flow – a situation which had impact on working hours in two opposing ways. At one extreme, handymen reported downtime and work stoppages, lasting from days to even weeks. At the other there were those for whom work was still relatively plentiful and kept them working full time, but uncertainty about the ability to secure job contracts in the near future meant that they could not afford to refuse work that was available at the time. These handymen worked long hours and hesitated in taking time off.

There was also a perception that clients demanded the same level and quality of service, but at a lower price, so working conditions have clearly deteriorated. And at the most extreme, a handful of handymen perceived increased levels of discrimination and prejudice against Polish workers in general, as the economic situation started to deteriorate and a tabloid-fuelled sense of migrant workers taking jobs when there was a lack of work for British nationals grew. This was one aspect in which migrant (and ethnic) status was acutely felt to have mattered as a direct outcome of the recession and competition for scarce jobs. The second migrant-specific factor was potential return migration back to Poland [see Table 1]. Generally, there were differences among our participants who came to the UK with the intention to stay there only temporarily as they were saving up for 'a nest' in Poland and prefer to raise children there and those who did not see a reason for returning because they were either satisfied with the way life has turned out in the UK or saw many obstacles to return, such as their children's schooling, difficulty of switching back to their previous professional occupation, or the impossibility of creating a livelihood out of handyman work in Poland. Finally, there were those who were both flexible and prepared to respond to the changing environment around them, or did not consider their evolving circumstances as sufficiently secure to make the decision either way.

4.4   Conclusion

Joining the European Union in 2004 gave Polish people free access to European labour markets and resulted in a number of positive and negative freedoms from which Polish handymen have benefited. Without a doubt, EU membership enlarges their political, social and economic rights and potentially brings them nearer to their desired model of the good life. Realization of the good life, however, remains limited in at least in two respects. First, advancements in some aspects of their personal and working lives have come at a cost to other aspects. Second, because some of the dreams they aspire to may be very difficult, if not impossible, to achieve.

As we have seen, the Polish handymen who participated in our study successfully negotiate the opportunity structures in patterns of development and migration legislation which form the background to their actions in pursuing their desires. Such interaction between agency and structure, illustrated for example by the process of migrant niching in the handyman sector, defies the construct of migrants as victims. Polish handymen respond to and actively shape the environment within which they operate. The main outcome is securing higher incomes, which allow saving, travel, or having a larger family – projects they feel outside of their reach back in Poland. But, migration to the UK also entails sacrifices. Loss of kin and social support networks and inability to take part in everyday family life with people as close to them as children from previous relationships, siblings or parents is one. Downward socio-occupational mobility, especially in the initial period, is another. And, the general longing for their more familiar way of life, working culture and hours, or even snow, moderate the positive assessment of their well-being. Finally, despite the sacrifices made, a range of dreams Polish handymen aspire to remain unrealized. One dimension is limited occupational mobility, especially when it is difficult to obtain time off from work for further education. Another is engaging in hands-on fathering, where the money-time nexus and breadwinning responsibilities, coupled with physical exhaustion from working long hours, poses difficult dilemmas. In these respects, the range of options available to Polish handymen are constrained and remain much narrower than those enjoyed by the middle class professional householders who rely on their labour.

While the European Union aims for economic and social cohesion within and between member states it is clear that, at present, wide asymmetries remain and stimulate the movement from low to higher income countries and reinforce unequal divisions based on gender, class, or migrant status. These inequalities mean that while people make the decision to migrate, they would rather be able to secure the same standard of living in Poland:

Q: If earnings in Poland were better, would you stay or would you
      go back?
A: I would go back without any hesitation.

                                        Interview with Wojtek, HM

Despite improvements in the life and opportunities that Polish handymen have gained through the enlargement of social, political and economic rights linked to the membership of the EU, then, a realization of their idea of the good life will remain restricted while the intra- and international inequalities that drive the process of migration remain. But despite the impossibility of a full realization of the good life, EU membership nonetheless gave Polish citizens migrating within Europe significant advantages over migrants elsewhere, who face much more rigorous migration legislation. The impact of this rigorous legislation on life-opportunities shall become clear in Chapter 6 when we discuss the cases of some undocumented immigrant gardeners in the USA. Before we do so, however, we turn to the employing households and consider how the help provided by the migrant handymen enables professional men to partially resolve some of the tensions they face between time with the family and commitment to work.

5
Connecting Men in the International Division of Domestic Work: The New 'Father Time-Bind', Global Divisions between Men and Gender Inequalities

> It's when time becomes precious and we've got the kind of disposable income to pay somebody else to do it.
>
> William, HH

5.1 Introduction

While the supply of appropriate migrants to work as handymen and gardeners in the UK and USA represents one side of an international division in male domestic labour, *demand* on the part of households for commoditized male domestic services represents the other. The current chapter explores this dimension by drawing on the interviews we conducted with households that buy in help for stereotypically masculine jobs on a repeated basis in the UK, mainly in London. Pahl (1984) has argued that for any one household, the patterns and rationale of self-provisioning and outsourcing are dynamic, shifting as households move through the 'domestic lifecycle'. We focus on just one stage of the domestic lifecycle – the childrearing phase – and within this on one type of household – those with a resident father. Such households consisting of dependent children and a resident father are among the most likely in the UK to outsource male domestic work (Kilkey and Perrons, 2010), and so represent a numerically important focus.[1]

The drivers underpinning demand among our householders for commoditized male domestic services are complex and multiple, reflecting different cultural norms and values, as well as material circumstances (Baxter, Hewitt and Western, 2008; de Ruijter and van der Lippe, 2009; Wallace, 2002). Indeed, those we interviewed revealed a range of reasons for outsourcing. They included, for some but certainly not all, a lack of skill and/or lassitude on the part of men, a subject we return to in Chapter 7. Another common set of reasons related to home ownership, and were bound up with the importance of the 'home' for the middle classes, in both monetary and status terms, noted in Chapter 2. Thus, becoming an owner-occupier and wanting a professional to do the job 'properly'; buying a house which is more maintenance-intensive than a flat; or upsizing the home to a scale where the tasks are deemed too large and/or difficult to manage without help, were all cited as triggers for using the services of handymen. The arrival of children was also an important trigger for outsourcing as it was difficult for parents to carry out noisy, messy and lengthy jobs in their presence.

The most frequent and almost universal rationale, as captured in the quote from a dual-earner father of three cited at the beginning of the chapter, related, however, to the combined effect of time and money. Time was more precisely an issue among our male, predominantly middle class professional and managerial, householders because of their time-greedy jobs combined with their high career orientation on the one hand, and their preference on the other to devote their remaining time to family and children:

> The primary reason that we do this is because I work very hard, very long hours. I'm away a lot. And when it comes to family time we want to have family quality time. If I don't make an effort I don't see my children from Monday to Friday at all. So this is a way of making sure that when I am there I've got time for them rather than running around changing light bulbs and cutting the grass.
>
> Richard, HH

As is the case for the sole breadwinner father of four just quoted, such perceptions of fathers' time-squeeze are generally endorsed by female partners. Thus, Richard's partner explains:

> Time is a big issue ... he works really long hours. He leaves about six in the morning and works right through, gets home about 7.30 every day. That's when he's around. When he's not in London he's travelling. So come the weekend, he's been working these crazy hours during the week, the last thing that we want to do is waste family time fixing things.
>
> Fiona, HH

While long working hours are not solely the preserve of professional men, high earnings are more so, and allowed the men in our study a large degree of autonomy over non-work time; in effect they were able to 'make' their child/family-time by outsourcing their domestic work to handymen. As the father of three next acknowledges, however, it is more precisely the differential between his earnings and those of the handymen that is the key factor:

> [I]t was really a judgement; my time is limited and I can earn £4000 a day doing my job, so I need to pay other people to do stuff which costs less than that.
>
> Ted, HH

In this chapter, we explore in greater depth the underpinnings and dynamics of the time/money equation driving the outsourcing of male domestic work, as well as the implications of outsourcing for economic and social divisions. We first examine the source of men's time-squeeze, arguing that it lies in what might be termed a new 'father time-bind' arising from tensions between a shifting set of social expectations around fathering that emphasizes presence and active involvement, economic expectations regarding working hours and work commitment, and a highly gendered and neoliberal social policy regime. We move on to examine the economic divisions upon which the outsourcing of male domestic work is predicated, arguing that the father time-bind is in part resolved for labour-using households by extending economic and class divisions across national boundaries; a process that parallels the classed divisions that can be reinforced between middle class mothers and their female migrant domestic workers. Through an exploration of migrant handymen's fathering norms and practices, we suggest that a key feature of those divisions relates to the ability to conform to the new social expectations around active and involved fatherhood. While the findings contribute to our knowledge of how men are connected in the international division of domestic work, we reflect finally on what the study reveals about the implications for gender inequalities of the outsourcing of male domestic work. Similarly to the outsourcing of feminized domestic labour and care, our evidence on the gendered distribution of labour within households shows that gender divisions are changed but not transformed.

5.2   Householder fathers and the father time-bind

5.2.1   The 'new father': Norms and realities

Dominant constructions of the 'good father' are subject to change (Cabrera et al., 2000). The discourse of the 'New Father' (Pleck, 1997) is widely identified as the latest fathering paradigm to dominate in 'Western' societies. Emerging in the latter years of the twentieth century, the 'new fathering' ideal constructs fathers as active and engaged with their children, and attributes to fathering a multidimensional role, incorporating financial provision, hands-on physical care-giving and emotional involvement (Lamb, 1987; Pleck, 1997). The contemporary paradigm of the 'new father' differs from models that dominated previous periods in history. Writing about the USA, Lamb (1987), for example, charts the evolution from father as 'Moral Teacher' in the 18th and early 19th centuries, through father as 'Breadwinner' in the early nineteenth century to the Second World War, and father as 'Sex-role Model' following WW2 to the 1970s and the emergence of what he terms the 'New Nurturant Father'.[2]

Each of those transitions has been bound up with wider structural and ideological changes, which have also been associated with corresponding shifts in dominant constructions of motherhood and childhood, masculinity and femininity, as well as gender and parental relations. Thus, the 'new father' ideal has emerged in part in response to concerns about men's detachment from families as a result of changing family forms and patterns of childbearing, including rising divorce rates and the increasing prevalence of lone mother families. It is in part also a response to women's, and especially mothers', increased rates of employment and an associated shift towards the value of gender equality. This in turn has contributed to more fluidity in the boundaries between masculinity and femininity, and given rise to constructions of masculinity which can incorporate emotion, empathy and care – traits long associated with essentialized constructions of mothering. Changing understandings of the meanings of childhood and parenting practices are also implicated in the emergence of the 'new father'. Writing about contemporary USA, Cindi Katz (2008: 6–9) argues that for society at large children have become a 'bulwark against ontological insecurity and other anxieties about the future', leading to an emphasis on 'securing children's futures and producing perfect childhoods'. In the context of neoliberalism and the ensuing privatization of social reproduction, the responsibility for achieving this, however, is increasingly an individual rather than a collective one. The result is, especially among the privileged classes, a shift in parenting practices towards what Katz (2008: 10–11) terms 'parental involution' – 'the over-elaboration of the work (and play) of childrearing', the doing of which 'absorb[s] parents almost to the limits of absorption'.

While the 'new father' has no doubt become part of the popular imagery of contemporary fatherhood in the UK and elsewhere, as both a normative construction and a lived reality its rise is far from being unequivocal. Thus, researches in the UK (Flouri, 2005) and the USA (Pleck, 1987) point to not one model of fatherhood in contemporary times but many, which collectively rest on the ethnic, cultural and class diversity of those societies. There is also much debate about the scale, spread and meaning of the key marker of the 'new father' – men's increased involvement in day-to-day childrearing. As is evidenced in time-use surveys, fathers in countries such as the UK (O'Brien, 2005) and the USA (Bianchi, Robinson and Milkie, 2006) are spending more time caring for their children than previously. In the UK, this has been most pronounced for fathers with children under five years for whom absolute involvement in child-related activities is up from an average of 15 minutes a day in the mid-1970s to two hours a day in the late 1990s. Averages, though, can obscure differences within the population, and in the UK social class and ethnicity have been identified as key variables influencing the amount of father involvement (Dex and Ward, 2007). Indeed, based on evidence of the amount of time fathers spend with their children, the activities they undertake with them and the role they adopt in childrearing, evidence which was gained through their in depth interviews with 61 fathers and their partners, Hatter, Vinter and Williams (2002) identified not one, but four, 'types' of father – 'enforcer dad', 'entertainer dad', 'useful dad' and 'fully involved dad'.

The significance of the 'new father's' involvement in childrearing is also questioned when measured against mothers'. Thus, UK data indicate that father-time still lags behind that of mothers, even when both are in full-time paid work such that among dual full-time earner couples with dependent children father-time amounts to only 75 per cent of mother-time on weekdays (O'Brien, 2005: 13). Gender gaps of a similar order exist in the USA and elsewhere, suggesting that while the 'new father' may be associated with increasing gender convergence in time spent with children, it has not resulted in equality (Kay, 2009). The persistence of such gender inequality in quantitative indicators of parental involvement has led Esther Dermott (2008) to suggest that the 'new father' should be more accurately understood as 'intimate fatherhood'. Such an understanding, she argues, centres on emotions, the expression of affection and the uniqueness and importance of the father-child dyad, rather than on participation in the work of childcare, and is compatible with a persistent asymmetry in the roles and responsibilities of mothers and fathers. Similarly, Liz Such (2009) suggests that the notion of the 'new father' centres on 'being with' children, the context for which is often provided through leisure. While 'being with' is different from the notion of 'providing for' children, it is also, Such argues, different from 'being there'. The latter, she suggests, is what is expected of mothers, and implies an ethic of care which is achieved through work rather than shared leisure. In other words, 'new fathering' does not necessarily entail a disruption to the gendered division of domestic work among couples, which, as we saw in Chapter 2, remains sharply unequal in the UK and elsewhere. Williams (2008) meanwhile suggests that fatherhood is increasingly individualized in its norms and practice, since it is highly contingent on situational circumstances. In this context he argues that reflexivity, more than anything else, has come to define contemporary fathering.

The householder fathers we interviewed were generally reflexive about the type of dad they felt they ought to be and how their performance was measuring up against those ideals. Their own fathers provided the main fathering reference, and their aspiration almost universally was to do things differently from them. While their own fathers tended to be described with terms such as 'distant', 'uninvolved', 'breadwinner' and 'disciplinarian', our fathers mostly set out to be 'present', 'engaged', 'involved' and 'hands-on'. Confirming the wider literature, there was diversity, though, in how such ideals translated into practice. Drawing on Hatter and colleagues' (2002) fourfold typology of fathers mentioned before, our householder fathers could be categorized as either 'useful' or 'entertainer dads.' None were 'enforcer dads' – characterized as being hands-off, except in the area of discipline. Nonetheless, while one or two approximated it, none could be said to be a 'fully involved dad,' that is one who is as equally involved as his partner in running the home and family, such that his role as father is virtually interchangeable with his partner's role as mother (Hatter, Vinter and Williams, 2002).

Among our householder fathers, 'useful dads' were actively involved in everyday childcare tasks, such as taking children to school, preparing meals for them, or giving them baths and putting them to bed. While such activities implied some redistribution of domestic work, this was limited since as the following quotes from a father of three and his wife indicate, the involvement of 'useful dads' took the form of singular, definable and time-limited engagement:

I take the kids to school every day and I spend time with them then. I really like that, because it means I go to work thinking I've seen them today, we've spent 15, 10 to 15, minutes walking up there together having a bit of a chat etc. So if I don't see them in the evening, by which time they're tired at 7 anyway, it's not the end of the world.

(Oliver, HH)

My husband comes home at 10-past-7, quarter-past-7, so that's when he will have his ten minutes of fathering, whereby he perhaps reads them a story and perhaps just puts them to bed.

Martha, HH

Contrast that with the wife's evening routine, which is more akin to the constant, repetitive and unrelenting care and household work of mothers (Kilkey and Perrons, 2010: 245):

Um, at 5.45 I'm returning from work, should be here at 6.10, seeing off the nanny, get the kids, talk to the kids, get them ready, read them stories, they read me stories, at 7.30 the younger two should be in their beds, I then probably under normal circumstances, tidy up the kitchen, the rest that has not been tidied before, probably do a wash load, do the stuff for the school bags, and hopefully, fingers crossed, can sit down with a glass of wine at around 9, 9 o'clock.

Martha, HH

Moreover, as another mother with two kids and a full-time job that netted more income than her husband's indicates, the female partners of 'useful dads' maintained overall responsibility for the care of children:

He does know them well, he knows what our older daughter's reading, he's, you know, like he helps the younger daughter do her homework, you know, it's not that he's not involved, but it's like that, that I feel like I have the responsibility to sort out the childcare and what they wear and their shoes and parties. He's very good with them, do you know what I mean, he's very involved with them, but there's none of the organizational stuff of having children would he do.

Laura, HH

'Entertainer dads' among our interviewees defined their involvement with their children mostly in terms of play and leisure; activities which could be undertaken without any engagement with the domestic work that accompanies care-giving. These were also predominantly what could be termed 'weekend dads' (Hatter, Vinter and Williams, 2002); as the father of two next indicates, paid work required a long daily commute or being away from home during the week, and weekends (and vacations) were the main opportunity for involved fathering, and tended to be ring-fenced for this purpose:

I try to protect the weekends, which means during the week, generally long days, quite often away ... staying away in the week. Sometimes there's weekend work but I'd rather be away all week and be home the weekends, rather than work weekends. I try and set the weekend for family time. So mostly, weekend's family time and the weeks are um … are busy.

Mathew, HH

Weekends, however, were clearly differentiated from 'rest of week' for most of the households we interviewed. Weekend-time tended to be family-centred and dominated by the tasks of 'parental involution' (Katz, 2008) that, as we argued earlier, have become an integral but time consuming part of middle class parenting. As the father next indicates, it was common, even among 'useful dads', for fathering over the weekend to take place predominantly through what Shaw and Dawson (2001) term 'purposive leisure' – leisure designed to achieve goals around family functioning and child development:

[I]n the weekends we're quite busy with the children, so we took them ice skating at the weekend, we take them to exhibitions, we try and do things with them rather than just sit at home, and if we are at home then normally one of them will go to a party or to a theatre group or whatever so, I think that it's quite conscious that we're actively using it, I think. It's rare, well lately it's been rare for us to kind of sit in front of the TV and stuff like that. We do do that, but not very often.

Oliver, HH

5.2.2   Work pressure and work commitment among professional and managerial fathers

Despite widespread endorsement among the householder fathers we interviewed of the 'new fathering' ideal, the dominance of 'useful' and 'entertainer dad' categories of involvement, combined with the prevalence of 'weekend fathering', highlights how in the main, as Halford (2006: 387) argues 'the embodied practices of fathering children, take place outside the time-space of the working day'. This is because, as we found, involved fathering must be squeezed into male-breadwinner working practices and cultures. Among professional and managerial workers, especially in sectors such as IT (James, 2011), law (Collier, 2010) and finance (Crompton, 2006) and in 'global cities' such as London (Sassen, 2010a), these breadwinning practices entail long working hours and treat 'face-time' as a key indicator of performance (Reindl, Kaiser and Stolz, 2010). Consistent with the data on the impact of parenthood on employment (EC, 2010), there was little evidence among the householder fathers interviewed of any scaling back of hours devoted to paid work, nor of other alterations to working patterns. For the limited few who reported adjustments, these took the form of a late start or early finish one or two days a week, with the purpose, as has been found in other studies (Working Families, 2011), of supporting partners' employment. Such flexibility, however, was not costless for our fathers: it inevitably entailed longer hours of work on other days of the week, thereby ruling out time with children on those evenings. Moreover, as we shall return to further on, there was also a degree of angst about what flexibility for 'family purposes' signalled to bosses and co-workers about their professional commitment. In contrast, the mothers we interviewed had almost all adapted their paid work practices to accommodate childcare responsibilities by, for example, reducing hours of work, working from home, using flexi-time, going self-employed or (temporarily) withdrawing from the labour market. Such strategies, of course, are not cost free either, being widely associated with lower pay, discrimination, reduced opportunities for promotion, lower lifetime earnings and reduced pension accumulation (Fagan, 2003).

The professional and managerial careers that the majority of our fathers were engaged in were time-greedy ones. Like the migrant handymen already discussed, householder fathers reported long and intensive working hours, with expectations from employers and clients for high levels of flexibility and availability. The increasing spatial and temporal flexibilization of paid work discussed in Chapter 2 also impacted our householder fathers. In some cases this impact was intensified by the international nature of their jobs, which required communication with clients and colleagues in different time zones. Many of the fathers described how work frequently spilled over into home and the rest of life, often through new mobile technologies:

I've got a Blackberry and, you know, it's your friend and it's your enemy, right, because it lets you leave the office early if you need to, but it means that you're expected, if a deal is live, the client is demanding that you sort of have to respond within a couple of hours, or flick it to a team mate to make sure that they're dealing with it.

Bill, HH

And, later in the interview, the same investment banker father of four told us with no hint of irony:

I just came back from a very relaxing holiday that was very compartmentalized where we didn't spend much time thinking about work.

I mean I had to check emails, I had to respond to a few emails, but I was able to sort of keep that away from the kids. We had a similar bike holiday in May where I actually was taking calls on the tandem bicycle. They were calls that I needed to monitor rather than lead, so otherwise I wouldn't have been doing them on a bicycle.

Bill, HH

As we noted in the introduction to the chapter, female partners generally confirmed fathers' accounts of long working hours. In the main, they also endorsed such working patterns, although not unreservedly. Thus, women considered their partners' long hours of work as a necessary evil to sustain the specific career they were engaged in, their role as primary breadwinner, and/or the standard of living the family was accustomed to. A minority of women, however, reported that they actively challenged their partners' working practices, as is the case with this mother of four:

I would change my husband's approach to work/life balance, if I could. Because I mean one of the big issues I have with him is he doesn't think to say 'Okay, it's the school holidays, or it's Easter holidays, perhaps maybe I should book leave over the Easter break'. You know, and it's something we talk about all the time, or I have to say 'Have you booked leave'? 'Well no I can't now because everybody else is going and somebody needs to stay in the office'. And my answer to that is 'Well, that's because they know that you haven't booked, and you're not going to do it, so therefore they take, they book before you do'. But it doesn't seem to bother him as much as it bothers me that he doesn't take his leave time seriously.

Fiona, HH

For some fathers the ethic of 'presentism' implicit in the culture of many organizations (Reindl, Kaiser and Stolz, 2010) was a source of pressure contributing to long working hours. Even those who actively negotiated this culture in order to meet parental responsibilities found that to do so was stressful, as the following quote from a father who leaves his central London office early (4.30 pm) two days a week to collect his three kids from the childminder indicates:

I get good reports. I always get high values on any ranking, so I'm seen as doing a very good job and seen, I think, as doing enough work, that's not an issue. As I say, I think it's the visibility issue, the fact that I'm not necessarily available during core hours, or what some people would call core hours. So they would call meetings and I'd have to leave those, I think that's where the problems arise. And there is a ... You know, there is a feeling that you will get if you are in a team of six people, you arrive at 8:45, 8:30 in the morning and they're all there, and then you leave at four-thirty in the evening and they're all there. Then you do feel that maybe you're not pulling your weight as much as you should be for that ... just that time reason.

Trevor, HH

Trevor demonstrates an acute sensibility towards the fact that the 'good worker' is widely constructed by employers in abstract and disembodied terms as a 'worker only, with no other demands on their time or energies' (Halford, 2006: 387). There were indications that his sensibility was informed by his recent experience of living and working in Denmark with his wife and children. As his wife commented:

He was very content because the attitude there to work-life balance is very good. The facilities are in place for women to work full-time and for men to be equally involved in their children's lives. Everybody leaves the office at four o'clock. They start work at eight and they leave at four and go and pick the kids up from childcare and childcare is subsidised ... to the extent that anyone could afford it.

Carol, HH

In contrast to the Danish approach, many of the fathers we interviewed suggested that in the UK any challenge to working practices in order to accommodate parental responsibilities could lead to 'career-death' (Reeves, 2002) for men, and, in some industries, for women too:

A man asking for reduced working hours may find themselves made redundant at the first opportunity. And, no woman in my industry would ask. Women suffer enough discrimination in investment banking anyway. The few that actually get in and survive have to appear or have to behave in a more macho way than many of the men do. Therefore, they can never do anything that shows a degree of weakness. And a large number of them give up work when they have children. They just can't ... they just can't do it.

Sam, HH

The role of workplace culture was also highlighted by this mother of two, a full-time marketing manager in the communications industry:

> It's the culture of the organization. So for me it's the first time that I've worked in an organization that has those flexible working patterns and because I hold a fairly senior role I guess I'm trusted because I'll be measured on my output. So as long as I get the job done by the time nobody seems to really mind about the hours. I don't think I could actually put a price on that flexibility. So if I was offered another job where I had to go back into a more 9 to 5 routine, I don't know how much more money somebody would have to pay me in order to make that shift. I can't, it's a value, it's something that's intrinsic ... And I find that quite, quite difficult because sometimes it's quite tempting to look at other jobs and I think no, no, no I like my whole lifestyle. So work-life balance thing I guess.
>
> Alice, HH

Interestingly, Alice seems to have chosen her current job because of the opportunities it offers for work-family balance. In adapting working practices in order to reconcile paid work and family responsibilities, she was similar, therefore, to all the working mothers we interviewed.

Fathers, on the other hand, tended to trade-off work-family balance for professional fulfilment. Thus, fathers were not necessarily critical of employer expectations, and across the interviews explicit reference to demanding employers was made less frequently than to their own expectations about what they wanted to achieve within work. As professional workers the fathers were highly committed to their jobs. For them, the meaning of work went beyond its breadwinning function; it seemed intrinsic to their identity and self-worth, and was something to be enjoyed and somewhere where they wanted to be (James, 2011; Reindl, Kaiser and Stolz, 2010). In sharp contrast to Alice's aforesaid statement, their preferences in this respect were voiced by comments such as:

> You need to work that many hours, right? No one's forcing you at the end of the day and there are periods where the hours, as I say, I would rather do less, but you know, the cost of doing that would be being in a less ambitious and less research orientated place and it's not a cost overall that I'm willing to bear, so overall I think we have a pretty nice life.
>
> Dermott, HH

I guess I'd like to have a job that's more predictable, but part of why I enjoy my job is the adrenalin of having deals that come and having clients that demand you to be available when they need you to be available.

Bill, HH

I enjoy my work mostly. It's very demanding but it's enjoyable.

Richard, HH

I like what I do in work as well so I don't think I would like to reduce that.

Stefan, HH

5.2.3   Work-family conflict among professional and managerial fathers

Householder fathers nonetheless expressed anxieties about the space, both mental and physical, their jobs left for their 'new fathering' aspirations. In this respect, they confirmed the wider research which finds that work-family conflict is highest for those holding both a strong work and a strong family commitment (Crompton and Lyonette, 2007; Reindl, Kaiser and Stolz, 2010). Thus, this father of three expresses frustration because the thoughts of unfinished work tasks distract him from properly playing with his youngest son:

I am particularly bad at where you're kind of sitting on the floor pretending to be, you know, a big bad wolf blowing down a house and [my youngest son] will want that of course to be a hundred per cent full on and I'm trying to do it, but also thinking 'damn, I've got that email … so how am I gonna do that, ooh, right, yeah, I'm a wolf, yes, sorry', and I do get angry with myself about that. I wish I could switch off from work at that kind of level to engage with mucking about kind of stuff.

James, HH

Another, a father of two, reported similar tensions:

I wish I wouldn't worry about work when I'm with them. That pressure to do whatever, that's always slightly at the back of my mind, even when I'm with them. So, you know, when I'm putting them to bed I sometimes hurry to put them to bed a bit because then I can read just while they're dropping off to sleep.

George, HH

And a number described their commitment to work and family as a no-win situation, paralleling the popular refrain that 'women can't have it all':

> I'd like to spend more time with them and still have my job here working at the same level, doing the same things, right, you can't have it all.
>
> Dermott, HH

> I need to spend more time at work and I need to spend more time with my children, which is a depressing place to be in. I can't give either the time that they require.
>
> Sam, HH

Women largely acknowledged the constraints that professional commitments imposed on their partners' ability to translate their desire for more father-time into actual practice. While some were sympathetic to their partners' dilemmas, others, as we saw earlier (section 5.2.2) with Fiona, were more critical, highlighting partners' complicity in the situation. Thus, the following mother of three seems to question how deep her husband's expressed desire for involved fathering actually goes:

> I mean he sometimes says things like 'oh it'd be nice to take you to school one day'. You know, he'll talk to the children and say 'one day I'll take you to school in the morning' or 'one day I'll pick you up from school'. But then he doesn't ... I mean I guess he would like to do it but probably he can't need to do it enough to make it happen very readily.
>
> Victoria, HH

5.2.4 Fathering in a gendered and neoliberal social policy regime

Work-family balance (WFB) policies, in so far as they are designed to (re)organize the distribution and scheduling of workers' time between labour market and family commitments, might be expected to address precisely the kind of tensions expressed previously, even for those men who are highly career oriented. Indeed, there is evidence from the Nordic countries (Haas and Rostgaard, 2011) and more widely (O'Brien, 2009) that appropriately designed parental leave policies can help fathers alter their work-care arrangements in such a way as to facilitate increased father-involvement. As noted in Chapter 2, the influence of liberalism with its non-interventionist stance towards both the market and 'the family' meant, however, that compared to many of its European neighbours, and especially its Nordic ones, the UK was slow to develop WFB policies. Under a succession of New Labour administrations from the late 1990s until 2010, however, a series of policy developments relating to the availability, affordability and quality of childcare services, care leave entitlements and working time regulations, has resulted in the emergence of an explicit WFB policy package in the UK (Lewis and Campbell, 2007). This happened in the context of New Labour's 'Third Way' philosophy with its emphasis on the 'productive' capacity of social policy; within this framework WFB policies were constructed in instrumental terms as being good for business as well as families (Kilkey, 2006). Indeed, the government department responsible at the time for WFB policies was the Department of Trade and Industry (DTI), and its inaugural Green Paper in this policy area was titled *Work and Parents: Competitiveness and Choice* (DTI, 2000). The framing of WFB policies in the UK, therefore, contrasts sharply with that in the Nordic countries; historically those countries have been less economistic in their rationale emphasising both gender equality and child welfare as goals of WFB policies irrespective of economic imperatives (Nyberg, 2006).

Accompanying the development of WFB policies in the UK during the late 1990s and 2000s was a reframing of the notion of the 'good father' across a number of policy agendas and in such a way that was in line with the shift from the 'breadwinner father' towards the 'new father' ideal – fathering as breadwinning and involvement – espoused by our householder fathers. From a policy perspective, 'new fathering' was advocated during the New Labour years as part of a 'child-centred social investment strategy' (Esping-Andersen, 2002), and was valued in instrumental terms because of its potential benefits for children's development, particularly in early years (Kilkey, 2006). As with WFB policies, the focus on children was itself an economistic one; as Lister (2003) notes in analysing New Labour's social investment strategy more broadly, children were a concern only in so far as they were 'citizen-workers of the future'. Thus in consulting in 2005 on proposals to extend fathers' care-leave entitlements, the DTI stated:

[W]hen mothers work during the first year of their child's life and fathers play a greater role in bringing up children, this can lead to strong, positive educational effects later on in the child's life … The new law enabling mothers to transfer a proportion of their maternity leave and pay to fathers will help give children the best start in life by supporting fathers' involvement in their care.

DTI (2005, cited in Kilkey, 2006: 172)

Despite the strong rhetoric on making WFB the business of fathers, the resulting policy package in the UK is comparatively weak when it comes to providing support for involved fathering. The care-leave entitlements that have emerged have been maternalist in their overall thrust (Daly, 2010). Thus, maternity leave has been extended at the expense of parental leave, and at 12 months, it is the longest in Europe (Lewis, 2009).[3] Viewed in its entirety the care-leave package currently available to fathers in the UK – two weeks flat-rate paternity leave and pay, 13 weeks unpaid parental leave and up to six months additional paternity leave and pay transferable from the mother[4] – lacks the features associated in other countries with comparatively high take-up rates. Such features include an individualized and non-transferable (use it or lose it) right, an absolute non-negotiable right to leave, flexibility, and critically, a high income replacement rate (Haas and Rostgaard, 2011). Norway, along with other Nordic countries, has been a pioneer of father-friendly parental leave schemes. There, since 1993, a proportion of leave (initially four weeks but now 12 weeks), paid at 80 per cent of salary, has been reserved for fathers only – the father quota – and has led to significant increases in fathers' take-up. Prior to 1993 when fathers were entitled only to *share* their partners' leave, the take-up rate was 4 per cent; in 2007 under the father quota, 75 per cent of eligible fathers took five or more weeks leave (Brandth and Kvande, 2009; Moss, 2012). In contrast, a survey of UK fathers found that 45 per cent fail to take up their two-week paternity-leave entitlement, with most saying they do not do so because they cannot afford to (EHRC, 2009).

The highly maternalist and gendered package of care-leave provisions to have emerged in the UK lies in New Labour's prioritising of the business case over all others. To the extent that employers bought into WFB policies it was in relation to mothers rather than fathers. While employers could be persuaded that there might be some economic return (e.g. in terms of retention) in supporting policies designed to strengthen mothers' attachment to the labour market, it was more difficult to convince them to support policies which challenged gendered assumptions about the provision of care and male norms of employment, especially when the only purported rationale for them was a long-term one relating to the next generation of workers (Kilkey, 2006; Milner, 2010). It is also worth noting that New Labour's policy package was developed in a period of relative economic growth; it remains to be seen what will happen to it in the context of a protracted recession, and in the hands of the Conservative-Liberal coalition government elected in 2010 (Grimshaw and Rubery, 2012).

New Labour's desire to placate business also led to weaknesses in another element of the WFB policy package – the regulation of working hours. In adopting the EU Working Time Directive in 1998, the government introduced an opt-out, allowing employees to work beyond the statutory maximum of 48 hours per week. Some two years later a proposal to give parents a right to work flexibly was diluted to a right to *request* to work flexibly following the business response that the original proposal went a 'step too far' (Kilkey, 2006: 171). The result is that WFB policies have not impacted the UK's working time regime in such a way as to facilitate father-time.

Current working patterns in the UK maintain all the features of the 'liberal flexibilization' regime Mutari and Figart (2001) identified in the UK more than a decade ago. For them, 'liberal flexibilization' was characterized by de-standardization of the 40-hour working week and a gendered polarization in working hours, with men working long hours and women working short hours. As we have already seen in respect of the households we interviewed, this pattern prevails today. Thus at 43.6 hours in 2009, UK male full-time employees worked the longest hours on average per week in the EU (EC, 2010). The average for the EU as a whole was 41.2 hours (ibid.). The shortest hours meanwhile were in Denmark (38 hours per week), where as we noted before (section 5.2.2), Trevor and Carol – two of our research participants – had recently lived and found reconciling work and family life for both women and men much easier than in the UK. The UK also has a problem with *very* long working hours among men: in 2008 25 per cent of men worked more than 50 hours per week, and of those over a third were working more than 60 hours; only Austria had higher rates of male very long working hours with 28 per cent working more than 50 hours per week. The lowest rate meanwhile was in Norway with 8 per cent (Relationships Foundation, 2011). The gendered division of working time also persists in the UK. Thus, rates of part-time working are high among women (43 per cent in 2012; ONS, 2012c). Moreover, when in full-time work, women tend to work shorter hours than men (40.1 in 2009; EC, 2010), and the incidence of very long working hours (50+ hours per week) is less at 7 per cent in 2008 (Relationships Foundation, 2011).

Mutari and Figart (2001) were predominantly concerned with the gender of working time, but it is important to note that there is a class dimension to the UK's 'liberal flexibilization' work time regime too: high wage earners work longer hours than low wage earners, and the gap has been widening since the mid-1980s as working hours for the high paid have risen while those of the low paid have remained more or less stable (OECD, 2011b).[5] Thus, in both gendered and classed terms the work patterns of the households we interviewed were not specific to them. Rather, they reflected the general characteristics of the UK working time regime.

5.3   'Making time' strategies: Globalization, economic inequalities and fathering

5.3.1   Reliance on handymen as a 'making time' strategy

In the context of minimal state support for involved fathering, the fathers we interviewed sought private resolutions to their work-family conflicts. Similar to mothers who 'to spend time ... first have to make it' (Everingham, 2002: 338–9), fathers developed what we might call 'making time' strategies. These included the ring-fencing of weekends for family-child time that we reported before, and a stretching of the waking day in order to squeeze in both work and family commitments, as in the case of this father of two:

> [G]enerally I try and see them, even if it means working in the evenings more, or working before they get up, so sometimes I'll start the day at sort of 4.30, 5 in the mornings, so that I can see the boys when they wake up at 7, spend some time with them, come in, work, go home, see the kids, have their bath, work again.
>
> Dermott, HH

Time is not just made in an individualized manner though; time has a relational quality, and its making occurs in and through social relations. It is more precisely in this sense that the outsourcing of male domestic work can also be understood as a 'making time' strategy. Male householders made time to resolve, or at least ease, the conflict between their time priorities – career on the one hand, family/children on the other – by relying on the time of handymen. Handymen, therefore, could be considered as constituting another component of the 'strategic infrastructure maintenance' workforce; the workforce that Sassen regarded advanced sectors of the economy in richer countries depend upon in light of increasing demands on professional households to commit long and flexible hours to the job. More specifically, what our study reveals is how households, where fathers have often internalized long hours of work as necessary and as a key part of their masculine identity, have also come to depend on such workers. As one father acknowledged: 'Our handymen and hired help are a key part of our coping strategy' (Bill, HH). As we shall see, however, they are also highly classed components of households' coping strategies.

Inequality is a key dimension of the relationality of time: some 'times' are valued more than other 'times'. In particular, time devoted to the market ('productive time') is more highly valued, monetarily and in terms of status and prestige, than non-market social reproductive time (see Chapter 7). And, some people's times are valued more than others'. In the context of globalization the net of social relations within which time is made has widened, stretching across international borders. This has implications for inequalities in the social relations of time, which have both widened and become more complex as within-country social and economic divisions are inflected by new positionings related to nation, race, ethnicity and migration status.

Income inequality among those of working age has risen faster in the UK over the last three-to four decades than in any other OECD country. The income share ratio between the top and bottom 10 per cent in the UK increased from 8 to 1 in 1985 to 12 to 1 in 2008 (the OECD average was 9 to 1 in 2008), with significantly faster than average growth at the top of the income distribution fuelling the widening gap (OECD, 2011b). As we noted in Chapter 2, London as a 'global city', has experienced a particularly sharp rise in income inequality, and with the highest proportion of people in both the top and the bottom deciles of the national income distribution, it is more unequal than any other region in the UK (Walker, 2010). Our householders, the majority of whom had incomes in the top decile, have been on the winning side of such growing polarization, and as the following quotes illustrate, they have consequently come to occupy a privileged position in the relational net of time:

I think the more you start earning, the more you know, the proportion of what you pay for handymen becomes negligible ... okay, not necessary negligible because I think labour is still expensive in England, but it's when you start working out taking a day off ... you can earn more money working that day and paying somebody to do the work.

Rose, HH

I think I'd save a lot of money if my husband would do a lot of things, but then again, he makes enough money to pay somebody else to do it. So, and the way I look at it, his time is worth more. His time per hour is worth more than what I'm paying people coming in to work.

Fiona, HH

Did the increasing availability of *migrant* handymen specifically contribute to making outsourcing of male domestic work more affordable for householders? In a review of the evidence on the impact of migration in the UK, Ruhs (2012) argues that in the short run, while the aggregate impact of migration on the wages of existing workers is negligible, the effect is more significant along the wage distribution, with those in the middle and top gaining and those at the bottom losing. But any decline, he argues, is offset over the long run by rising wages.[6] The findings from our study would seem to match that aggregate picture. Householders and British handymen reported that in the early stages, the arrival of Polish migrants working in the sector exerted a downward pressure on handyman rates, but that this was short term as over time the rates charged by Polish handymen increased. Thus, it is difficult to be conclusive as to whether the increasing density of migrants in the sector is implicated in the increasing affordability of handyman services that our householders reported. What is more clear, though, is that paralleling the outsourcing of feminized domestic and care work, the increasing presence of migrants in the handyman sector signals a stretching across national borders of the classed social relations within which UK male householders 'make their time'. Resolution of the father time-bind through the outsourcing of masculinized domestic work, therefore, takes on a transnational, as well as a class dimension.

With the purpose of deepening the analytical pursuit of connecting men in the international division of domestic work, the chapter next turns to a discussion of the implications of this transnational reconfiguration of male domestic responsibilities from the perspective of the Polish handymen. While Chapter 4 focused on their experiences as migrant workers, here, as with the final section of the discussion of *jardineros* in Chapter 6 that follows, the concern turns to what their positioning as migrants within the new international division of male domestic labour implied for their lives beyond the role of worker, and specifically for their role as fathers.

5.3.2   Migrant handymen and the father time-bind

While physical controls at the border and internally, and related practices such as detention, expulsion and deportation, remain important tools in the UK's current approach to migration management, the main instrument it has come to adopt operates through allocating differential rights to different categories of migrants in terms of entry, residence, labour market access and social/welfare entitlements (Bolderson, 2011; Wills et al., 2010). This has resulted in a hierarchy of stratified rights among migrants – what Morris (2002) refers to as 'civic stratification' – whose particular positioning within which is a critical factor shaping their life experiences. We have already seen in Chapter 4 that since 2004 Polish nationals, along with those of other EU8 countries, have come to occupy a relatively privileged place within the UK's system of civic stratification, and while not the only factor, this has impacted on their opportunities for integration into the UK economy. Embedded within patterns of civic stratification for labour migrants is also a hierarchy of family-related rights, producing what Kraler (2010: 15) terms 'stratified reproduction' – 'the ability of migrant families to reconstitute their families during processes of migration'. In this respect too, Polish nationals migrating to the UK for work after 2004 have been positioned relatively favourably. Following 12 months of continuous employment as a WRS-registered worker, they were entitled to European Economic Area (EEA) residency status, which conferred a right of residence in the UK on the worker's family-members, whom under EU law include ascendant and descendant dependent relatives regardless of their nationality. EEA residency status also extended eligibility to many of the UK's social provisions, including child-related benefits. The result has been a shift in the migration strategies of Polish families, at least as they relate to the UK; while in the past, the dominant pattern was one of 'incomplete migration', taking the form of a male breadwinner migrant with wife and children remaining at home – a pattern which led to transnational families, today whole family migration has become more common (White, 2011).

This broad pattern was found among the Polish handymen that we interviewed. All who had dependent children and who were in a relationship with the mother of the child or children were living with their families in the UK at the time of interview. That is not to say that there were no instances of transnational fathering. This was restricted, though, to divorced men whose children were in the care of former partners back home, and men with grown-up children who had independent lives in Poland or elsewhere. In some cases, those men had children in the UK as well, usually as part of new second families, and were simultaneously engaged in transnational and proximate fathering. Transnational fathering was also a specific stage in the family migration strategy of those men who ultimately experienced family reunification. Thus it was common to leave children behind in Poland temporarily in order to get settled in London. Although planned as a short-term arrangement, we found that this could last longer than expected because of difficulties encountered in securing the resources – time, money and home – required for the proximate care of children. Without exception, however, migration ultimately expanded the fathers' livelihood opportunities and facilitated successful breadwinning, something that had been limited in Poland, as the following father of two (one born in Poland pre-migration, the other in London) testifies:

I was a mechanic and there wasn't much money for it. I was earning 200 zloty per week. Especially when the child was born, pampers, nappies were expensive because it cost 60 zloty for the nappies. Buying the nappies and some milk and my money was gone, you don't have enough.

Jan, HM

The growth in whole family migration among recent Polish migrants is not solely a product of their positioning within the UK's migration regime. Additionally, it reflects new social norms in Polish society around the valuing of partner and father-child relations (White, 2011). Indeed, research indicates that Polish fathers are just as likely as their UK counterparts to subscribe to 'new fathering' ideals: of Polish and UK fathers responding to the European Social Survey, more than 90 per cent in each group said that it was important to find a job that 'enables them to reconcile employment with family life' (Hobson and Fahlén, 2009). In line with those broader findings, fathers among the Polish handymen, just like the fathers in their labour-using households, expressed a desire to be more involved and nurturing with their own children than their fathers had been with them. Thus, a father of four commented: '[I]t's different, you know. I spend more time with the children. I give them more love. Definitely more love. I show more love to them because that's what I was missing' (Adam, HM). His wife, who also worked as a 'handywoman', endorsed this, adding immediately: 'You play with them' (Marta, HW).[7]

Many of the migrant fathers interviewed, however, reported that the pressures of paid work constrained the time available for more involved fathering. The same couple went on to report:

We leave the house at 7 or 8 am and work till 9 pm and the children when we come back home we see them for an hour and they go to sleep. We are very tired. Sometimes we don't even have the energy to play with the children. It is so. And, unfortunately, people expect more and more.

Marta, HW

Q: Your customers?
A: Yes, the customers.

Marta, HW

It's because there is a big competition. You know it well yourself, that there is a big competition on the market. To get the job you have to be very flexible, at the cost of the family.

Adam, HM

Of note in the aforesaid comments is the contrast with James, the labour-using householder quoted earlier in this chapter (section 5.2.3). For James, the constraint imposed by the job was a cerebral one as thoughts about work intruded into his father-child playtime. For Adam, it was the physical tiredness wrought by the job which restricted involved fathering.

While the migrant handymen fathers experienced a father time-bind, the 'making time' strategies available to them to resolve it were more limited than in the case of their labour-using householders. In particular, they were less able to ring fence weekends and holidays for active and involved father time:

Work often takes up most of the time in the week as well as during the weekend, so it limits the amount of time for the family and that makes things difficult.

Piotr, HM

I don't know, so far the work has taken me a bit too much time. I tried to have a holiday, I didn't have any holiday this year because I don't know what I am going to do from August, from September.

Fryderyk, HM

The comparative disadvantage of migrant handymen in finding ways to 'make time' arose from their relative positioning in London's post-industrial service economy. The migrants' incomes were more precarious than those of labour-using households, and while, as we saw in Chapter 4, some reported earnings in the top decile, most had incomes at or below the median. To improve their economic position, some of those we interviewed did handyman work for private households in the evenings and weekends on top of other jobs, usually in the construction and building sector. Work flows were also precarious, and had become more so in the context of the recession. Handymen were, therefore, reluctant to turn down work when opportunities arose. As a result they had less scope than the fathers in labour-using households to plan and strategize their time in order to resolve work-family tensions. Additionally, those who were self-employed and/or whose labour market status was in some way irregular had no access to employee rights such as paid holidays.

As the quote earlier from the handyman couple – Marta and Adam – revealed, the relative absence of 'time sovereignty' (Reisch, 2001) also arose because the handyman role as 'strategic infrastructure maintenance workers' (Sassen, 2010a) required that they respond to and fit in with the complex work-family configurations of their labour-using households. With parallels to the problems female domestic workers encounter as a result of being thought of as 'one of the family' (Anderson, 2000; Hondagneu-Sotelo, 2001), one Polish handyman father explained:

It suits them that I am flexible because actually nearly every time when they call, on a Sunday, there is a special situation. The boss is having a party and something needs to be done or if something is jammed.

Filip, HM

Indeed, this handyman's flexibility was expected to extend into the realm of 'parental involution' (Katz, 2008):

One of the boys plays football and the daughter rides a horse. My duties include chauffeuring them to specific destinations where they attend their training. I wait for them and then drive them home.

Filip, HM

Later in the interview, he expressed regret that he was unable to do the same for his own son:

You come from work tired and there are other things to do and you have to dedicate your free time to the child and you don't always have that time ... I would like to have time to do what I do with the boss's children. Whatever my son would like to do, whether he wants to play football or guitar or go swimming, so I had time to do it with my child too, as much as he wants.

Filip, HM

Overall, therefore, despite their endorsement of involved fathering, while migrant handymen seemed able to fulfil the earning dimension of the ideal, this was to a certain extent at the expense of its caring dimension. The ability to realize the expectations of involved fathering is not, therefore, universal; rather, it is highly dependent on one's economic and geopolitical positioning. Moreover, through the lens of the international division in male domestic work, it becomes apparent that it is precisely as a result of their comparatively privileged economic and geopolitical positioning that some men are able exploit the labour of other less privileged men in order to 'make time' for 'new fathering'; a situation which puts at risk the commitment of the those less privileged men to more active and involved fathering. As noted in Chapter 1, therefore, Esping-Andersen's (2009) observation of the social inequalities produced by the pursuit of gender equality among the middle classes is equally applicable to fathers as to mothers.

5.4 The international division of male domestic work and gender inequalities

The UK study set out to examine the ways in which men are connected in the relationship between globalization, migration and social reproduction. An unexpected finding, though, was that, in the main, there was rarely any physical connection between fathers in labour using households and the handymen to whom 'their' domestic work was outsourced. This was because upon the transfer of the doing of male domestic work from the household to the market, there was a further transfer within the household of its management from male to female partners. All three sets of interviews – male householders, their partners and handymen – suggested that more often than not, it was women who initiated the organization of handyman work by drawing up lists of tasks needing attention, contacting and selecting appropriate tradesmen, negotiating payments, and overseeing the completion of the various jobs. As one mother concluded:

It's almost as if he's let off the hook completely, and he just doesn't, he doesn't even … He might disagree, he might think he does, but I think he just kind of doesn't even think about it anymore.

Rachel, HH

Women take responsibility because they are at home more, because their work is deemed more flexible, or because it is more important to them than their partners that the jobs get done. As one father commented:

> In a way it's shifted pressure from me to her because a lot of the organizing of these things and the need to be here for when the handyman comes falls on her shoulders ... it's a *natural* division of duties because I'm just not here. So it's not like I'm sort of shirking the responsibility, it's just practical.
>
> Richard, HH (our emphasis)

In the previous comments Richard unquestioningly normalizes his household's gender division of labour. This stands in contrast to his wife Fiona, whom as we reported previously (section 5.2.2), challenged his lack of attention to work-family balance (but not the use of handymen).

Thus, somewhat paradoxically the outsourcing of male domestic work could lead to an increase in the burden of women's domestic responsibilities. This occurred not just because women took over responsibility for managing their partners' domestic work, but because men did not significantly use the time they gained from being freed from these responsibilities to address the gendered division of feminized domestic work and care. We have already discussed before that none of our fathers could be said to be 'fully involved dads' – dads who were virtually interchangeable with partners as mothers. While the work of 'useful dads' led to some redistribution of traditionally more feminized tasks, as we saw this was in specific areas and was time-bounded, leading one mother to observe of her 'useful dad' husband:

> It's not a traditional relationship in the sense that Pete has no expectations that I would do all the housework and he would mend the car because he knows that he can't mend the car. And so he doesn't have any expectations overtly about those gender roles, those traditional roles about me doing the cleaning and him putting his feet up with the newspaper. But he does pick and choose what he will do, so he's actually more traditional than he thinks.
>
> Rachel, HH

The result of such patterns is less change in the gender division of labour than might have been expected.

5.5 Conclusion

In this chapter, we focused on the demand side of the international division in male domestic work. Drawing on our UK householder interviews we examined the underpinnings and dynamics of the outsourcing of male domestic work. We also drew on our interviews with migrant handymen to reflect on the implications of outsourcing for economic and social divisions. A key finding is that tensions between 'competing work-life scenarios' (Hobson and Fahlén, 2009: 214) at the personal and societal level created a time-bind for the fathers we interviewed. At the personal level, while fathers subscribed to new social norms around active involved fathering, they were highly committed to their careers and did little to alter their working practices in order to realize their 'new fathering' aspirations. At the societal level, there has been much rhetoric from recent UK governments about the value of involved fatherhood, especially for child development. Work-family balance policies, however, have been developed in the context of a neoliberal and gendered social policy regime, and have not effectively challenged employers' construction of the 'good worker' as disembodied and abstracted units of labour. While our fathers' positioning as professional and managerial workers in a 'global city' labour market may have exacerbated their time-bind, they were able to utilize the monetary wealth derived from their occupational positioning to ring fence nonwork times for child- and family-centred activities by displacing 'their' domestic work onto handymen.

Paralleling the literature on the outsourcing of feminized domestic work, we found that such a 'making time' strategy, however, had consequences for social and economic divisions. We considered firstly the implications for divisions among men by examining migrant handymen's experience of work and family life. We found that migrant handymen also faced tensions between 'competing work-life scenarios' (Hobson and Fahlén, op. cit.), but positioned on the other side of the new international division of male domestic work, they had less scope for developing strategies to resolve, or at least ease, them and prioritized breadwinning over active and involved fathering. What is apparent, therefore, is that fathers' ability to conform to 'new fathering' norms is highly dependent on their position within the international social and economic order. Finally, we examined whether and how the outsourcing of male domestic work impacted the gender division of labour in our UK households, and found some changes but not transformation. Thus, while fathers are playing a greater role in childcare during the working week and/or over weekends, there was little redistribution of domestic work in general. Moreover, women often took over responsibility for the organization of male domestic work once it was outsourced, adding to their overall volume of domestic work. As a consequence, women continued to adapt their paid work to fit around domestic responsibilities, and the assumption of flexibility that ensued, or in the case of Richard, as mentioned before, was considered natural, reinforced the rationale underpinning households' gender division of labour.

6
Mexican Gardeners in the USA

Hernan Ramirez and Pierrette Hondagneu-Sotelo

6.1 Introduction

Today, visitors to Los Angeles and to other leafy suburban residential neighbourhoods in California are greeted by visual panoramas of pristinely manicured lawns and the constant hum of machinery, as gas-powered blowers, mowers, and trimmers are used to prune, manage, and manicure foliage and dispose of debris around private homes. Not long ago, mowing the front lawn was a weekly chore performed without pay by the man of the house, or by a teenage son who might have received a modest allowance for the task. The family man mowing the lawn was an iconic American image seen in scores of television shows and American front lawns on Saturday afternoons. Today it is rare to see male homeowners or family members mowing or raking their lawns in the middle class neighbourhoods of California. Unpaid male family labour has been replaced by Latino immigrant *jardineros*, who work six days a week, and often, on Sundays too. Gardening is the masculine counterpart of interior domestic work. Latino immigrant men, most of them from Mexico, now prevail in the occupational niche of suburban maintenance gardening.

For the reader who has not visited Los Angeles, it is important to recognize the spatial scale of the city and its residential neighbourhoods. Los Angeles is a very spread out, horizontal place. The County of Los Angeles, where many of the middle class and more affluent homes are located, includes 4061 square miles (10,517 km²) with a population of nearly 10 million people. By contrast, Greater London is more densely populated, with around eight million people living in 607 square miles (1572 km²). Some Angelenos live in apartments and condominiums, but since the turn of the twentieth century, when real estate boosters developed the city, single detached homes with ample front yards and backyards have prevailed as the cultural norm. Even modest homes feature expanses of lawn, with shrubs and flowers surrounding the perimeter of the house, and *jardineros* in Los Angeles service everything from small bungalows, to expansive ranch-style homes and estates. The California dream house includes a patio, pool and garden, and the temperate climate, together with ample applications of chemical fertilizers and imported water, ensures that lawn and plants grow year-round.

The tools and technology of gardening have changed over time, and the gas-powered blowers which were introduced in the 1970s are now necessary tools of the trade for the gardeners who must quickly and efficiently perform their gardening duties. Gardeners are paid by the job, and a crew of two men may tend up to 15 or 20 residential gardens in one day. At the low end, homeowner residents may pay as little as $50 a month to have their yard 'mowed and blowed' weekly, but upmarket clients pay substantially more – $300 a month – for services that include annual planting, fertilizing, pruning and even more for 'extras' such as putting in irrigation or hardscape. Grass lawn and shrubs grow easily in LA's hospitable climate, creating a Sisyphean cycle of fertilizing, watering, mowing, blowing and disposing of copious amounts of grass and leaves. Recently, a new environmentalist-inspired anti-lawnism has emerged (Bormann, Balmori and Gebelle, 2001; Haeg, 2008), but Angelenos have adopted it sparingly – and why shouldn't they, when Mexican immigrant gardeners are doing the work? If time-strapped homeowners had to mow their own lawns, the lawns would disappear (or at the very least, they would likely become overgrown). Instead, the standards for lawn care have risen, and with the exception of neighbourhoods full of foreclosures due to the sub-prime mortgage crisis which began in 2008 (most of which is not concentrated in Los Angeles County), in Los Angeles and nearby cities, it is extremely rare to see a dead, dried-out or overgrown lawn. Lawn veneration prevails with some municipalities imposing fines on residents who fail to follow the cultural standards of lawn upkeep.

Latino immigrant gardeners work around the exterior of the home, a space gendered as men's domestic area. No one refers to them as 'male domestic workers' but this would not be inaccurate, as they are contracted by the homeowner residents to do household maintenance gardening work. Unlike domestic workers who do interior cleaning and caring for children or the elderly, and unlike the Polish handymen in the UK, the immigrant gardeners never enter the interior of the homes. Thus, they have little, if any contact with the residents who employ them. Social invisibility prevails, yet since they work outdoors and move around residential neighbourhoods in pickup trucks laden with tools and gas-powered machinery, they have high public visibility and audibility. This last trait has become a source of irritation and contention with some LA residents who sought to ban the blowers, and this prompted a movement towards collective organizing among Latino immigrant gardeners in the 1990s.

In this chapter, we contend that Latino immigrant gardeners constitute the most significant group of male domestic workers in the contemporary USA. Latino immigrant gardeners are pervasive in California, Texas, Florida, Georgia, North Carolina and even in cold weather states such as New Jersey and New York. As we have already noted, they do the work that husbands and sons once did for free, and they work in the domestic areas traditionally defined as male spaces. They also perform tasks socially constructed as men's work, including lifting and using heavy machinery, mowing, pruning, and doing yard clean up, with fallen leaves and dirt swirling about them. This sort of men's work is dedicated to the upkeep of residential real estate values and appearances, not the human social reproduction of caring for bodies and domestic interiors. As such, suburban maintenance gardening labour is better remunerated and rewarded than the work of Latina immigrant nannies and housekeepers. Yet, as we will see, the gardening occupation is part of the informal sector of the economy, and it is deeply stratified, offering ladders of mobility to the route owners, and marginal wages for the employed *ayudantes*.

In this chapter, we discuss the historical trajectory of the occupation, and its transformation from a Japanese occupational niche to a largely Mexican immigrant occupational niche. After reviewing the processes of ethnic succession and the relevant immigration regimes, we adopt an intersectionalities approach to show how gardening labour is a stratified occupation. We discuss the dynamics of gardeners' family relations in regard to occupational exploitation and self-exploitation, and show how stratification in the occupation affects the *jardineros*' family relations.

6.2   Legacies of conquest, labour migration and ethnic succession: From Japanese gardeners to Mexican gardeners

The residential maintenance gardening occupation as we know it today was innovated by Japanese immigrant men in early twentieth century California. Japanese men had come to the USA from rural backgrounds and with little money. In California, they first worked in other jobs, not gardening. From the end of the nineteenth to the early twentieth century, young Japanese men in Los Angeles could be found working as domestic 'houseboys' for Anglo families, who had flooded into California, drawn by the prospect of quick riches in the gold rush that followed the Mexican American war and the USA conquest of approximately one-third of Mexico's territory (Glenn, 1986). Many Japanese migrant men viewed working as domestics as temporary first jobs, and they shifted to agriculture and eventually suburban gardening, as soon as they could (España-Maram, 2006: 23). When they were allowed to buy real estate property, the Japanese also developed a related industry, plant and flower nurseries, cultivating carnations and chrysanthemums for sale as cut flowers, or plants for sale to local residents looking to spruce up their yards. As 'truck farmers' selling their produce in cities, they thus ascended into the ranks of the petite bourgeoisie (Bonacich and Modell, 1980: 45).

Although the *Issei* (first generation Japanese immigrant) gardeners had been tending to their employers' yards as early as the 1890s, it was in the 1920s that the maintenance gardening occupation began developing rapidly among Japanese Americans in Los Angeles (Bloom and Riemer, 1949; Hirahara, 2000). Los Angeles by then had an expanding number of suburban neighbourhoods with detached homes and garden-filled yards, and the more affluent homeowners began hiring Japanese gardeners to do maintenance upkeep. The gardeners worked in various yards, developing a route of paying customers. A push factor was, however, also implicated in this expansion of Japanese men's involvement in domestic gardening services. Anglo American fear, hatred and anxiety about the growing economic power of the Japanese resulted in legislation that pushed the Japanese from land ownership and into the labouring class. We can see this as a racially defined restrictionist movement. The California Alien Land Law, which was passed in 1913, denied aliens ineligible for citizenship the right to own land in the state of California, but historians agree that the law targeted primarily the Japanese. The intent of the law, and of its subsequent amendment in 1920, was to drive the Japanese out of agriculture and truck farming, thus eliminating white farmers' competition (Gaines and Cho, 2004; Henry, 1978: 26). Many of these Japanese people then moved into boarding houses in Los Angeles's early Japanese ethnic enclaves. As they were dispossessed of their land and moved to the cities and suburbs, many went on to start their own suburban maintenance gardening businesses (Tsuchida, 1984; Tsukashima, 1991, 1995/1996, 1998).

Although an exhausting job, suburban maintenance gardening could be undertaken with modest amounts of start-up capital, knowledge of English, or special skills (Bonacich and Modell, 1980: 45; Tsuchida, 1984: 443). Coming from rural Japan and having worked on agricultural farms, most immigrant men were able to handle the rigours of horticultural work. Their farming experience in Japan or the USA, as well as their ability to leverage images associated with Japanese horticultural aesthetics and artistic talent, facilitated Japanese immigrant men's entry into the gardening occupation in Southern California. Simultaneously, a context of racial discrimination and hostility emanating from the surrounding society prevented them from finding opportunities for advancement in the general economy. In this regard, racism and exclusion helped pull them towards domestic gardening (Daniels, 1966: 11–12). By the 1930s, maintenance gardening was institutionalized as a Japanese American man's job not only in California but also in the West Coast states of Oregon and Washington.

The steady income they derived from gardening work allowed many *Issei* gardeners to own a house, a pickup truck, and a passenger car, and to provide for their families (Tsuchida, 1984: 445). Many *Nisei* (second generation) men learnt the trade while helping their fathers during their free time, particularly during summer vacations from school, providing unpaid family labour in support of the family business. Sometimes wives and daughters also worked alongside their male kin, but this was somewhat rare (Jiobu, 1988: 362). Even after the *Nisei* obtained high school and college education, many remained in gardening because of racial discrimination (Japanese American National Museum, 2007).

Japanese immigrant men entered the gardening occupation with help from their fellow immigrants who had already established a foothold in the occupation, and that pattern holds true among Latino immigrants today. Gendered network hiring prevailed, with small gardening crews consisting of brothers, uncles, cousins, and men from the same Japanese prefectures working in clusters of two or three throughout the city. Newly arrived Japanese immigrants would begin working as helpers, earning relatively low wages while performing menial tasks and learning how to maintain lawns and gardens under the supervision of a more experienced maintenance gardener, typically an older, self-employed co-ethnic immigrant (often a male relative) who had spent years building up a route of paying customers and developing his skills as a gardener.

After a period of informal apprenticeship, which could last a few years, helpers went into business for themselves, buying their own truck and equipment and landing new clients, typically through word-of-mouth referrals. They also bought established routes from their fellow gardeners, or might be handed a few clients from a route owner grateful for his helper's years of hard work. This reliance on recruiting through informal channels to secure 'cheap' labour from within the ethnic group, as well as the reliance on unpaid family labour, contributed to the rise of maintenance gardening among the Japanese (Bonacich and Modell, 1980: 48).

Distinctive immigration histories are also bound up with the development of the gardening occupation. Most of the Japanese immigration to the USA occurred during a short span of time, unlike Mexican immigration, which has remained more or less constant from the late nineteenth century until 2011, when net flows stopped. The Japanese were recruited to replace Chinese immigrant workers after the Chinese Exclusion Act of 1882, but passage of the 1907 Gentlemen's Agreement and later the 1924 ban on immigration of 'Orientals' from the Eastern hemisphere stopped Japanese immigration. By the late twentieth century, when the racial exclusion bans were lifted, Japan had become a modern, industrialized nation, and few Japanese looked to the USA for better life opportunities.

Without newer waves of compatriots to hire, Japanese gardeners began hiring Mexican immigrant men to work for them. Evidence suggests that Japanese American gardeners in Los Angeles employed Mexican helpers as far back as the 1930s (Tsuchida, 1984), but it was not until the late 1960s that the Mexican immigrant population began growing in urban and suburban locales throughout the USA Southwest. USA-born Mexican workers and labour migrants had been present in the West since 1848, but deportation campaigns, seasonal agricultural work, and labour recruitment programmes sponsored by both the USA government and employers ensured that a significant proportion of Mexican immigrants during the early twentieth century remained in the USA only temporarily (Garcia y Griego, 1983). The Second World War brought Mexican male workers back to the USA when the USA government initiated the Bracero Programme, a massive labour recruitment programme that was initially designed to meet wartime labour shortages in agriculture, but which lasted for more than 20 years. Between 1942 and 1964 nearly five million temporary work contracts went to Mexican migrant workers, and nearly all of these contracts went to men. This Bracero Programme officially ended in 1964, but it sowed the seeds for the rapid expansion and large-scale permanent settlement of Mexican immigrants in the 1970s and 1980s. As former

Braceros legalized their status through employer certification or family reunification provisions of the 1965 Immigration Act, many of them brought their families to the USA and moved out of the fields and into cities and suburbs. Social network migration prevailed, and the demand for Mexican immigrant labour diversified out of agricultural jobs in rural areas and into manufacturing, services, and construction – jobs located in cities and suburbs.

It is in this post-1965 era, beginning in the 1970s and consolidating in the 1980s, that gardening shifted from being a Japanese American occupational niche to a Mexican one in Los Angeles and elsewhere in the USA (Ramirez and Hondagneu-Sotelo, 2009). By the 1970s, the numbers of *Nisei* gardeners in Los Angeles had begun to dwindle, as succeeding generations of Japanese Americans experienced upward mobility and embarked on professional careers. *Nisei* gardeners who had more customers than they could handle themselves generally hired Mexican helpers, for *Nisei* labour was in short supply, more expensive and less compliant (Tsuchida, 1984: 448). These Mexican helpers, in turn, followed in the time honoured tradition of their Japanese predecessors and went on to establish their own gardening routes. At around the same time, Los Angeles experienced the effects of growing income inequality, globalization and the rise of time-starved dual income households hiring and outsourcing more domestic services. The result was a rapid increase in the number of Mexican immigrant gardeners in the city.

6.3   A growing occupational sector, the institutionalization of Mexican gardeners and the migration regime

It is notoriously difficult to measure informal sector growth, as census data tend to undercount both informal economic activity and the employment of unauthorized immigrant workers. Nevertheless, Integrated Public Use Microdata Series data show that in 1980 there were 8000 Mexican foreign-born men working as gardeners in the Los Angeles-Long Beach metropolitan area. By 1990, this had more than doubled to 19,886, and by 2000, there were 31,000 foreign-born Mexican gardeners counted. The numbers nearly quadrupled in 20 years (Ruggles et al., 2004). It is likely that many remain uncounted. Of course the population of Los Angeles County has grown immensely in recent decades, but so has the widespread employment of gardeners in private residential homes. While paying for gardening services was once a privilege enjoyed by the wealthy, in Los Angeles today, like interior domestic service, gardening service is routinely accessible to the middle class and to dual-income families.

This expansion in gardening occurred during the 1980s and 1990s, decades when Mexican immigration increased dramatically. Since 1980 Mexico has become the largest source country for immigrants to the USA, and in 2006 there were 11.5 million foreign-born Mexican immigrants in the USA, accounting for approximately 30 per cent of the total immigrant population (Batalova, 2008). This is a labour migration, as opposed to the migration of professionals or refugees, and Mexican immigrants are characterized by very low levels of formal schooling, rural backgrounds with traditions of working the land, and during the early years of migration and settlement, limited English proficiency (Portes and Rumbaut, 2006). These are traits very similar to those of the Japanese immigrants who innovated maintenance gardening.

The changing immigration regime is also critical. While former Braceros were able to legalize their immigration status in the late 1960s and 1970s, unauthorized migration from Mexico has since grown. After many years of legislative negotiation the federal government passed the Immigration Reform and Control Act in 1986, which criminalized the employment of undocumented immigrant workers, but also made available a one-time amnesty-legalization programme, allowing approximately 3.1 million formerly undocumented immigrants to regularize their status. This affected the gardening sector in Los Angeles, as many formerly undocumented *ayudantes* used their new legal resource to start their own independent route-owning businesses. Since 1986, however, there has been no legalization programme and it is very difficult, in fact nearly impossible, for Mexican undocumented immigrants to legalize their status. In the 1990s and the first decade of the new millennium the USA government militarized the USA-Mexico border, prompting deaths, violence and fewer trips back home to Mexico. More recently, the government has accelerated deportations and detentions of undocumented immigrants. Thus, Mexican immigrant gardeners have diverse immigration statuses. Among the route owners, we find many men who have been in the country for several decades, and who are naturalized citizens or legal permanent residents. The *ayudantes* include many undocumented immigrant men who have not been able to secure authorization to work.

Today, the gradual process of ethnic succession that began several decades ago is complete, as relatively few Japanese American gardeners remain. In Los Angeles, suburban maintenance gardening is now institutionalized as a Mexican immigrant man's job. There are some Central American immigrant men in the occupation, but they seem to have had a harder time breaking into the ranks of an occupation that is dominated by Mexican immigrant social networks. Mexican immigrant men – those with legal status and those without it – provide an institutionalized source of labour in many industries and occupations, in construction, hotels, restaurants, and as painters, parking valets, and *carwasheros*. Gardening is simply one of the many diverse service occupations in which they work, serving as part of a new caste-like labour force in a post-industrial plantation-like economy.

Unlike the aforementioned occupations, however, the gardening niche has a long history of offering immigrant men the promise of upward mobility through self-employment and independent small business ownership. In the following section, we examine how the occupation is stratified. As we will see, this stratification, involving legal status, earnings and position in the occupation, has lasting consequences for the men's relationships with their families.

6.4 Intersectional inequalities in the gardening occupation and masculinized human capital

Suburban maintenance gardening is a racialized and gendered immigrant job, one undertaken primarily by working class Mexican immigrant men, many of whom have origins in central western rural Mexico. These men grew up in *ranchos*, cultivating corn and beans alongside their fathers and siblings as part of a peasant family agricultural system. When they arrive in Los Angeles, they are exposed to suburban residential gardens for the first time. They encounter vast, expansive lawns and an array of ornamental flowers, trees and bushes, all of which require different tending and cultivation techniques than those they used back home in the fields. There is both continuity and discontinuity with the cultivation techniques, as they are still working with plants and soil, but they must learn to operate machinery, such as lawnmowers and leaf blowers, that they might have never seen in their *ranchos* or villages of origin. However, the social organization of the work is similar to what the men experienced in Mexico, because gardeners generally work in small homo-social groups, with a route owner who oversees and is assisted by one or two *ayudantes*. These men are often relatives or *paisanos* from the same town.

In central western Mexico the work of cultivating crops in the fields is men's work, one that men begin learning as young boys. Mexican immigrant gardeners' backgrounds working in the fields alongside their fathers and older brothers endow them with masculine human capital well-suited for the way that residential gardening is organized in the

USA. The men are accustomed to getting dirty and performing manual labour under the sun. They consider a pair of rough and callused hands to be a sign of an honoured working class masculinity (Ramirez, 2011). They take pride in getting their work done, but few of them know the names of all the plants they tend. One *jardinero* recalled that an Anglo female garden designer he once worked for seemed to know the scientific name of every plant she encountered. When asked what he thought about that, he simply replied, 'that's girl stuff.'

They view gardening as a masculine job that takes place in a masculine milieu. It involves manual work that is performed outdoors and is coded as masculine. It is performed by men, and organized through social networks of male kin and friends; in fact, in Los Angeles, 97 per cent of non-USA citizen gardeners are men (Klowden et al., 2005). As we indicated in the introduction to this chapter, gardening work is also masculinized because it provides the commoditized version of labour that substitutes for the work of husbands and sons.

While it is seen as a masculine and honourable job, the gardening occupation also reflects racial and legal status hierarchies. It is rare to find white men in the occupation as self-employed gardeners, although Vietnamese refugees, French Basques and other European migrants from rural peasant societies also broke into gardening in the mid and late twentieth century California. As we will see in the next section, legal citizenship status differentiates route owners and their *ayudantes*.

6.5 The social organization of gardening and gardeners' agency

Given their history of migration, direct labour recruitment, and economic incorporation in the United States, and their low levels of education and occupational skills, most Mexican immigrants in the USA work as manual labourers, and not as credentialed professionals. Other immigrant groups, particularly Koreans, Cubans, Chinese, and in an earlier era, Jewish immigrants, have been over-represented among entrepreneurial immigrants (Portes and Rumbaut, 2006). We argue, however, that self-employed *jardineros* represent a hybrid form of worker-entrepreneur: they run their own small businesses, employ one or more co-ethnic workers, own their trucks, tools, and equipment, and independently build a clientele and negotiate prices and terms of service with their clients, who tend to be white homeowners. Yet, even as small business owners, they continue performing the sorts of tasks that are typically associated with manual labour migrants.

In order to understand the distinctiveness of the position these men occupy as worker-entrepreneurs, it is instructive to build on insights from the literature on ethnic enclave entrepreneurship more broadly. The concept of immigrant ethnic enclaves captures spatial sites where immigrant co-ethnics constitute a singular commercial sphere of business owners, employees, and customers (Light, 1972; Light and Bonacich, 1988; Valdez, 2008b; Zhou, 1992). Chinatown and Cuban Miami are classic ethnic enclaves. An ethnic enclave economy provides immigrants with refuge from otherwise hostile labour markets, endowing a spatially concentrated ethnic community with social capital and social networks, enabling the development of thriving ethnic businesses (Valdez, 2008b). Immigrants without valuable employment credentials, job skills, education, and English language fluency, and who face racial discrimination in the formal, non-ethnic economy, may seek work in the ethnic enclave and discover that it serves as an 'employment buffer' (Light and Gold, 2000), or that it prevents 'downward assimilation' (Valdez, 2008b). In the most optimistic rendering, the ethnic enclave leads to expanding opportunities and upward mobility (Lee, 2002; Light, 1972). Unpaid family labour, social capital, and ethnic solidarity bolster business. Sectoral specialization is a key feature of immigrant businesses. As Kaplan and Li (2006: 3) summarize, this specialization stems from 'the skills that ethnics bring with them, the opportunities available in a particular context, the legacy of longstanding activity in a sector, and the structural barriers set by hosting societies'.

For Mexican immigrant men, the gardening business has become a sector of gendered specialization. As we will show in this section, Mexican immigrant men possess skills, experience, and the predisposition required for residential maintenance gardening, and through informal apprenticeships they learn from one another how to operate these businesses.

By definition, the workplaces are spatially dispersed. Gardeners go to work in other people's neighbourhoods and yards. In Los Angeles, many of them travel daily from the more heavily Latino eastside to the more affluent white majority neighbourhoods. Like paid domestic workers and nannies, the gardening industry is integrated into the mainstream suburban society and economy, allowing Latino immigrant workers passage into neighbourhoods where they might not otherwise be welcome. Here, the 'landscapes of the ethnic economy', a term that geographers introduced to refer to Chinatowns or ethnic commercial neighbourhoods (Kaplan and Li, 2006), are simultaneously visible and invisible throughout white suburbia. While black men in Los Angeles' white, affluent neighbourhoods may be racially profiled, Mexican men in trucks with tools are common sights.

We find that occupational stratification and an informal organizational system mediate residential gardening jobs. Most gardeners, however, do a variety of tasks, including driving, mowing, blowing leaves, pruning, clipping, planting annuals, fertilizing, and so on. The primary differentiation among the gardeners is determined not by the tasks they do, but according to occupational social relations. There are basically two sub-occupations, route owners or independent gardeners and *ayudantes*, the waged employees who work for the independent gardeners.

6.5.1 The *ayudante* apprenticeship

There is a linear progression of mobility in the job, and while not everyone becomes a financially solvent route owner, all newcomers begin by working as *ayudantes* or employees. These are not advertised job positions. Rather, gendered social networks provide an 'in'. The men typically start off working for male family members or for acquaintances from their *ranchos* or towns of origin. A few are hired from day labourer hiring sites, but generally, social networks and social capital assure the independent route owners of a trusted, loyal workforce (Huerta, 2007; Pisani and Yoskowitz, 2005, 2006).

Social network hiring and social capital are institutionalized mechanisms of immigrant occupational niches and ethnic enclave employment (Light, 1972; Waldinger and Lichter, 2003), and social networks may in fact help regulate informal sector occupations (Hondagneu-Sotelo, 1994a). It is not just solidarity among co-ethnics, however, but a familial and localized sense of trust and obligation that allows newly arrived Mexican men to work as gardening helpers for their family members and close acquaintances. At the point of occupational entry, informality and social capital rule.

Wages are generally paid in cash. During the summer of 2007, the daily wages averaged between $75 and $80, with drivers earning slightly more ($100 to $110). With the minimum wage in California set at $7.50 an hour in 2007, the *ayudantes* were earning just slightly better than minimum wage. Most of them earned from $450 to $480 for a six-day workweek – and they typically worked long days, especially in summer. Whenever possible, the *ayudantes* earned additional pay (typically $100 a day) by working weekend 'extras'. Tree trimmers, a job that involves more danger and skill, might earn $200 a day. Informality prevails, and part of their wages may even be paid in kind, as room and board to men who are newly arrived from Mexico.

When discussing their earlier experiences as *ayudantes*, some of the men – now route owners – recounted narratives of gratitude while some expressed resentment, but they all agreed that working as a gardener's helper served as an apprenticeship and an important entry into residential maintenance gardening. As one man recalled: 'I started working [in 1974] as a gardener's helper with some relatives, but really, it was practically out of appreciation for food and everything, and I worked that way for four months. And that's what allowed me to learn [about gardening].' Previously, newcomers to the job may have worked as helpers for several months or years before they broke out on their own. As we see further on, however, the opportunity for progression from *ayudante* to route owner is now tighter in the context of more restrictive immigration laws.

Migrant social networks among family and friends constitute powerful channels pulling the men into gardening. Thirty-seven out of the 47 gardeners interviewed reported finding their first job with family members or friends. One interviewee said that he had initially shown an interest in construction work, but this proved impossible to break into because his brothers and uncles all worked in gardening jobs. 'So, well, okay, gardening it is', he conceded. Another gardener explained the magnet of family networks this way: 'All of my paisanos [countrymen] that are here, those from the rancho, my friends, the brothers of my friends, my ancestors, all of them came here to work in this [gardening].' Recognizing the powerful tug of these ties, but the arbitrary job sector to which they connect, he explained: 'If they had all worked in restaurants, I would assure you that today we'd all be working in restaurants.'

Mexican immigrant gardeners have low levels of formal education, few job skills, and backgrounds rooted in rural, peasant agriculture in central western Mexico. The majority of our interviewees grew up in *ranchos*, or rural villages, and as adolescents many of them cultivated and harvested corn, beans, and other crops in small plots of land, working alongside their fathers, as described earlier. All of the gardeners interviewed, except one, had previous experience working in small-scale agriculture in Mexico (the one exception was an engineer who was pulled into gardening, he said, because 'my relatives were gardeners'). Some had also worked in the agri-business fields in California. In this regard, they have a similar human capital profile to earlier generations of Japanese gardeners who brought farming experience with them from Japan, which Tsuchida (1984: 440) suggests facilitated entry into the occupation but also made a hard job 'relatively easy for them'. The Mexican gardeners echoed this assessment. Residential maintenance gardening is hard physical work, but the gardeners were unanimous that it was easier and *menos matado* (less backbreaking, but literally, less killing), than either peasant cultivation on Mexican *ranchos* or fieldwork in Californian agriculture. When asked about what they liked best about their job, they said it was the ability to work outdoors, in *aire libre* (open air), as they had been accustomed to doing in Mexico. They saw working outdoors, and among plants, as preferable to the limited opportunities and stifling work sites available to them in factories, sweatshops, or restaurant kitchens.

6.5.2 Becoming an independent gardener

The potential for higher earnings increases for independent gardeners who maintain a 'route' of regular customers. The independent gardeners act as worker/entrepreneurs. They continue to do the manual work of gardening maintenance, but they also own their own trucks, machinery, and tools, and, importantly, they negotiate the price and collect fees for services from the customers. In essence, they own a route of paying jobs. Most *ayudantes* eventually try to venture out on their own as route owners.

Mexican immigrant men become independent gardeners both by building on the gendered human and social capital that they have already accumulated and by cobbling together help from family members and friends who give or lend them equipment and sometimes *casas*, or customers. The route of regular customers is the primary business commodity that these gardeners own (Huerta, 2007), and the gifting and sharing of routes poses an interesting sociological dilemma. The gardeners talk about the size of their business not in relation to how many *ayudantes* or employees they have working, nor how much they own in tools and machinery, but rather by reference to the amount they gross from their route of paying customers each month. '*Traigo una ruta de $7000*' or 'I've got a route worth $7000 [a month]' is the common lingo they use to discuss their businesses. Why would they give away part of their business? Some well-established gardeners want to downsize their routes, or they want to get rid of their lowest paying clients, but they also do it to help newcomer relatives. An uncle or father may give his nephew or son a portion of a route as a wedding gift. One gardener offered this analysis of the social network chains that initially absorb men as *ayudantes* or employees, and then spawn new, independent gardeners by giving them portions of routes:

For example, my nephew arrived and I got him in working with me. One day soon he'll want to become independent, and I'll help him.

I'll say, 'Here are a few houses', and then it will be one more who is separating [to become an independent route owner] and then his brother will come, and he'll put him to work. And that's how it grows.

Adrian

Even with assistance from friends and family, the men need financial capital to become independent route owners. According to our interviewees, breaking into independent gardening in 2007 required a financial investment of about $5000. Gardeners need a truck, tools, equipment, and a list of paying customers. Gardeners agree that becoming an independent route owner is harder than it used to be because there are too many gardeners, and because equipment is now more expensive. Careful calculations of investment are in order. As one gardener said:

If you're going to start from the bottom, you need a truck. You need your equipment, and all of that. Just your maquina [mower], how much is that going to cost you? Brand new, it'll cost more than $1000. That's just to cut, and then maybe another $500 for the blower. And then the edger, let's say another $400 and some. And you have to buy your truck, your rakes, all of it – hoes, rakes, hoses, oil, and gasoline every day. You have to spend a lot.

Salvador

Before inflation, it was cheaper. In the 1980s, one gardener recalled spending $1100 on a used Datsun pickup, and going to the swap meet to buy used equipment. 'Back then, 20 years ago, it wasn't that expensive', he said. 'You could buy a lawnmower for $160, a weeder for $60, a blower for $40' (Antonio). Although no one spoke about buying stolen machinery or equipment, just about every gardener told a story of having had a blower or power mower stolen from his truck. This suggests a lively underground market at swap meets for low-priced gardening equipment, a market that lowers the entrance fee for becoming a route owner. With a strong route, a successful route owner can gross $5000 monthly, so the initial costs can be quickly recouped.

Routes are also bought and sold, usually for two to three times what they generate in monthly earnings, and this too is an informal practice. Typically the transaction occurs between friends and acquaintances, but at least one LA lawnmower repair shop features a corkboard with notices of routes for sale. These are delicate negotiations. While social capital and trust prevail, the buyer still risks purchasing a route where the customers may be habitually late payers or too picky, or where the homes are distantly located.

Finally, mobility in household gardening requires legal immigrant status. Legal immigrant status is technically required for route own-ers because they own and drive trucks, and since 1993, applicants for driver's licences in California must present Social Security numbers. All of the *ayudantes* we interviewed were undocumented immigrants, and most of the route owners (32 of 36) were legal permanent residents or naturalized USA citizens. Still, a few interviewees had ventured into independent gardening in spite of undocumented status, and like many of the estimated 12 million undocumented immigrants in the USA, they lived and worked in fear. They fear not only deportation, but also hav-ing their trucks impounded and losing their investments. 'I don't have a driver's licence so I must drive very carefully', said one man who had his truck registered under his wife's name. Besides driver's licences, garden-ers are also required to have work permits to do gardening in particular municipalities. These are generally not enforced, and gardeners seek permits if they have many houses in one city, and forego the permit fees if they only have one or two houses in the city limits. Undocumented gardeners also fear inspectors who may issue tickets for using loud, gas-powered blowers. Gas-powered blowers are banned in 20 California cities, many of which are in Southern California, but this is haphazardly enforced and blowers are widely used.

6.5.3 Managing the route: Shades of grey

Once they own a route, Mexican immigrant gardeners innovate busi-ness strategies along a continuum of economic informality and for-mality. First, it is important to note the many practices of formality in which the gardeners engage. Most of the independent route owners are legal permanent residents or naturalized USA citizens. This means that they can, and usually do, abide by the rules that regulate the roads. They generally hold valid California driver's licences, pay state regis-tration fees for their pickup trucks, buy auto insurance, and carefully abide by traffic laws. They also pay income tax as well as the annual municipal permits in cities where they have a concentrated number of customers. Moreover, they act as formal business agents by submit-ting monthly bills in writing to their customers. The customers pay by check, not cash. The gardeners cash these checks at banks, and they pay income tax, although they may underreport their earnings.

Still, informality characterizes other dimensions of their jobs, particu-larly those involving their paid helpers and paying customers. Most hire informally, through family and migrant networks, and they pay these *ayudantes* in cash. Some even try to maintain good relations with their workers by providing lunch for them, a paternalistic practice of informality. While the gardeners bill their customers in writing, mailing the bill or leaving it in the mailbox, they do the jobs based on verbal agreements. There is typically no signed contract between the gardener and client. When the gardeners encounter clients who are months late in paying their bills, they do not penalize these late bill payers or go to small claims court, but they informally handle it by patiently waiting for payment. It is not uncommon for a gardener to keep working at a home where he has not been paid for three months. Independent route owners thus navigate their businesses by abiding by some rules and practices of the formal economy, but they also rely on informal occupational practices.

6.5.4 Managing competition

The biggest complaint, repeated by every independent route owner interviewed, is that customer fees have remained stagnant while competition and underbidding from new independent route-owner gardeners has become fierce. '*Estamos entre la espada y la pared* ... We're caught in between a rock and a hard place', is how one gardener summarized the situation of being caught between rising costs and stagnant fees. Also, more gardeners willing to work for less are crowding the field. Independent route owners who had been in business for many years said that the Immigration Reform and Control Act of 1986, which as noted previously offered amnesty-legalization to many formerly undocumented Mexican migrants, had acted as a catalyst for helpers to venture out on their own as route owners. Amnesty-legalization freed the *ayudantes* from the yoke of working for someone else, and it emboldened those who remained as helpers to be more demanding about their working conditions and pay. Labour costs, and the cost for equipment and maintenance had steadily increased, and during the summer of 2007, gasoline soared to over $3 a gallon. All of this created competitive pressures.

> The clients don't go with the first estimate they get, but they get two, three, maybe four estimates from different *jardineros*. They tend to go with the lowest bidder. If you charge $300 [a month] for a place, there will be people who will charge $250.
>
> Salvador

> Things have gotten tougher for *jardineros*. Clients today look for the lowest price, and they almost always go for the lowest bid. This has

been the change I've noticed over the last 15 years. Lots of new *jardineros* have entered the field ... They charge lower prices, and as a result, the work is going downhill for all *jardineros*.

Raul

I think *jardinería* is still a good line of work. It's good to be your own boss. But I don't like it when younger *jardineros* undercut each other ... clients take advantage of the situation and pay the lowest possible price.

Fernando

Veteran gardeners who have been working for the last 30 years in Los Angeles said the market was now flooded with competitors. 'For every *jardinero* who retires, there must be two new guys who enter *jardinería*. In the 1980s, there were half as many as today,' said Alberto. While their periodization varied, many of these veteran gardeners portrayed the 1970s and 1980s as the 'golden age' of gardening in Los Angeles.

Managing the route of customers is the top business skill required of successful gardeners, and Mexican immigrant gardeners innovate various approaches to doing this in the increasingly competitive environment. Route size varies, but most keep a route of about 40 to 60 clients. One route-managing business strategy is to simply increase the route size, to obtain and keep as many clients and jobs as possible, regardless of what they pay. One interviewee maintained a route of between 200 and 250 customers, but he owned four trucks, each manned by different crews. This gardener's strategy was to build the business and route size to the maximum, and his customers included ones that he'd had since he first began in the business. 'I'm not going to leave them just because they pay little', he reasoned. Rather, he said his business philosophy was *'No te fijes en lo que te da uno, sino fijate en lo que juntes de todos* ... Don't pay attention to what you make from one, but rather to what you make from all of them'. This jumbo-sized route yielded him gross monthly earnings of $18,000 to $20,000, but after labour costs, machine maintenance and gas, he said he reported annual income of $120,000 to the IRS. This places him among high-income earners, on par with well-remunerated professionals and managers.[1]

Maximizing route size, however, was not a favoured business strategy with most gardeners because it involves managing more customers and a larger workforce, and both may entail problems. The route owners generally reported that they had good employees, and they said they were thankful for their many good clients, but they also complained that clients have become cheaper, while the *ayudantes* have become less reliable. Here, their thinking follows that of many business people, they want to keep their labour costs down and they want to increase the price of their service. Instead, the opposite seems to be happening and they expressed complaints such as the following:

> If you used to have an *ayudante*, you would put him to work, and he'd work. There wasn't a problem. But after that [1986 amnesty-legalization], they got finicky. They'd say, 'Oh, I'm not going to start work at such and such time', or 'I don't want to work late'.
>
> Ramon

> Nowadays, *ayudantes* don't want to be paid too little, but clients don't want to pay well either ... I've always tried to carry worker's compensation insurance, in case something happens, but it has become an added burden.
>
> Horacio

> The clients are sometimes too demanding. They ask for too much. They pay too little. And sometimes the workers – there are days they know how to do the work, and there are days that they don't.
>
> Juan

> I don't like it when clients are impatient ... and they call you to come out for some silly reason, and then they don't want to pay [extra].
>
> Teodoro

In this context of stagnant fees and higher labour costs, most gardeners do not want to build jumbo-sized routes. Once they reach what they consider an optimal route size, they pass jobs onto friends or relatives who are starting out in the business. They also try to minimize risk and costs by guardedly, and cautiously, taking on new customers. These route owners are selective about whom they will accept and keep as their paying customers. Some gardeners deliberately 'downsize', doing away with *ayudantes* altogether in order to save on labour costs and avoid labour management headaches.

Gardeners complained of stagnant fees, but by asking the clients for a raise, they risk being fired and losing the job. In this aspect, they are in the same position as domestic workers who may work at the same house without a raise for many years. As workers, they feel the inflationary pressures. As one gardener explained: 'You get home and each month you've got bills to pay ... but they [customers] don't ask you if your [gardening service] fees are going up. They don't ask that.' He had concluded, as had other route owners, that 'then you have to resort to other tactics ... not to depend solely on maintenance gardening'. Longstanding customers, he said, *'ya no dejan* ... no longer leave a profit'.

The proven strategy cited by all the route owners involved taking on extras. They keep their route of steady residential garden maintenance jobs, even if fee levels remain flat, in hope that the clients will approach them for the more lucrative extra jobs. These extras involve special tasks, such as the seasonal pruning of big trees, laying sod, cleaning brush on hillsides, putting in sprinklers or walkways, or planting annual flowerbeds or bulbs. Many gardeners said this is where they earned real money.

> What generates a profit is [extra] planting ... I've had the same fees for a long time. But like I tell you, what helps me out are the extra jobs I do for them. They never, never haggle [over prices for extras].
>
> Juan

> With the route you make enough to get by, you make enough to pay the rent and to cover your basic expenses. And the extras, you know, are the ones that generate profit ... [the route] is where you make enough to sustain yourself, but the extras are the ones that leave you enough money for savings.
>
> Miguel

> The good thing about having the route is that it provides a base [of work], and it's always stable ... You make a bit more money when there are extras. The route itself doesn't make you as much money as the extras.
>
> Mario

Extras can yield the route owners anywhere from $2000 to $4000 a month. Good ones might pay $500 to $1000 a day. 'It's better business' and 'you make more money and you work less' were common refrains about the extras. One gardener said he even targeted the earnings from extras to his savings account. 'I notice that when I get checks from [the route], I don't deposit anything into my savings account. When I do make deposits to my savings is whenever I do extra jobs.'

Keeping the maintenance route allows the gardeners access to the more lucrative extras, and it allows them to balance the reliability and predictability of steady earnings with the opportunities of the extras. In lieu of asking for raises or charging higher fees, they count on the extras. When they charge for extras, gardeners position themselves as independent contractors, such as professional painters, roofers, or appliance vendors. They name a price, and most clients go for it. Also, the fees may involve selection, purchase, delivery, and installation of plants or materials. The gardener charges the clients more than his expenses, so he profits from both labour and the markup on material. This is how they navigate the turbulence of saturated labour markets.

6.6   The exploitation of co-ethnic employees (*ayudantes*)

Gardening route owners' ability to generate profits stems from the difference between their fees and their costs. Whether or not they recognize it, the truth is that their upward mobility hinges in part on their ability to exploit an undocumented, relatively docile workforce. Most route owners described having generally positive working relationships with their employees. Because most gardening route owners got their start as *ayudantes* – and went though the same informal, on-the-job apprenticeship that today's *ayudantes* go through – it stands to reason that they might see a little bit of themselves in their workers, and be inclined to treat them justly as a result.

Nevertheless, route owners typically pay their employees a flat daily rate, which – as noted earlier – can be anywhere from $75 to $110, with truck drivers making the most. When *ayudantes'* workdays are extended, as they typically are during the summer months, their pay does not increase accordingly. As a result, they may end up making less than the minimum wage. Though route owners might be fair, scrupulous individuals, the nature of the job is such that they often find themselves working longer than expected. In such cases, they do not adjust their employees' pay accordingly; *ayudantes* are left with no choice but to soldier on through their workdays, recognizing that their only immediate alternatives might be day labour or, indeed, unemployment.

The exploitation of co-ethnic workers that we see in suburban maintenance gardening is certainly not a new phenomenon. We know that immigrant employers have privileged access to low-wage co-ethnic labour (Evans, 1989; Hum, 2000: 283). Research has shown that immigrant employers benefit from the fact that their workers share a common culture and language, as this reduces their operating, recruitment, and on-the-job communication costs (Ong, 1984). The exploitation of co-ethnic labour generates the marginal profit that typically enables migrant firms to survive (Kim, 1996; Kwong, 1996). Meanwhile, in exchange for substandard work conditions, employees benefit from a flexible work environment, one that provides cultural continuity, informal training, and opportunities for promotion (Portes and Stepick, 1985; Zhou, 1992). Thus, gardening routes are like other migrant-owned businesses that provide employment opportunities and avenues for upward mobility, yet rely on the exploitation of co-ethnic labour (Hum, 2000: 283). As we will see further, they also rely on the exploitation of family labour.

6.7 The impact of gardening work on the gardeners' family lives

In this section, we discuss two aspects of family life. First, we examine the integration of family labour in the gardening occupation. Second, we discuss how the Mexican immigrant gardeners' family relations are affected by their jobs. With respect to the second, we focus predominantly on the route owners, since the *ayudantes* are mostly young and unmarried. The family situation of the route owners is less diverse than that observed for Polish handymen. Most of the former have their children with them in the USA, and although transnational parenting is a feature of Mexican-USA immigration (Dreby, 2010), it was not prevalent among the gardeners we interviewed. This can be explained by the historical development of the USA's immigration regime and the positioning of our *jardineros* within it.[2] Like the Guest Worker Programmes in Europe, the Bracero Programme recruited male immigrant labour and mandated long-term family separations. Towards the end of the Bracero Programme, many Mexican men immigrated without authorized labour contracts (and were readily hired by employers). With new immigration legislation in 1965, many former Braceros were able to apply for legal permanent residency, and they were subsequently joined by family members. The 1986 Immigration Reform and Control Act, by allowing undocumented immigrants to regularize their status, provided a further one-off opportunity for legal family reunification. Today there is a small agricultural visa programme in effect between Mexico and the USA, but none of the gardeners in Los Angeles are on these visas. Instead, we see mostly intact families among the route owners.

As with many ethnic enterprises, family labour plays an important role in the smooth functioning of more than a few *jardineros'* businesses, in part by driving down their labour costs. There are clearly gendered patterns in the sorts of work that the USA-born sons and daughters of *jardineros* do to contribute to the smooth functioning of their fathers' gardening routes. Many of the sons of *jardineros* grow up going to work with their fathers during weekends or summer vacations from school, directly engaging in dirty gardening work, while daughters and spouses tend to contribute by translating, assisting with billing, the packing of hot lunches, and so on. These forms of labour contribute to the route owners' maximization of profit.

The sons play a particularly important role, working on the job with their fathers on weekends and school vacations. Some of the sons begin working at very young ages, ten or twelve, but it is rare that they would be pulled out of school to do so. Besides valuable manual labour, older sons provide special skills that their fathers or their fathers' *ayudantes* might lack. For example, because of their mainly undocumented status, not all *ayudantes* possess driver's licences. Those *ayudantes* who *are* licenced to drive are valuable because they can be hired to drive a work truck, thus they command a premium over their unlicensed peers (they might be paid, say, $110 or $100 a day, as opposed to $80). But a son who is able to drive a truck and who can do garden maintenance work can mean that one less *ayudante* is necessary.

Family relations at home are also affected by the gardening occupation, but the patterns that emerge for route owners and *ayudantes* are very different. Both route owners and *ayudantes* work long hours and typically six days a week. During summer months, the days are long and the workday might extend for 12 hours, until 7 pm. Like their paid employees, route owners spend their days working on the gardens themselves – mowing lawns, raking or blowing leaves, weeding and cultivating flowerbeds, pruning rosebushes, fertilizing and watering plants, and trimming trees or hedges. They must go through the daily grind of loading and unloading equipment from their pickup trucks, and commuting from one house to the next, as efficiently as possible. But unlike their *ayudantes*, self-employed route owners are never really 'off the clock'. Even during weekends and evenings, they are constantly strategizing and thinking about upcoming jobs. As one route owner explained, 'I'll get out tomorrow, Monday, and as I'll be driving back home, I'll have to be planning for Tuesday. And the difference with the workers is – you just drop them off, and that's it.'

Self-employed *jardineros* must shoulder the burden of building and managing the route, maintaining regular communication with their client base, and dealing with angry or unpleasant customers. They are, as we saw in the previous section, a hybrid form of worker and entrepreneur, performing the same type of manual labour that their paid employees do, while simultaneously performing the role of a small business owner. This affects both route owners and *ayudantes*, but for the latter, like live-out domestic workers, the workday has an end to it. There are long hours, to be sure, but the work hours end every day. Many *ayudantes* are unmarried men, and they might return to a home that is a cramped apartment shared with other men.

Route owners are more likely than the *ayudantes* to have legal status, to be married with children, and to own their own homes. As explained before, they generally live with their wives and children. The work day and work week is not so finite for the route owners, who like doctors, remain on call, and who like entrepreneurs, stay mentally focused on upcoming work and business plans. Customers may call to complain about hedges that were sheared in a particular way, or they may be expected to sacrifice their weekends for emergency fixes of sprinkler irrigation. Gardeners fear losing customers so they try to respond to these requests. This takes a toll on family life. One route owner recounted the following experience:

> There are no vacations, not even on Sundays, because the clients overpower you so much sometimes that they feel you belong to them. And whatever comes up, 'Ah!' They call me. In other words, they don't care if you're in bed, or if you're going to take the day off tomorrow. On Saturday, in fact, I was thinking about taking my kids to the beach, on a bicycle ride; I wasn't going to work. And somebody called me from Malibu, and said, 'Why don't you come fix this sprinkler head?' Imagine that. So I took my kids with me to the beach and I told them, 'Go!' I'm going to see them in the water, while I'm over here working.
>
> Adrian

This route owner solved the family versus work conflict by taking his kids along with him to the job, but of course few customers live in beachfront homes. Work and family are not always so seamlessly matched.

Even when the route owners are home with their families, they may be on the phone negotiating with customers, or thinking and worrying about the upcoming week's tasks. They arrive home exhausted after a day of driving around LA streets and highways, repeatedly loading and unloading heavy machinery, and physically bending, pushing, pulling and pruning. Arriving home physically exhausted, in dirty clothes, and hungry, they are not likely to be in shape for playing with the children or overseeing homework. Another *jardinero* described what this was like:

> I get home late. I get home late from work, tired. Sometimes, I can't describe what I feel ... My kids even tell me, 'You don't want to play with us, papi'. I tell them, 'No, son, it's because I get back home really tired. You want me to start playing with you, to play, to run, to play basketball. Son, don't you know how tired I am when I return home from work? And you still want to keep playing ...' I tell them, 'No, it's because I can't'.
>
> Gustavo

Similar to the Polish handymen in the UK, the job allows many of them to excel as breadwinner fathers, but not as the 'hands-on' dads that are so idealized in popular discourse today.

6.8   Conclusion

To conclude, we discuss the social causes and consequences of the institutionalization of commoditized garden services of Mexican immigrant *jardineros*. There are several primary social causes that explain the expansion of the gardening occupational niche. As in the UK, the rise of time-squeezed professional class households, and new standards of involved fatherhood are social processes that have driven the outsourcing of male domestic work, in this case gardening and yard cleaning. As we observed in the previous chapter in relation to London householders, just as cultural norms of 'intensive motherhood' (Hays, 1996) and parental 'concerted cultivation' and supervision and structuring of American middle class children (Lareau, 2003) have taken hold, so too the new ideals of what we might call 'intensive fatherhood' have arisen. The good father in the USA is now highly involved in the lives of his children, and youth sports coaching is a popular outlet for public displays of this behaviour. Sociologist Michael Messner (2009) refers to this as 'plug-in volunteerism', and while the cultural standards for fathers' involvement are lower than for mothers, the good father in professional class communities is one who takes his kids to their athletic practices and games. These games are usually scheduled on Saturday, traditionally a day when many middle class men used to mow the lawn. The suburban man of the house now has new duties, and those who are fathers of young children are expected to be attending soccer games and perhaps coaching little league baseball teams. Meanwhile, Mexican immigrant *jardineros*, the route owners, may bring their sons along with them to work on Saturdays and during school vacations.

The outsourcing of household gardening is also fuelled by the increased labour supply of Mexican immigrant workers, who work in a myriad of services in California. As we saw, Mexican labour migration to the USA increased exponentially in the 1980s and 1990s, and Mexican immigrant labour markets diversified outside of agricultural work into the diverse service industries. This is now an institutionalized part of the culture and taken for granted.

Finally, rising real estate values and the importance of image help explain the rise of gardening services, especially in affluent Los Angeles where home values are among the highest in the nation and where capital circulates out of many dynamic sectors. A well-groomed garden adds to what the real estate agents call 'curb appeal', which boosts the investment value of a home. Image is an important product in Los Angeles, and in some of the more affluent neighbourhoods, the homes look as though they might be part of a movie set, with flowers always in bloom and scarcely a leaf or blade of grass out of place.

There are two primary social consequences to the outsourcing of household gardening. First, it is important to underscore that in contrast with female immigrant domestic workers and Polish immigrant handymen, the Mexican immigrant gardeners have very little contact with the residents in the employer households. There is no indoor intimacy, and the gardeners might rarely even see the residents for whom they work. The route owners send their bills, and most employer householders mail their payment. Unlike female domestic workers who clean and care in intimate spaces, the gardeners remain outside, cleaning the yard. They are tending to plant life, not human lives and bodies. No one ever says of the gardeners as one hears about the female nannies, 'Oh, he is just like one of the family', although it is true that in some cases, long-term route owners may establish relationships that extend beyond employment to include obligations of support (e.g. employers offering advice on legal matters or helping the child of a gardener obtain a job in the formal sector of the labour force). The gardeners remain outside of the family/domestic sphere both physically and metaphorically. As brown-skinned, working class immigrant men working in predominantly white and some Asian American neighbourhoods, they remain permanent outsiders.

Another major difference with the female *domesticas* of Los Angeles, but similar to Polish handyman-work in the UK, is that the occupation is stratified. Some route-owner gardeners experience substantial upward mobility for themselves, and for their children. While working in residential gardening offers no direct pathway to jobs in the formal sector, there is occupational differentiation and mobility within the occupation, and this mobility track leads towards economic formality and higher earnings. For some men, this internal occupational mobility is nothing short of stunning. Within several years, a newcomer rookie can gather his apprenticeship knowledge, a driver's licence, a truck, and modest savings, and use these to become an independent route-owner gardener. There is differentiation among the route owners in Los Angeles, but most of them do quite well in terms of their earnings. Few occupations in the contemporary, post-industrial service economy offer Mexican immigrant men with less than primary school education and limited English fluency this opportunity.

We are less sanguine, however, about current mobility opportunities for the *ayudantes*. Competition is stiff, and given the hostile immigration climate described earlier in this chapter, and the distinct possibility that comprehensive immigration reform and a new legalization programme will not appear soon, the current population of undocumented wage labourer *ayudantes* are likely to face roadblocks in their mobility pathways.

Finally, it is important to note that in the case of *jardineros*, the route to upward mobility is paved with steep costs. Route-owner gardeners act as both workers and entrepreneurs, and both roles require extreme self-exploitation. As workers, the route owners put in long hours, working 12-hour work days in the summer months, and usually working six days a week. Repetitive stress injuries, the occasional accident with a gasoline-powered hedge trimmer or sharp blade, physical exhaustion, and no vacation are routine parts of the job. As small entrepreneurs, the route owners experience the constant stress of calculating costs and fees, planning and scheduling their extra jobs, and managing the routes and clients so as to minimize risk. Even when they rest at night or on Sunday afternoons, they must plan upcoming logistics. *Jardinería* allows some route owner men to achieve idealized breadwinner status, but in many cases the rigours of taking on both entrepreneurial risk and stress, and worker injuries and physical exhaustion, can prevent them from spending time with their children. In the end, the route-owner gardeners face many of the family-work conflicts of successful breadwinners.

7
Gender Identity and Work: Migrant Domestic Work and Masculinity

Ladies (& Gentlemen) if your husband won't do it ...
I will!!
Postcard advert for handyman services (2011)

7.1 Introduction

Owing to its growing scale and association with various forms of exploitation and harassment, feminist analysts have focused on women working in stereotypically feminized forms of domestic work such as cleaning, caring and catering. The focus on male migrant domestic workers raises interesting parallels, but also highlights key differences. These differences have significance for understanding how the processes of globalization, migration and social reproduction are gendered, how they manifest themselves in daily life, and, in particular, on the way that varying normative gendered expectations shape decisions people make about what work to do and what work to outsource to others. Gendered social norms also shape the economic and social status of occupations, and thereby structure the well-being and opportunities of both migrant domestic workers and the people for whom they work. These norms and practices are neither uniform nor static. Rather, they change over time and space and vary by social identity, level of economic development, migration legislation and citizenship regimes, rendering specific understandings and outcomes contingent and varied. What becomes clear, however, is that while the way that 'gender matters in a particular location ... is variable and contingent', the fact 'that gender matters is not' (Bair, 2010: 204).

In traditional understandings of the gendered division of labour, paid work forms a central aspect of men's masculine identities. Paid work plays a significant role in shaping how they think about themselves and

149

how they relate to other men and women. We begin this chapter, which forms the conclusion to the book, with a brief review of the varied and dynamic character of masculinity, before considering how these different understandings are reflected in decisions regarding work made by *jardineros* – route-owners and *ayudantes* – in the USA and migrants working as handymen in the UK. In the latter case, we also study how understandings of masculinity shape the behaviour of the householders using handyman services. In so doing, we recognize workers as embodied and gender as performance, and examine how and why different forms of work are constructed as masculine or feminine, what implications this has for their economic valuation and social status, and how the work environment itself permits and constrains different expressions of masculinity. We consider how this gendering of work influences the householders' decisions regarding both what work to do and what work to outsource to others; decisions that affect the way in which they allocate time between paid work, parenting and domestic work. We consider, further, how these decisions impact on subjectivities, the gender division of labour and understandings of masculinity and femininity. We examine how the migrant handymen and *jardineros* conceptualize their work and what opportunities it provides in terms of social mobility. In addition, we compare the decisions to migrate and how their experience meets their expectations, how it affects their family relationships, and how these experiences vary by citizenship status. With a particular emphasis on the handymen working in the UK, we examine how the migrants perceive and relate to the householders, as this too provides insights into how work is gendered. Gender is influenced by other social divisions including social class, ethnicity and migrant status, and we look at how these different dimensions intersect and have profound implications for both the comparative well-being of the migrant handymen and *jardineros* and the relationship between the householders and migrants. Finally, we contrast our findings with feminized domestic work by reference to the literature on feminized domestic services reviewed in Chapter 2. We conclude by showing how our findings contribute to discussions of gender identity and social reproduction in a global context.

7.2   Varied and dynamic understandings of masculinity

The first thing that needs to be said is that few of our workers, handymen or *jardineros,* would recognize themselves as or wish to be termed domestic workers. This is because such a term has feminine and homely connotations – connotations which resonate poorly with stereotypical masculine qualities of strength, toughness, competitiveness and the public world of paid work. The terms *jardinero* and handyman are more acceptable because the former is linked to strenuous manual outdoor work and the latter is widely understood as skilled work associated with making and repairing things in and around the house. In both cases the work is defined as male and multi-skilled, thereby conforming to stereo-typical understandings of muscular and skilled masculinity. Advertising, whether on websites or postcards, endorses this conceptualization of masculinity through images of prime aged, physically fit men, wearing fully equipped body-belts and carrying power tools. The larger agencies supplying these services show men on powerful shiny black motorbikes, suggestive of skill, strength and speed of response.[1] The 'Dial a Hubby' website (2012), while following the sentiments quoted at the beginning of the chapter by claiming 'Anything your husband Can't or Won't Do, WE DO!'[2] differed by portraying an older man smiling like a genial grandfather. But despite this difference, the man still conveyed techni-cal ability via the wearing of a tool-belt.

This view of the masculinized character of the work carried out in and around middle and upper class households was largely endorsed by the workers in our study, who saw their work as difficult, sometimes dirty, and even dangerous, but always manly. The *jardineros* in particular, while not identifying completely with the traditional *ranchero* machismo (a hard drinking and sexually dominant form of masculinity), took pride in their fit physique and calloused hands as visible signifiers of their hard mascu-line labour (Ramirez, 2011; see also Chapter 6).[3] Even though there was a profound change in the work environment, as lawn mowing, leaf blow-ing and pool cleaning in the Los Angeles suburbs was quite different from peasant agriculture, there were some parallels – it was outdoor, required physical strength and use of machines, and was carried out in a team and therefore allowed for homosociality (see Chapter 6). These teams were important for transferring skills, which were predominantly learnt on the job and provided the social networks through which work was acquired. In the main, handymen too saw their work as inherently masculine, more as a consequence of the stereotypically masculinized skills involved than through manual strength alone. At the same time there was some ambivalence. They sometimes discussed being called out to do 'silly jobs' such as fixing a shower – 'something that we in Poland would do ourselves without thinking about calling someone' (Mateusz, HM), but at other times reported having to consult books and the Internet or call their friends in Poland to check techniques. As Daniel explains:

> There was a moment when I was working for myself ... I had to read up, I bought books and all that so that I would know because

it became clear to me that I could get a lot more of these jobs if I'm able to do them ... if I did not know something I would quickly call Poland in the afternoon, to a plumber. 'Listen, I have this job how do I do this?' And then he'd give me material for the evening and by the morning I'm all clever, right?

Daniel, HM

Some tasks clearly required specific material competencies and conscious learning, but in general many of the necessary skills were considered 'natural', learnt from their fathers and commonly practised in Poland, where low incomes meant it was often necessary to make do and mend rather than buy and replace.

Men in labour-using households in the UK had a rather different understanding of masculinity. Generally, they expressed little sense of loss as a consequence of either outsourcing work to handymen or disclosing that they did traditionally feminine tasks such as childcare and shopping. Here, our findings differ from Rosie Cox's (2012) study of 'Hubbys' in New Zealand, where the householders saw this DIY work as central to the their masculine identity, confirming their status as regular 'Kiwi blokes' and providing a way of contributing to the family that reaffirmed their masculine identity and sociality. Accordingly, employing others, the 'Hubbys,' to do *their* work was associated primarily with lack, laziness and failure.[4] By contrast, the UK male householders valued their professional work and their role as hands-on fathers, thereby reflecting the connection between masculinity and professional work (Goffman, 1968; Kimmel, 2011) while simultaneously endorsing a broader conception of fatherhood which involves nurturing in addition to traditional breadwinning roles (Brannen and Nielson, 2006). As outlined in Chapter 5, fathering became an important aspect of their self-identity, and one they prioritized over and above household tasks. One householder, Oliver, justified this priority by saying:

I'm *lucky* enough to be quite a high income earner and, when I'm not working then I want to spend time with my family, not putting up shelves.

Oliver, HH (our emphasis)[5]

Oliver refers to his luck in being a high earner and his resulting ability to pay someone else to carry out the male household work in order to ease his father time-bind. What he refers to as luck could equally be referred to as the power and privilege associated with his gender and social class (Hondagneu-Sotelo and Messner, 1997). In Oliver's situation, a case which reflects the position of other male householders, ability to play this fathering role depends not only on high income but, crucially, on the ability to withdraw from traditional areas of male domestic responsibility by outsourcing these roles to less privileged others.

This outsourcing also enabled the male householders to be complicit with expectations regarding long working hours. These expectations had an impact upon the gender division of labour in the home. Invariably, it was the women who adjusted their working hours in order to manage reproductive work (see Chapter 5). In addition, they arranged and oversaw the work of the handymen, leading to a double displacement of responsibilities from the man to both his female partner and to a less privileged man. While there was a clear expansion of nurturing among the male householders compared to their own fathers, this nurturing tended to be specific and time-bounded. It would involve, for example, getting breakfast and taking children to the nursery or dealing with bath time, and would not involve a full range of responsibilities. This limited, time-bounded nurturing is reflected in Rachel's claim, referred to in Chapter 5, that her partner 'does pick and choose what he will do, so he's actually more traditional than he thinks' (Rachel, HH). Similarly to Rachel, many women noted this arrangement, often with a hint of irony, but they did not question it fundamentally. Their decision was influenced by prevailing social norms and practices, including, in most cases, a gendered pay differential. This pay differential ensured that economic penalties would have been incurred had a less traditional gender arrangement been adopted. Given the financial penalties associated with even a short term absence from the labour market (Metcalf, 2009; Manning and Petrongolo, 2008), while their decision is rational in the short term from the perspective of the household unit, it is questionable whether it is beneficial for the woman in the longer term, as it has a detrimental impact on their individual lifetime earnings and pension arrangements.

Some male householders admitted to being incapable of handyman work, but this was largely considered a matter of difference rather than failure. Others assumed capability, but as Oliver's previous remark indicates, expressed a preference for family time. In other cases regret at losing a traditional sense of masculinity was outweighed by efficiency arguments related to the cost and speed of the work. This was indicated by Sam:

I've always tried to do the manly thing. Like many men of my generation, I think there's a residual feeling of guilt if you don't do it

yourself, passed down from father to son. I never learnt the skills and
I have no interest in doing them.

Sam, HH

Sam's comments were endorsed by his wife, who noted that:

I know when we first did it, one of the reasons he was so reluctant
was because he felt it was his role, he felt as though he was the provider and he was supposed to do these sorts of things.

Elaine, HH

This lack of attachment to manual domestic work reflects a different
understanding of masculinity. Two issues are at stake here. The first concerns the possession or otherwise of what are assumed to be masculine
skills, and the second concerns the physical bodily capacity to be able
to do this work, with the idea of 'skilled bodily activity' often being a
'prime indicator of masculinity' (Connell and Messerschmidt, 2005:
851). In this respect, contemporary social practices like working out at
the gym and eating a healthy diet, now the province of men as well
as women, may more than substitute for maintaining bodily prowess
through manual paid work.

Holding on to traditional ideas of muscular masculinity, as in the case
of the *jardineros,* may be an expression of limited social mobility. For
example, the one householder in our study who, like Cox's interviewees
in New Zealand (Cox, 2012), reported being laughed at by his peers for
lack of handyman skills, was the only non–middle class householder we
interviewed. Even so, traditional ideas of masculinity surfaced occasionally in the householders' musings on other men doing *their* domestic
work. Jeff, for instance, commented that:

If it was some hot young stud every time who was doing it shirtless
then I don't know, who knows maybe it'd make me feel slightly
emasculated but, but, I kind of doubt that.

Jeff, HH

More often, however, the householders indicated an awareness of but
lack of identity with traditional notions of masculinity. This is reflected
in Rachel's comments on the views of her partner and father:

It doesn't bother him at all. I think it bothers my dad. I think ...
I think he knows ... he knows that in my dad's eyes he is found

wanting as a man in the masculine sense, but my dad respects him because he's this kind of, you know ... he's an academic.

Rachel, HH

Overall, these varied expressions and understandings indicate how masculinity is a plural and complex concept that changes over time and space and varies between different social groups. Despite these variations, not all ideas of masculinity have equal status. Here the concept hegemonic masculinity (Connell, 1987) can be useful, especially in its revised formulations (Connell, 2011; Connell and Messerschmidt, 2005). Raewyn Connell (2011) uses the term hegemonic in the Gramscian sense, understanding hegemonic masculinity as the form of masculinity that emerges from struggles for dominance between variant masculine identities.[6] The emergent hegemonic form then becomes the prevailing idea or ideal of masculine identity against which other masculinities are compared. It is, furthermore, a form of identity to which understandings of appropriate femininity are invariably subordinate, albeit in different ways. Hegemonic masculinity, then, is not necessarily universally or numerically dominant. Rather, it has the form of a prevailing ideal or exemplar in relation to which other men, indeed perhaps even the majority of men, may be subordinate, marginalized or complicit (Connell, 1995). Accordingly, the *jardineros*, handymen and householders may each hold concepts of masculinity to which they aspire, but these can be different from one another. Consequently, the prevailing form of masculinity may change over time and vary between and within different societies, for example, by social class and by generation. But these different forms of masculinity are not merely lifestyle choices. Rather, they reflect prevailing power relations (Connell, 1995) and may contribute towards the broader creation of one dominant or hegemonic form of masculinity that reigns supreme in the sense of shaping the overall economic, social and political power structures within which all social groups reside.

Resonating with the notion of hegemonic masculinity, but predating Connell (1987), Erving Goffman, writing about the USA, argued that:

> in an important sense there is only one complete unblushing male in America: a young, married, white, urban, northern, heterosexual Protestant father of college education, fully employed, of good complexion, weight and height and a recent record in sports ... Any male who fails to qualify in any of these ways is likely to view himself – during moments at least – as unworthy, incomplete and inferior; at

times he is likely to pass and at times he is likely to find himself being apologetic or aggressive concerning known-about aspects of himself he knows are probably seen as undesirable. *The general identity-values of a society may be fully entrenched nowhere, and yet they can cast some kind of shadow on the encounters encountered everywhere in daily living.*
Goffman (1968: 153; also partially cited by Kimmel, 2011; our emphasis)

Michael Kimmel (2011: 2), recognising masculinity as a 'changing, fluid assemblage of meanings and behaviours that vary dramatically,' contrasts Goffman's image with what he terms the 'emergent global hegemonic version of masculinity'. This man

sits in first class waiting rooms or in elegant business hotels the world over in a designer business suit, speaking English, eating "continental" cuisine, talking on his cell phone, his laptop computer plugged into any electrical outlet, while he watches CNN International on television. Temperamentally, he is increasingly cosmopolitan, with liberal tastes in consumption (and sexuality) and conservative political ideas of limited government control of the economy. This has the additional effect of increasing the power of the hegemonic countries within the global political and economic arena, since everyone, no matter where they are from, talks and acts like they do.
Kimmel (2011: 4)

Many men fitting Goffman's (1968: 153) image might fall into Kimmel's category alongside elite men from other world regions. Kimmel's (2011) characterization also parallels Leslie Sklair's (2001) concept of the transnational capitalist class and expresses a form of masculinity that can be considered hegemonic in the sense that men matching this description are enormously powerful in terms of influencing economic and social policies within their companies, states of residence, and international institutions. This economic and social power makes them the contemporary mandarins or Davos men (Benería, 1999). Their decisions have profound influence over economic, political and institutional arrangements. Among other things, their decisions work to uphold the prevalence of neoliberal thinking, which reinforces the uneven development between and widening class inequalities within countries and, in so doing, upholds the power and incomes of already privileged people, including themselves, while also providing the material foundation for both migration and commoditized domestic labour.

While, hegemonic understandings are both embedded in state, institutional and company policies and convey the everyday realities of social and cultural practice, they are ideals to which few men can live up to consistently. Furthermore, most men have wider dimensions to their personalities that remain hidden from these hegemonic portrayals (Connell and Messerschmidt, 2005: 838). Some of the London professionals we interviewed could, on occasion, match Kimmel's description earlier. They would carry the demeanour of competitive, disembodied workers available for work 24/7 (Hobson and Fahlén, 2009), but this image would not encapsulate their totality. On other occasions, they would be found pouring out cornflakes, running baths and changing nappies. On these occasions their identity would resonate more closely with ideas of companionate partnership or the 'new man', rather than the Victorian patriarch (Connell and Messerschmidt, 2005: 846). In a parallel vein, the tough, strong, weather beaten *jardineros* bearing all the hallmarks of muscular masculinity are rendered tender in moments reflecting on their home and families, and docile in moments in which their minority ethnic position and servile and precarious employment relations become clear (Ramirez, 2011). The *jardineros* and, in particular, the *ayudantes* lacking legal status, are very conscious of their powerlessness, but are willing to pay this price in return for their comparatively high USA earnings. It is, in turn, these comparatively high earnings that facilitate their provider role, another critical component of their masculine identity, enabling them to maintain honour and pride. Here, we see an example of the ambiguities of masculinity, and the manner in which numerous different forms of masculinity can nonetheless all uphold a hegemonic form of masculinity to which both women and other masculinities are subordinate. The *jardineros*, especially the *ayudantes*, in effect inhabit a subordinate masculine position of precarity, minority ethnic status, and dependence on doing work passed on by other men, but they inhabit this subordinate position in order to secure the very resources that enable them to perform the dominant breadwinning role typical of hegemonic forms of masculinity.

More broadly, while Kimmel's (2011) image of global masculinity is hegemonic in the sense that it influences overall power structures, it is doubtful whether it is quite so hegemonic at the personal level, in the sense of shaping taste and style universally and possessing attributes to which all men aspire. As Connell and Messerschmidt (2005: 841) argue, 'the concept of hegemonic masculinity is not intended as a catchall ... [rather] it is a means of grasping a certain dynamic within the social process'. This dynamic is arguably similar to Goffman's (1968: 153) idea of casting 'some kind of shadow on the encounters encountered every-where in daily living'. These understandings can induce feelings of guilt and conflict as people are aware of their failure to live up to all of the ideals simultaneously. The male householders expressed concerns about being inadequate as workers and as fathers. They showed a sense of guilt about not being present sufficiently either at home or at work, think-ing of work while playing games with their children, or leaving work before colleagues to see their children before bedtime.[7] These concerns echo the well-known tensions experienced by working mothers. Some householders, however, had the necessary confidence and status within their organizations to secure some flexibility. Trevor, while reflecting on the more favourable working hours and recognition of parental roles in Denmark, (see Chapter 5) nonetheless points out that:

A: I always leave on time at work and work know that two days a week I will leave at 4:30 to 4:45.

Q: And is that alright with your employers, with your colleagues?

A: I've made it clear that it was part of my working week and my boss was happy with that. I'm reasonably high up the company, so I have freedom like that.

Interview with Trevor, HH

In some exceptional cases, those with high earnings were able to resolve these tensions through expensive technologies, as reflected in Ted's (HH) remark that 'the big thing was the ability to be able to buy an all weather helicopter that means that, um, I can fly in the dark and all weather and get home at 6 o'clock'. This strategy is clearly one only accessible to the highly wealthy elite.

Feelings of inadequacy may be countered by attachment or partial attachment to marginal understandings of masculinity, like the exag-gerated masculinity of machismo in the case of the *jardineros* or the new caring form of masculinity in the case of UK householders. Alternatively, great emphasis might be placed on one of the multifaceted aspects of the dominant form of masculinity, as in the case of some handymen who focus on their provider role. Arguably, such understandings may become hegemonic within particular groups as people focus more on acceptability within their immediate social surroundings, those beyond being too distant to matter on a daily basis. But the manner in which even these different masculinities can contribute to the creation of hegemonic forms discussed earlier, with both the *jardineros* and the handymen willing to accept precarious work that subordinates them to the householders that employ them in order to perform their breadwinning role, shows that the 'emergent global hegemonic version of masculinity' (Kimmel, 2011) continues to mould the economic and political environment and, in so doing, continues to constrain the conditions of the migrants' daily lives.

Even though the dimensions and meaning of hegemonic masculinity may vary and change, possibly leading to subtle changes in the patterns of gender relations, what is also clear is that a gender hierarchy remains premised on a form of masculine superiority. As we shall see further on this superiority influences the economic value of the work done, the self-identity of the handymen and *jardineros*, the relations between handymen and householders, and the division of labour between the men and the women householders. Patterns of 'masculinity are socially defined in contradistinction from some model (whether real or imaginary) of femininity' (Connell and Messerschmidt, 2005: 845). What this means is that, implicitly or explicitly, the majority of the men are complicit with hegemonic understandings of masculinity and benefit to some degree from the inherent gender power imbalance without necessarily having to exert a strong form of masculinity themselves, though the extent of this benefit varies according to differences in other aspects of their identity, in this case, social position, citizenship status and their specific economic and social context (Connell and Messerschmidt, 2005: 832, 848; Hearn, 2004).

Having discussed some of the varied and dynamic understandings of masculinity in the rest of the chapter we consider how these different understandings of masculinity are reflected in the gendering of work and in the work experiences of the route-owner *jardineros*, *ayudantes*, migrant handymen and, in the case of the UK study, the householders.

7.3   Gender, work and identity

For many adults and especially for men, paid work provides the main source of income, establishes social status, and shapes their integration into the economic and social system (Weeks, 2011). Work is hierarchically and horizontally segregated in a variety of ways, and people are selected for different positions on the basis of their existing identities, which are, in turn, shaped further by their work. The characteristics of work and workers are thus mutually constitutive and mutually reinforcing.

Professional salaried employees with stable employment, paid holidays, pensions, high incomes and a clear career trajectory are distinguished from the regularly employed working class by income. But while both groups benefit from permanency, paid holidays, and social security rights, a third broad grouping, the 'new precariat', have no employment contract and little protection from arbitrary dismissal, and therefore lack security with regard to work and income. In addition, the new precariat have little protection with respect to health and safety, and is character- ized by a lack of social mobility (Standing, 2011). Recent and low quali- fied migrants figure prominently in this last group.

This threefold categorization of the employment structure in late cap- italist societies partially corresponds to the different groups of workers in our study. Householders experience the benefits of professional work, and at the other extreme the *ayudantes* match the characteristics of the new precariat. The handymen and route-owner *jardineros*, however, are more diverse. The majority of our handymen were formally registered as self-employed, but what this means in practice varies. Some were entre- preneurs, operating as one-man bands; a small minority would hire or subcontract work to other handymen, some of whom might also be self-employed though, in fact they were working for someone else but without the protection of an employment contract. In practice, then, the positions of the handymen varied considerably. A small minority had incomes similar to salaried professionals, others had incomes com- parable with the working classes, but few had equivalent job security or reliability of employment. Those dependent on occasional subcon- tracted work, a situation many migrants found themselves in when they first arrived,[8] were in an analogous position to the *ayudantes* and the new precariat, but as EU citizens, they could all draw on social benefits when out of work. Similarly to the route-owner *jardineros*, individual well-being varied a great deal depending on length of residency and the scale and regularity of work. In addition, language and citizenship status were important factors in determining the different positions of the (im)migrant workers.

This hierarchical employment structure intersects with the horizontal segregation of work, which is similarly associated with different earn- ings based upon different gender and racialized ascriptions. Even in the twenty-first century, and arguably universally, women continue to be over represented in the five C's: cleaning, catering, caring, clerking and cashiering, while men are over represented in four M's: manage- ment, money, materials and machinery. While there are exceptions, for example, some of the middle class women householders in our study enter management and the professions, as do some migrant ethnic and racial minorities from higher social classes, in the main social mobility is limited and occupations become associated with particular social groups. Just as leadership positions in management and the professions are linked predominantly to ethnic majority men, contract gardening and handyman work have become associated with Mexicans and Poles, respectively, creating the migrant niches and ethnic enclaves discussed in Chapters 4 and 6, respectively. These niches and enclaves have led to the stereotypical portrayal of contract gardeners in the USA as Mexican, so much so that when Gargamel (the 'baddie' in the Smurfs cartoon series and recent movie) steals a leaf blower, it is from a Mexican gardener (The Smurfs, directed by Gonell 2011). In the UK, the Polish plumber has become a common caricature.

These associations have mixed impacts. The high public visibility and audibility of the *jardineros* as they mow the lawns and drive their trucks through predominantly white suburban America provides acceptability for an ethnic minority that might otherwise be questioned (see Chapter 6). At the same time, the work is often dirty, which, in the minds of the ethnic majority population, can mark *jardineros* as inferior subjects, suited only to hard manual labour. In the UK, the caricature of the Polish plumber has been used to establish credentials and quality and is reinforced by the dual recognition (by both suppliers and buyers) of 'Polish Handymen' as polite, hardworking, flexible, skilled and reliable, in contrast to British handymen who are often denigrated as unreliable and lazy workers. As Jeff comments:

> I am completely against these [British] cowboys ... whereas ... I trust Poles and Eastern European immigrants hugely. I just don't trust Brits. But on the other hand I have a British handyman who does our work who's a lovely old bloke.
>
> Jeff, HH

The Polish handymen took pride in these ascriptions and drew on them to market their services as high quality and reliable (Datta and Brickell, 2009; Garapich, 2008a; Brannen, 2012). There is also a sense in which this superiority of Polish handymen is recognized as a stereotype – as householders, similarly to Jeff, mentioned before refer to their own handymen as being British, but old and reliable, and the Polish migrants speak of poor shoddy work and exploitation by their compatriots.

The handymen's work is relational, insofar as they work inside the home and have direct encounters with the consumer. The *jardineros* work is also relational but to a lesser extent; while they must negotiate arrangements with their clients, they tend to do so over the phone, and their work is predominantly performed outdoors. For the handymen, the relational nature of the work ensures that bodily appearance and the manner of service delivery matters.[9] Negotiating contracts successfully very much depends on the rapport the workers establish with potential clients. As a result, personal qualities influence the propensity to be hired, and attributes of race, ethnicity or gender can come into play in a potentially discriminatory manner (Hochschild, 1983; McDowell, 2009b; Wright Mills, 1953). Some kind of affective relationship has to be established with the potential clients, with the workers expected to portray both authoritative professional competency and a measure of personal deference (Hochschild, 1983).

Neither the handymen (nor the *jardineros*) have any training in this respect. Instead, they have to rely on their personal charms, social skills and professionalism. In contrast to care work, these personal attributes bear little relation to the specific purpose of the work; it is doubtful whether shelves go up more easily if the wood is handled by someone graced with social skills, and quite often, workers work alone in the house or garden. Nonetheless, the home is a very personal space, so not only do image and demeanour matter but also poor quality work could have lasting and costly implications. Being able to trust and feel at ease in the presence of the handymen was therefore crucial for householders, and the Polish were often considered more appropriate, as well as more skilled, than others. Typically, they were both more educated than their British counterparts, more alert to middle class tastes and sensitivities, some having experienced downward social mobility, so in some ways there was a closer cultural proximity, as discussed in Chapter 4. In addition their ethnicity would, to some extent, make them immune to class prejudices surrounding British handymen as 'cowboys'. British working class men, especially young men, were considered sexist and racist as well as unreliable and untrustworthy, perhaps reflecting the wider middle class 'demonization of the working class' (Jones, 2012; Skeggs, 1997).

Positioning within this hierarchical and horizontal work structure builds from and reinforces individual identity with respect to age, social class, gender, ethnicity and citizenship. Jobs and their attributes tend to become identified with particular social groups, and other groups then become unsuitable by virtue of not having had the necessary practice, experience or appropriate social networks. Accordingly, the gender and ethnicity of people holding particular positions becomes identified with those positions, such that leadership and authority 'stick'[10] to and become equated with white men who, in turn, shape the notion of leadership as male and white. Likewise, aptitudes for work which is perceived to be physically but not intellectually challenging become associated with ethnic and racialized minorities, who are believed to have the apposite natural predisposition and personality type. In this respect, jobs 'are not neutral slots but are, instead, socially constructed definitions, created to attract differently raced and gendered workers' (McDowell, Batnitzky and Dyer, 2009: 7). Women, racial and ethnic minorities and migrants become underrepresented in higher and over-represented in lower status jobs even when there are no formal barriers and when equal opportunities and anti-discrimination legislation are in place. When people lack citizenship status, are ethnic minorities and are subject to discrimination, as is the case with the *ayudantes*, propensity for employment in marginal and precarious work is intensified. The *ayudantes* tolerate these living and working conditions largely because the work provides higher earnings compared to other options open to them. For the Polish migrants, especially the more highly qualified, the situation is often very different. Working as a handyman is often seen as a temporary stage in a longer-term life and career strategy.

Numerous studies have pointed out the horizontal gendering of domestic work, rightly noting the considerable difference in pay between feminized and masculinized manual work.[11] Important in this regard is a hierarchical dualism between mind and body, with feminine work deemed lower value on the basis that the work involves emotional and physical care rather than rational thinking. But this hierarchal dualism between mind and body also applies to masculine domestic work (McDowell, 2009b; Wolkowitz, 2006). For neither the *jardineros* nor (except in very rare cases) the handymen, was the employment relationship with clients seen as one between equals. The question of deference was somewhat different between the two cases. In their relatively rare encounters with householders, the Mexican gardeners found it difficult to deal with the way that class, citizenship and ethnicity could supersede the gender order, rendering their masculinity redundant. They had little choice but to act deferentially when receiving instructions from the women householders, some of whom were considered very disrespectful (Chapter 6; Ramirez, 2011).[12] On occasion, however, closer relations develop between householders and *jardineros* of long standing. *Jardineros* may be asked to do additional jobs inside as well as outside the house, and householders have been known to help with education or by providing information and advice (Ramirez, 2011). While indicating some degree of human empathy, the relationship still reflects inequality in the sense that it is one-sided. The *jardinero* is always paid for the labour and does not help the employers in other ways. The *jardinero,* for example, does not offer to give cast off clothing, and he would probably be met with surprise were he to do so.[13] Even were the *jardineros* to be 'treated as one of the family', then, the relationship would remain unequal.

In the UK, deference to householders was gendered. Handymen rarely met the male householders, but where they did, they were generally deferential, despite on occasion presuming a shared masculinity on the basis of knowledge and understanding of the work to be done. With the female householders, handymen were more likely to assume superior technical knowledge. The British ones in particular could be bold and flirtatious, drawing on the wider authority associated with being male. This 'sexual banter' with the woman of the household, which is often understood to be politically incorrect but nonetheless passes as a socially normalized behaviour across gender and social class divides, would be totally unacceptable in the presence of the male owner. With the male owner present, an authoritative professionalism was more likely to hold sway, showing how 'men do gender in different ways in different circumstances' (McDowell, 2009b: 131). Such performances are not consciously planned. Instead, they signal the enactment of hegemonic norms learned through social observation and reiteration (Butler, 1990).

In this way traditional understandings of masculine strength and technical capability were used to deny any possible sense of inferiority based on social class or migrant status. As some of the female householders commented, these assumptions about technical ability were made independently of their actual knowledge. Often, it was in fact the women householders rather than their male partners who had greater understanding of the work involved. As Chapter 5 points out, it was invariably the women householders who made arrangements with the handymen and decided what needed to be done, a pattern picked up by the handymen agencies in their advertising which is very much addressed towards women. The terms themselves, 'hire', 'rent', or 'dial a hubby', imply not only that it was male domestic work that was neglected but also that it would be the 'wife' who would be looking for a replacement service.

Occupations become gender, race and class stereotyped, and while the boundaries are socially and culturally constructed and always permeable, they remain deeply embedded in thought and reality. Occupational or work segregation is perpetuated from one generation to the next through repeated performances which shape expectations of who is appropriate for what job[14] and how it is valued both socially and in money terms. In the next section, we consider how the work of handymen and *jardineros* is valued and how it compares to feminized domestic work. The section begins by comparing the situation of the male domestic workers in our two case studies and their decision-making rationale, before contrasting their work and pay with the work and pay of feminized domestic workers.

7.4   Migrant domestic work and pay

One of the key factors underlying both migration and the growth of commoditized domestic labour is the continuing uneven development between and widening income divisions within countries (discussed in Chapter 1). With the financial crisis, recession and subsequent low economic growth starting in 2008, net migration from Mexico to the USA and from Poland to the UK has fallen. In the case of Mexico this decline has been attributed to the weakening of the USA job market, stronger border controls, and harsher treatment of illegal migrants, and also to economic growth in Mexico (Passel, Cohn and Gonzalez-Barrera, 2012).[15] The economic advantage of the UK relative to Poland has also declined. While the UK entered a period of prolonged depression from 2008,[16] employment, earnings and the value of the Zloty all increased in Poland. Net migration to the UK from Poland decreased accordingly, though it remained positive.[17] Some handymen reported that colleagues had returned to Poland owing to the difficulty of finding work, yet demand for handyman services remained, as regardless of some job losses, earnings in the top decile, especially in London, continued to increase while those in lower deciles stagnated.[18] Despite the recession, significant absolute economic differentials remain between Poland and the UK and between Mexico and the USA, providing a continuing economic incentive for migration.

The Polish handymen often migrated in the knowledge that they would experience downward occupational mobility or take up jobs for which they were over qualified, but their strategy was motivated by a realistic desire to earn more income in addition to fulfilling more varied personal goals. Migration was legal once Poland became a member of the EU, and travel was cheap, so migrants could come and go as they pleased. In this respect the casual and temporary character of handyman work was almost an advantage, as it was something that could be taken up and put down relatively easily as Jacek explains: And they're temporary jobs so you can always come here for a few months, earn some money and go back. It's not very … It doesn't keep you here;

you can always leave whenever you want' (Jacek, HM). This casual and temporary work, together with the fall back position of social benefits, also gave the migrants some flexibility in terms of which jobs to accept and which to reject. But for the undocumented *ayudantes* (as well as undocumented migrants in the UK, see Chapter 4) the situation could not have been more different. Migration was difficult and dangerous and yet more necessary as a survival strategy, given the fewer opportunities and substantially lower earnings available to them in Mexico. The independent route-owning *jardineros*, in contrast, were generally immigrants of long standing, and most had established a viable way of life in the USA (see Chapters 3 and 6).

Migration was so engrained in Zacatecanos, the state from which most of the *jardineros* came, that it was almost a rite of passage to adulthood (Ramirez, 2011 and Chapter 3). As we saw in Chapter 4, there was also a culture of outward migration in Poland, but the Polish migrants expressed a whole series of motivations for moving, including love, adventure, learning a language and escaping failed business ventures and failed relationships. While specific motivations always vary, it is unlikely that migration on the current scale would have taken place without a steep economic gradient and the associated possibilities for creating a new life. Earnings of both the *jardineros* and handymen were unpredictable, but were potentially ten times higher in the USA and UK than they would have been in Mexico or Poland, providing a major migration incentive for both groups.

In the USA, *ayudantes* generally earned just above the USA minimum wage, but working hours were irregular and often extended in the summer months. Similarly to the migrant handymen, a minority of route-owner *jardineros* reported earnings in the top decile. These *jardineros* would have been in the USA for a long time, have resident status and may have become citizens through one of the many amnesties. Typically, they would own several trucks, have a number of regular routes and do some of the more lucrative, specialized work discussed in Chapter 6. In the UK, differentiation among migrant handymen is linked more to language ability, necessary for advertising services and for negotiating with clients. As Patryk explains:

> they can't find jobs because they can't speak the language. They can't put their adverts on Gumtree or other English websites ... and these people I take to do jobs ... I charge approximately £180 or £190 for the work, and ask workers whether they would agree to work for £50.
>
> Patryk, HM

Through these margins Patryk would be able to accumulate capital and potentially expand his operations. Likewise, the route-owner *jardineros* gained from the margin between their costs (labour and equipment) and the fees paid by householders. As their work was more standardized and more publicly visible than that of the handymen, competition was greater, making it difficult to charge more for their services. As a consequence their margins were squeezed and often secured through very long working hours, resulting in co-ethnic, family and self-exploitation (see Chapter 6).

Invariably, a wider gap in earnings would exist between the migrant handymen and the householders for whom they worked than between the worker entrepreneur and their employees. This wide differential provided a key motivation for householders to outsource. Dermott was quite explicit on this issue:

> well, you know, my day rate's a thousand quid, right, so anything that's less than that is fine, you know [laughs] within reason it's kinda fine, so you know, 200 quid, 200 quid a day to have someone to come and decorate the house doesn't seem very expensive, really, I mean, fine it's after tax income but, you know, if I was doing a brutal calculation I could've, we could afford to pay more than we currently do, I wouldn't say a lot more, but we can certainly afford to pay more than we currently do.
>
> Dermott, HH

Interestingly this householder also commented that they paid their cleaner above the minimum wage, but on a daily basis this amounted to only half the handyman rate, a difference he did not question. Nor did he question the wage gap between himself and the handyman.

Reward structures are influenced by prevailing labour market conditions and regulations, the work itself, and how the work is organized. Arguably, pay is also influenced by the identity characteristics of the worker, revealing social understandings of what is deserving or undeserving, what is skilful and what is simply 'natural' talent, and what is worthy of financial recompense and what merits less than a living wage. Such notions are gendered, racialized and ethnicized, but have become sedimented in the social imagination as natural and difficult to challenge. Less well explained are the reasons as to why different social and monetary values are attached to different forms of work and how this gendered hierarchy has come into being. We now explore these issues, beginning with Adam Smith's (1976: 351–2) theoretical exposition before examining the differences between the masculinized domestic work from our case studies and the feminized domestic work discussed in Chapter 2.

In 1776, Adam Smith contrasted manufacturing work with the work of domestic servants, arguing that the former was productive and the latter unproductive. His rationale was that the services of the domestic servant 'generally perish in the very instant of their performance, and seldom leave any trace of value behind them for which an equal quantity of service could afterwards be procured' (Smith, 1976: 351–2). Smith's point is not to say that the labour of the servant is without value in the sense of being useless. Indeed, he places many 'public servants' in this category, from the 'churchmen, lawyers, physicians [and] men of letters' performing the 'gravest and most important' services to the 'buffoons, musicians, opera singers, etc.' that perform services which are 'frivolous'. Rather, his point is to emphasize that the value of the servants' work 'perish[es] in the very instance of its production' (Smith, 1976: 352), while manufacturing produces a product whose value can be realized when sold. This difference arises because the worker in manufacturing adds value to the 'materials which he [sic] works upon' over and above that necessary to cover the wages. While someone employing many workers (in manufacturing) could become rich by realising this value or profit, therefore, those who employ many servants will become poor, as money is spent but no new value is created. In a footnote to this remark Smith acknowledges that an innkeeper could become rich by employing servants to run the inn, but his argument relates to the economy as a whole and to the fact that a certain amount of value has to be created in manufacturing before it can be spent on services (Smith, 1976: 352).

The binary between productive and reproductive work has always been challenged by feminists, but often on moral grounds relating to the intrinsic or use value of the work, and not on technical, economic grounds within the exigencies of a capitalist society, where profit rather than well-being are the order of the day. Thinking through the implications of the technical distinction between productive and unproductive work can be helpful because it shows that there are important similarities and differences in the work done by handymen, *jardineros,* maids and nannies. Potentially, they could all be termed unproductive services, as none recoup the expenditure laid out on them directly, if at all. Handyman work has greater durability because it generally adds value by increasing the worth of the house. Likewise garden design and reconstruction, for example, through decking, paving and water features (the more specialized work occasionally done by *jardinero*s) arguably enhance real estate values, while the more regular lawn mowing and leaf blowing perhaps contributes more to upholding the status or social capital of householders within the neighbourhood as the impact is more transitory and, like household cleaning and caring, has to be redone constantly. It therefore 'seldom leave[s] any [or perhaps more accurately much] trace of value behind' (Smith, 1976: 351).

What this means is that male commoditized services (similar to feminized services) only indirectly (through maintaining house prices), and to varying degrees, contribute to the buyers' economic wealth. In general, they represent a deduction from the buyers' income. This limits the level of demand for their services and the prices people are willing to pay, thus affecting the profitability of the work and, in turn, the workers' earnings. The fact that handyman work potentially contributes more to economic wealth than that of either *jardineros* or maids perhaps explains the comparatively lower migrant density of this sector (see Chapter 4 and Kilkey and Perrons, 2010).

A further common feature of commoditized services that similarly limits the market size and earnings of any individual producer relates to other shared economic properties (Folbre and Nelson, 2000; Himmelweit, 2007). To varying degrees, these services have limited economies of scale and limited expansibility. Such properties arise because the services have to be delivered personally on a one to one basis and in situ, so the capacity for productivity increases, expanding market share, and increasing profits and earnings are again very limited. More specifically, it is very difficult to increase the quantity of work that any individual *jardinero* or handyman can supply – one *jardinero* can only mow one lawn at a time, albeit with a powerful machine, just as a handyman can only fix one tap at once, or a carer put one person to bed before moving on to the next.

While a worker entrepreneur may own several trucks and employ a number of *ayudantes,* economies of scale remain limited – each team can only complete so much work in a day, and our case study showed that the *jardineros* sought to secure an optimally sized route with regular and reliable clients rather than a 'jumbo route'. Given the limited possibilities for productivity increases, having large routes or a large number of routes simply meant that they had to employ more *ayudantes;* a strategy considered risky and difficult to manage (see Chapter 6). *Jardineros* would therefore downsize by passing less reliable clients and more difficult routes on to others. There are exceptions, however, and larger firms and web-based agencies exist in gardening just as they do in handyman work and in feminized domestic care and cleaning.[19] Many of these firms, though, focus on organizational or managerial arrangements, and make money either through initial design and landscape planning or by putting buyers and suppliers into contact with each other.[20] The actual physical work is generally subcontracted to independent producers – individual suppliers, worker entrepreneurs or small firms, who are the ones faced with the problems of profitability outlined previously and analysed further later.

William Baumol (1967) refers to the characteristics of these types of work or services as technologically unprogressive and argues that their real costs will rise over time in comparison to technologically progressive commodities, where there is scope for productivity increases through mass production. As a consequence, he argued that except for elite demand, these activities would tend to disappear from the market unless subsidized by the state. Corresponding to this analysis, the domestic servant population declined dramatically in the early-middle twentieth century, when alternative employment opportunities with significantly higher earnings became available through the expansion of mass-produced consumer goods. These employment opportunities led also to the 'great wage compression' – a trend towards an equalization of earnings – that took place through to the early 1970s (Krugman, 2002; Miller, 1991). Since, as we have argued, inequality generates a demand for and supply of domestic services, this compression inevitably resulted in a decline in domestic services; a decline intensified by virtue of the fact that the consumer goods produced were often household items that reduced the burden of domestic work (as discussed in Chapter 2). Today's neoliberal global economy, with liberalization, deregulation, widening inequalities and a growing international division of labour, has seen a resurgence of demand for (and supply of) commoditized services. These are rendered profitable as a result of a polarization of earnings through the re-emergence of both elite earners and low cost labour, the latter being secured through either a socially disadvantaged workforce (with the *ayudantes'* migration status rendering them disadvantaged, for instance) or worker entrepreneurs practising co-ethnic, self and family exploitation.

In addition to the economic properties of the work which limit earnings, the individualized character of domestic work also contributes to insecure and potentially exploitative conditions. The route-owner *jardineros* negotiate contracts with households to tend their gardens on a regular and repeated basis, but these contracts can be relatively informal and difficult to enforce. In addition, the sector is highly competitive and the route owners are exposed to the risk of non-payment and termination with very little possibility of effective legal redress. This insecurity is passed on to the *ayudantes*, so their 'contracts' too are informal and their wages insecure, varying with the uncertain volume of work done (see Chapter 6). By comparison, the handymen work for the same client on a much less frequent basis, largely because the work itself is bespoke or one-off meaning that they continually have to search for new jobs and clients. This uncertainty makes them reluctant to turn down work, for fear of having none at all, leading to periods of overwork. Once a price has been negotiated for a particular job it is generally respected on both sides, but these arrangements are not legally enforceable and there is often an element of uncertainty in household repair. Unexpected complications arise: holes can be found in the floorboards, walls can disintegrate when wallpaper is stripped away, etc., and handymen might find themselves with problems that are difficult and costly to resolve and for which clients may be reluctant to pay. The worker-entrepreneurs pass this uncertainty on to people who work for them who, consequently, do not have regular contracts:

> I didn't want to sign any contracts. My work is not regular enough so that I could ensure people that I'll have work for them for the next six months. No, I can't. There could be problems and I might not have any work for a week.
>
> Patryk, HM

Given their gender, neither the *jardineros* nor the handymen are likely to be exposed to the personal hazards and sexual abuse that some female domestic workers experience as a consequence of working in private homes (Anderson, 2000; Lutz, 2011). Even so, in all cases the individualized character of the work means that it is difficult to organize any collective action to improve the terms and conditions of their employment. Some female domestic workers have organized and campaigned for improved conditions leading to the ILO's Convention on Domestic Workers, which if ratified by all states, will in principle protect an estimated 53 to 100 million workers (ILO, 2011), though the individual character of the work still means that monitoring and enforcement remain extremely difficult. The *jardineros* might find it easier than would the handymen, whose work is much less visible, to follow the example of janitors in the USA (Sassen, 2010b) and office cleaners in the UK (Wills, 2008) and show their potential strength by downing tools, as before long, the ensuing unkempt lawns would become visible. Any form of protest, though, would be extremely hazardous for those without citizenship, and the high level of competition would make such action very risky for any individual worker entrepreneur.

On a more positive note, male (and female) domestic workers report favourably on some aspects of their experiences. The *jardineros* expressed pride in their work, and even more so in how they had used the skills they had acquired to construct their own gardens (see Chapter 3). Likewise the handymen commented on work satisfaction. Olek, who complains that people often want high quality outcomes for little money and have little understanding of the complexities of the work or processes involved, still expresses intrinsic pleasure in the work itself, especially when the results are appreciated:

> I like jobs when I have to start from the beginning ... I redecorated the foyer this way. Dust everywhere. I put new plaster panels, plaster, new lighting. I used ... an Italian material that looks like marble. It's a very good material, easy to use. I installed halogens in the ceiling. The woman was in seventh heaven. She went to fetch the camera and sent pictures of the ceiling to people.

> Olek, HM

In this respect there are some parallels with the affective elements of feminized domestic work, especially with respect to caring for children (Isaksen, Devi and Hochschild, 2008; Parreñas, 2005; 2012). In contrast to findings from some studies of female domestic workers, for example, Parreñas (2001), the Polish handymen, while being acutely aware of their lowly position within the increasingly inegalitarian UK society, (recall Daniel's remarks in Chapter 4), rarely reported any sense of despair or misery linked to a lack of social recognition or the low social standing of their work. In some cases, this was because they regarded the work as temporary and as something that did not therefore define their social identity, while in others no loss of social mobility was involved.[21]

While sharing many features of feminized domestic work in terms of limited scope for productivity (and pay) increases, with the individualized and domestic location of both forms of work leading to informality, precarity and few if any employment rights, the fact that stereotypically masculine domestic work is associated with male attributes of strength, use of machinery and, especially in the case of the handymen, with formal male skilled trades, means earnings are significantly higher than feminized domestic work. Lawn mowing does not fit into this category so well, but the work nonetheless becomes associated with machines and traditional masculinity. These higher returns enabled some of the long standing route-owner *jardineros* to have good quality housing and put their children through the USA education system, as discussed in

Chapter 3. It is too soon to know whether the migrant handymen will achieve similar outcomes, but many reported earnings that are significantly higher than those in the care and cleaning sectors. Studies of feminized domestic workers also report on how they have used their earnings to finance housing and finance their children's education, but this is generally through remittances sent to their countries of origin, and is only possible by virtue of the value of different currencies and costs of living. Unlike some *jardineros*, they were less able to finance these purchases in the country in which they are working.

The fact that masculine domestic services are linked with work in formal craft trades still leaves unanswered the question of why these predominantly male forms of work are regarded as skilled and are higher paid than care and cleaning work, where women are over represented. Since people are likely to value their children more highly than their homes or gardens, this question is particularly puzzling. Francesca Scrinzi (2010) suggests that feminized work is considered unskilled because similar work is carried out for free by women in the family. This explanation has the benefit of accounting for the gendering of care and handyman work, but given that lawn mowing and handyman work were similarly provided for free by men in the family, it cannot account for the fact that the male work is regarded as skilled and paid more highly. Adam Smith's technical distinction, discussed previously, between productive and unproductive work, can partially explain the difference by showing how masculine domestic work potentially has more lasting value by virtue of its contribution to real estate values. But this explanation is insufficient for two reasons. First, care work can be regarded as having some productive value, insofar as it can enable families to spend more time working and earning a wage and because it can help develop the human, cultural and social capital of the child, ensuring not only that they can make more money in the future but that they also become trusted and reliable citizens.[22] This productive effect is less tangible, and therefore easily overlooked using Smith's criteria, but a second, deeper problem remains: Smith's distinction does not explain why the different forms of work are gendered in the first place.

Crucial in explaining the different valuations of male and female work, then, are deeply embedded cultural practices and gendered social norms; norms which uphold and reinforce existing practices and understandings of appropriate roles for women and men and the value of different activities. These boundaries are deeply rooted and have arguably become naturalized through repeated practice (Butler, 1990; Epstein, 2006: 320). But simply pointing to these norms and their naturalization through repeated practice serves only to restate the problem, and does not get down to the roots of the question of how and why these gendered practices and gender differentiated rewards emerged in the first place. What must not be forgotten, therefore, is the question of the power that underlies these social norms. Masculine understandings of the economy prioritize markets and the publically visible, 'productive' and quantifiably profitable sector.[23] By contrast, feminist economics offers a broader understanding of the economy encompassing the importance of less visible and less quantifiably profitable forms of social provisioning. This broader feminist focus can contribute to an explanation of the low social priority given to the care sector, but once more, this does not account for how these understandings and values become dominant and, additionally, why care work is feminized in the first place. Questions regarding masculinity and power, focused on how masculine identities are produced and how masculine power is publically secured and revered such that oppressive forms of masculinity can become hegemonic, therefore become crucial. To explain the gendering of domestic work and their differential valuations consequently requires further work that links literature on masculinity with literature on the gendering of work.

7.5   Our final conclusion

Householders, the migrant handymen and immigrant *jardineros* are drawn together as a consequence of their different social positions, arising from uneven development and increasing inequality, to create the growing market in domestic labour. This growing market forms part of the broader process of the commoditization of social reproduction accompanying the displacement of the male breadwinner family model by the dual worker model in Europe and the USA (Crompton, 2006; Lewis, 2009). Drawing on our case study research of migrant domestic workers in the UK and USA we have considered the meanings associated with the performance of male domestic work, and assessed how these meanings contribute to our understanding of the contemporary masculinities of the migrant men and the people for whom they work. We indicated how these understandings are shaped by the various ways in which individual identity characteristics intersect both with each other and with broader socio-economic and political and cultural contexts.

Generalizations about the position of migrant domestic workers are complicated therefore by the specific ways in which identity characteristics intersect. As we have seen, gender cuts across other identity characteristics, as feminized domestic work is invariably valued less highly than work stereotypically done by men. Likewise citizenship and language ability provide possibilities for greater progression by enabling the migrants to become worker entrepreneurs. The question of ethnicity is more complex. While the ethnicity and nationality of the *jardineros* assisted finding work within this sector through social networking, thereby establishing an ethnic enclave, it limited their opportunities within the overall USA labour force owing to various forms of discrimination and exclusion. This situation was further exacerbated by their rural backgrounds and low levels of formal education. They expected that this limitation would be less serious for their sons and daughters, whose education formed one of the motivations for working long hours (see Chapter 6). The Polish ethnicity was, by contrast, largely seen as an advantage in handymen and perhaps other forms of work, so opportunities in the wider labour market are potentially less restrictive. In this respect their 'whiteness' or racial similarity with the majority may have been an advantage. Certainly, the UK turned towards Europe before looking to the former colonies to resolve labour shortages in the mid twentieth century post-war boom (McDowell, 2005).

We have seen how the existence of commoditized services is linked both to uneven development between Mexico and the USA and between Poland and the UK and rising inequality within the USA and UK. Migration can be seen as an individual response to the structural problem of inequality and, in the main, the individual migrants benefitted from their moves through increased incomes and wider opportunities for themselves and their children. But whether such migration reinforces or resolves the broader patterns of inequality that generate this phenomenon remains unclear. A further inequality arises in the extent to which men are able to realize their aspirations to be hands-on nurturing fathers. Many of the men we interviewed in the UK shared the aspiration to be a modern nurturing father, but the opportunities for so doing were very much shaped by social position, especially given the limited degree of state support for childcare, and the variation in corporate policies.[24] The higher incomes of the male householders in the UK gave them the privilege of being able to outsource domestic work to less wealthy others in order to simultaneously pursue their careers and engage in hands-on fathering. The migrant handymen similarly worked long hours, but lacked the income to outsource domestic work, leaving them with fewer opportunities to spend time with their children and meet their aspiration to be hands-on fathers. While the Polish handymen could at least be accompanied by families and could travel back and forth without border controls, the situation was worse for the *ayudantes* without citizenship, who lamented the long periods of time spent away from their families and children (Ramirez, 2011). The route-owner *jardineros* who had been in the USA for several decades had been able to secure a standard of living for their children that would not have been possible had they remained in Mexico, but this came at the cost of being unable to spend much time with them during their formative years. In many cases, therefore, the performance of a breadwinning masculine role was only possible at the expense of an alternative, nurturing identity. The most successful and affluent route owners could partially combine the two by virtue of the flexibility associated with their self-employed status; a flexibility which enabled them to occasionally make time for their children's special events (see Chapter 3). Later on, shared time would often take place in work as the male children acted as assistants during weekends and vacations.

While almost all of the UK professional fathers in the study demonstrated a strong commitment to their paid work, few fathers demonstrated any attachment towards handyman type tasks and were happy that their incomes allowed them to outsource these in order to spend more time with their children. In this respect, fathering clearly formed part of their masculinity identity, although there was little evidence to suggest a more profound change in gender roles or responsibilities. In this respect, our findings support Jennifer Bair's (2010) argument mentioned at the beginning of this chapter, namely, that gender continues to matter, even if the way in which it does so varies by time and place.

Our book has demonstrated how prevailing understandings of global hegemonic masculinity are associated with continuing uneven development between and rising inequalities within states, circumstances that have led to the demand for commoditized services, supplied in part, through migrant and immigrant labour. It has also shown how three groups of people: Mexican *jardineros* in the USA, Polish migrant handymen in the UK, and the UK householders drawing on handyman services, have managed their daily lives in this context of inequality. The householders have found a private but only partial resolution to the conflicting expectations relating to long working hours and their own aspirations to be hands-on nurturing parents. The handymen and route-owner *jardineros* we interviewed have shown how it is possible to develop better lives for themselves and their families through migration and long working hours.[25] What remains unexplained, however, is how the power of global hegemonic masculinity that makes these difficult life choices necessary is sustained.

While our account is by no means all encompassing, we have started to demonstrate the manner in which these difficult life choices relating to places of residence and work and family life balance are forced upon both householders and migrant workers by powerful notions of global hegemonic masculinity which underpin the current economic, political and social order. We have begun to illustrate, furthermore, how this form of masculinity is produced not only by dominant, wealthy householders, but also by the more subordinate migrant workers, whose life choices are shaped by but also reproduce notions of male strength, breadwinning and gender power. This dominant notion of masculinity was shown to modify but not transform gender relations, but also to generate difficult choices and constrain opportunities for a male work-life balance. But the men in our study rarely questioned the value of these power structures and identities, raising the question of how, where and when these constraining notions of masculinity might be displaced.

Notes

1 Gender, Migration and Domestic Work: An Introduction

1. This literature is reviewed in Chapter 2, but key writers include Anderson (2000), Hondagneu-Sotelo (2001), Lutz (2011) and Parreñas (2001) and for a review focusing on parallels with the global value chains, see Yeates (2012). One study that focuses on masculinized domestic work is Cox (2010; 2012).
2. Time Use Survey data show, albeit with cross-national variation in its extent, a gendered division of labour in the distribution of household tasks, with men more likely to do gardening, household repairs and maintenance, and women more likely to do food preparation, laundry, ironing, cleaning and childcare (Aliaga, 2006: Table 2; Miranda, 2011).
3. In the UK, net inward migration increased significantly in the 1990s and doubled again in the 2000s, reaching 184,000 in 2007–8 reflecting a permanent move to the UK (defined as staying for more than one year) of just over 0.5 million (554,000) and an outward movement of 371,000 people (ONS, 2012a).
4. Overall, in 2011 about 50 per cent of UK's foreign-born population were in London (37 per cent) and the South East (13 per cent) (Migration Observatory, 2012). Migrants from new EU member states show a wider spatial distribution, matching the demand for work in agriculture and food processing.
5. The terms 'accession' and 'enlargement' are used interchangeably throughout the book to refer to the process by which ten new countries, including Poland, joined the EU on 1 May 2004. For citizens of EU Member States of long standing there is free movement of labour. For countries joining the EU in 2004 such as Poland there was more gradual transition towards free movement of labour. The scale and timing of the migration is discussed in Chapter 4.
6. Details of the migration arrangements between the USA and Mexico are discussed in Chapter 6.
7. This definition is different from the Marxist understanding which refers to the reproduction of entire social systems.
8. The upper classes have a long history of outsourcing all forms of domestic work and care – issues discussed in more detail in Chapter 2.
9. In the UK between 1996 and 2010, there has been a 5.8 per cent increase in the proportion of mothers working full time from 23.1 per cent in 1996 to 29.0 per cent by the end of 2010. In addition 37.4 per cent of mothers work part time. This leaves 66.5 per cent of mothers in paid employment, compared to 67.3 per cent of women without dependent children (ONS, 2011a).
10. See Esping-Andersen (2009) who finds that educated parents devote on average 30 per cent more time to their children than the low educated – and this time is especially differentiated during the developmental parenting – where early skills are developed.

11. These findings, though, are not repeated across all cases, with our find-ings showing that in at least one case, aspects of new fathering were also outsourced to handymen. This case is discussed further in Chapter 5.
12. This literature is fully explored in Chapter 2.
13. This data comes from the UK Time Use Survey 2000 and is reported in more detail in Kilkey and Perrons (2010). We exclude window cleaning purchased by 30 per cent of households and vehicle repair (15 per cent) from our analysis, because they are supplied by specialists rather than handymen. Elderly care is purchased by 1 per cent of households (Kilkey and Perrons, 2010).
14. Quote from a postcard left in a Brighton hardware store.
15. See McDowell, Batnitzky and Dyer (2009).
16. Gumtree (2012) is a multipurpose site for people to buy and sell goods and services.
17. Palenga-Möllenbeck's current study of Polish handymen in Germany and their labour-using households replicates our UK study.
18. The work of Brannen (2012) and Ryan (2011) provide recent exceptions.

2 Globalization, Migration and Domestic Work: Gendering the Debate

1. See, for example, Búriková and Miller (2010), Cox (2006), Gregson and Lowe (1994), McDowell et al. (2005) on England; Degiuli (2007), Hochschild (2000), Lazaridis (2007), Pojmann (2006) on Southern Europe; Akalin (2007) on Turkey; Widding Isaksen (2010) on the Nordic countries; Lutz (2011) on Germany; Hondagneu-Sotelo (2001) on the USA; Moors and de Regt (2008) on the Middle East; Anderson (2000), Anderson and O'Connell Davidson (2003), Cancedda (2001), Gutiérrez-Rodríguez (2010), Lister et al. (2007), Parreñas (2001), Sarti (2006) on cross-national experiences; Lutz's (2008) edited collection covering a wide range of European countries. On time spent on the various tasks of social reproductive labour, see Miranda (2011).
2. In some parts of the world men still have a strong presence as domestic workers (see, for example, Qayum and Ray, 2010 on India and Bartolomei, 2010 on Africa).
3. There are cross-national differences, especially in the hours of paid work done by women. Comparing the UK and the USA for example, Mutari and Figart (2001) note that part-time working is more common among women in the former than in the latter. See also EC (2010).
4. In the UK, but not elsewhere, increasing women's employment has been advocated for other reasons too, including its potential to reduce child pov-erty, and to address consequences of poor parenting through the provision of childcare services (Lewis, 2009).
5. The language of 'consumer choice' is used to legitimize shifts towards direct payments for care (Glendinning, 2008; Land and Himmelweit, 2010).
6. One example of such a policy for domestic work in general is the *Chèque Emploi-Service Universel* in France. It was introduced in January 2006, although it had a series of predecessors dating from the early 1990s, and has the dual aims of helping families reconcile work and family life and creating jobs. The

scheme offers tax breaks to those who purchase domestic services or employ a domestic worker, and applies to areas of domestic work such as cleaning, shopping, repairs and maintenance, as well as care-giving (Windebank, 2007). For other examples from across Europe, see Cancedda (2001).

7. This has remained the case through the economic downturn, as house prices in both cities have continued to rise.

8. This theme is also apparent in a range of studies seeking to account for the patterns of labour market insertion of recent arrivals to the UK, including Datta and Brickell (2009) on Polish migrants working on London's building sites; Wills et al. (2010) on the concentration of migrants in London's bottom-end jobs and the creation of a 'migrant division of labour'; McDowell, Batnitzky and Dyer (2007) on segmentation and division within the hospitality sector; McDowell, Batnitzky and Dyer (2008) on the hospitality sector and the NHS; McGregor (2007) on the elder-care industry; and Anderson et al. (2006) on the agricultural, construction, hospitality and the au pair sectors.

9. For a comprehensive review of the transnational care literature, see Baldassar and Merla (eds) (2013).

3   Researching Men in the Relationship between Gender, Migration and Domestic Work

1. Throughout the book, 'partner' is the default term, and the one predominantly used; we use 'wife'/'husband' only when it reflects a self-identified marital status.

2. Participants' names have been recoded to ensure anonymity; throughout the book we distinguish among the groups of interviewees using the following codes: 'A' for agency, 'HH' for household, 'HM' for handyman, and 'HW' for handywoman.

3. Research Association's 'Ethical Guidelines', the British Sociological Association's 'Statement of Ethical Practice', and the Data Protection Act were applied as the study raised issues of informed consent, confidentiality and anonymity.

4. Three of the 79 interviews were conducted by telephone at the request of participants and due to time and location considerations.

5. Two interviews were not transcribed because of poor quality recording. Detailed notes were taken.

6. For consistency we refer to the eight Central and East European countries (Czech Republic, Estonia, Hungary, Latvia, Lithuania, Poland, Slovakia and Slovenia) which joined the EU in 2004 as EU8. The term A8 (Accession 8) is also commonly applied to this group.

7. Institutional Review Boards (IRBs) manage the 'Human Subjects Protection' process in research with human subjects with respect to informed consent; confidentiality, anonymity, privacy and deception; and compliance with federal laws (Lincoln and Tierney, 2004).

8. This aspect refers to such issues as funding and training resources as well as themes referring to time, productivity, and accountability in the prevailing research practice in contemporary neoliberal university settings, and is further elaborated upon elsewhere (Plomien, 2013).

9. The Construction Industry Scheme applies to contractors and subcontractors in construction work and regulates payment issues in the construction industry.

4 Migrants and Male Domestic Work in the UK: The Rise of the 'Polish Handyman'

1. In the 2004–10 period, 2007 represents the year with the highest stock of Polish nationals living abroad (2.27 million) for longer than two (up to 2006) or three months (from 2007 onwards) (GUS 2011).
2. Regulations defined 'no interruption' as periods of unemployment not exceeding 30 days in any 12-month period.
3. Signed in Brussels on 16 December 1991, ratified by Poland on 4 July 1992, in force since 1 February 1994 (Dziennik Ustaw 1994, nr 11, poz. 39).
4. See also Palenga-Möllenbeck (2012) whose recent study of Polish handymen and their labour-using households in Germany, which replicates our UK study in many aspects, reports high numbers of self-employed Polish handymen working in Germany.
5. One householder couple in our study, Laura and Mark, who reside in the North-East of England, both noted this, as Mark expressed: 'but you know, London is much easier. Everyone seems to have their house renovated by Polish builders in London' (Mark, HH).
6. It may, however, manifest itself more clearly at an institutional or policy level.
7. But see Burrell (2009) for a discussion of negative press coverage.
8. We also draw on Jeff's evaluation of British handymen in Chapter 7.
9. McDowell, Batnitzky and Dyer base their analysis on Burawoy (1979); their approach differs from the concept of interpellation as developed by Althusser (1970).
10. Similar processes occur among *jardineros* analysed in Chapter 6, and compared in Chapter 7.
11. Palenga-Möllenbeck (2012) reports a similar phenomenon in Germany.
12. Nationals of Bulgaria and Romania, countries which joined the EU in a further enlargement in 2007, are subject to stronger restrictions on working; in most cases non-EU rules apply, except for self-employment provisions of EC Association Agreement (UK Border Agency, 2011).
13. Throughout the last couple of decades asylum seekers have been subjected to ever harsher treatment in the UK migration regime (for an overview see Sales, 2007).

5 Connecting Men in the International Division of Domestic Work: The New 'Father Time-Bind', Global Divisions between Men and Gender Inequalities

1. It needs to be acknowledged, though, that as a result of the exclusion of other stages of the domestic lifecycle and other types of households – for example, elderly households and single parent households – our account of the source of demand for commoditized male domestic services will be incomplete.

2. Other, very similar mappings of the 'epochs' of fathering exist, largely based on the USA experience. See, for example, Pleck (1987) and Cabrera et al. (2000). But, see Burnett et al. (2010) for an application of these to the history of England.
3. This is not to suggest that UK maternity leave is generous on other dimensions; while it might be the longest, it is the worst paid (Moss, 2012).
4. Available only as a transferable right from the mother's maternity leave and pay entitlements if she returns to paid work before having exhausted these.
5. In the UK in 1986 the bottom quintile worked on average 21.6 hours per week and 1020 hours per year. In 2004 the respective figures were 22.8 and 1053. The top quintile worked on average 43.6 hours per week and 2224 hours per year in 1986. In 2004 the respective figures were 47.7 and 2451 (OECD, 2011b).
6. Ruhs (2012) draws this conclusion from a review of three studies, each conducted for a different time period: 1992–2006, 1997–2005 and 2000–7. He acknowledges that the effects of migration may have changed during the recession.
7. This is the only interview conducted with partners of handymen, and the only case where partners were interviewed together.

6   Mexican Gardeners in the USA

1. According to the United States Census Bureau (2012), the median household income in California for 2006–10 was $60,883.
2. Immigration law in the United States is complicated, but some of the gendered transitions these have involved for Mexican immigrant families and communities are analysed in the book *Gendered Transitions* (Hondagneu-Sotelo, 1994b).

7   Gender Identity and Work: Migrant Domestic Work and Masculinity

1. See, for example Hire a Hubby (2012); 0800 Handyman (2012); Hire a Hubby (2012); Rent a Hubby (2012); Handy Squad (2012); Polish Handyman (2012).
2. This provider also runs a service called 'Dump a Hubby' (2012), which is a waste disposal service.
3. In the traditional Latin American understanding, machismo, exaggerated masculinity or being a 'proper man', has been linked to past colonial cultural subordination (Chant with Craske, 2003) and in contemporary times is reinforced by their structural location in the USA, which affords only limited social mobility given the discriminatory environment, their minority racial position and, in some cases, their limited citizenship rights (Ramirez, 2011).
4. See also Gelber (1997) for similar findings in relation to the rise of DIY in early twentieth century USA.
5. Given that both studies were based on in depth interviews, we cannot say whether the contrasting findings reflect differences between countries or

just differences between the samples. In the UK our householders were all fathers, predominantly professionals living in London and users of handymen services, whereas in Rosie Cox's (2012) study the homeowners were more diverse.

6. See also Demetriou (2001).
7. Recall the comments of the householder James in Chapter 5 for example.
8. Recall the case of Olek, discussed in Chapter 4.
9. See McDowell (2009b) for a discussion of how bodily attributes influence the hiring process and how interactive workers are trained to behave in pleasing ways.
10. For a parallel comment relating to social identity more generally, see Ahmed (2004).
11. See for example Bradley (1989); Cohen (2007); Crompton and Sanderson (1990); EC (2011).
12. These direct encounters are comparatively rare and the masculine character of the work suggests their loss of self-esteem is perhaps less demeaning than the situation of male domestic workers from the Philippines in the Netherlands, who find themselves cleaning while the female owner sits on the sofa reading a magazine (Haile and Siegmann, 2013).
13. See Anderson (2000), who makes this comment in relation to female domestic workers.
14. These points are made more abstractly by Judith Butler (1990) and Pierre Bourdieu (2001).
15. Using a wide range of data sources, Passel, Cohn and Gonzalez Barrera (2012) show that in the last four decades 12 million people entered the USA from Mexico, mainly without documents, but that net migration has either stopped or even reversed.
16. In 2012 negative growth was recorded in the UK as austerity policies were intensified.
17. Since its high point in 2007 of 87,000 new migrants, migration from EU8 countries reached a low of 16,000 in 2009 but from then onwards until 2012 has been in the mid 40,000s per year, the majority from Poland (ONS, 2012a).
18. The High Pay Commission (2011: 9) reported that despite the continuing low growth rate in the UK, executive pay in the FTSE 100 rose on average by 49 per cent compared with an increase of just 2.7 per cent for the average employee. More broadly, the hourly earnings (excluding overtime, for full-time employees) of the top decile, where the majority of our householders were placed, grew at 1.8 per cent between 2010 and 2011, compared to an increase of only 0.8 per cent in the lowest decile (ONS, 2012d).
19. Groundworks Landscape (2012) provides one example. In addition there are firms that act as a gateway for a range of smaller firms, including Gardenseekers (2012).
20. In the case of gardening, some firms focus on the design aspects of landscaping but similarly the physical work is generally subcontracted.
21. Within the literature on nannies and maids there is a tension between accounts which portray the situation of migrant care workers as abject, exposed to long and unregulated working hours and abuse from the householders who entrap them by taking away their passports (Anderson, 2000)

and accounts which emphasize the care workers' agency and ability to fulfil migratory projects (Andrijasevic, 2010; Agustin, 2007).

22. As discussed in Chapters 2 and 5, this rationale formed the basis of the (albeit limited) state support for work-life balance policies.

23. This masculine priority afforded to the economy parallels some of our interviewees' commitment to paid work. For example, Richard, discussed in Chapter 5, clearly enjoys spending long hours working. He always leaves it too late to arrange holiday leave to coincide with school breaks, and while he outsources male domestic work to spend time with his children on weekends, he leaves the organization of handyman work to his wife, Fiona. Richard regards this division of labour as 'natural', 'because I'm just not here' (Richard, HH).

24. See Hochschild (2012).

25. Clearly we have an inevitable selection bias associated with qualitative research especially with respect to (im)migrants. We have not for example interviewed people whose migration strategies have failed.

References

0800 Handymen (2012) http://www.0800handyman.com/services/, date accessed 20 July 2012.

AA (2012) http://www.theaa.com/homeassist/london-handyman-service.html, date accessed 28 October 2012.

Agustín, L. (2003) 'A migrant world of services', *Social Politics* 10, 377–96.

Agustin, L. (2007) *Sex at the Margins, Migration, Labour Markets and the Rescue Industry*. London: Zed Books.

Ahmed, S. (2004) 'Affective economies', *Social Text* 22, 117–39.

Akalin, A. (2007) 'Hired as a caregiver, demanded as a housewife. Becoming a migrant domestic worker in Turkey', *European Journal of Women's Studies* 14, 209–25.

Aliaga, C. (2006) *How is the Time of Women and Men Distributed in Europe?* Statistics in Focus, Population and Social Conditions 4/2006. Luxembourg: Office for Official Publications of the European Communities.

Althusser, L. (1970) '"Lenin and Philosophy" and Other Essays', Monthly Review Press 1971, http://www.marxists.org/reference/archive/althusser/1970/ideology.htm, date accessed 17 July 2012.

Anderson, B. (2000) *Doing the Dirty Work? The Global Politics of Domestic Labour*. London: Zed Books.

Anderson, B. (2007) 'A very private business. Exploring the demand for migrant domestic workers', *European Journal of Women's Studies* 14, 247–64.

Anderson, B. and O'Connell Davidson, J. (2003) *Is Trafficking in Human Beings Demand Driven? A Multi-Cultural Pilot Study*. International Organisation for Migration Research Series No. 15. Geneva: International Organisation for Migration.

Anderson, C. A. and Bowman, M. J. (1953) 'The vanishing servant and the contemporary status system of the American south', *American Journal of Sociology* 59, 215–30.

Anderson, B., Ruhs, B. M., Rogaly, B. and Spencer, S. (2006) *Fair Enough? Central and East European Migrants in Low-Wage Employment in the UK*. York: JRF.

Andrijasevic, R. (2010) *Migration, Agency and Citizenship in Sex Trafficking*. London: Palgrave Macmillan.

Arendell, T. (1997) 'Reflections on the researcher-researched relationship: a woman interviewing men', *Qualitative Sociology* 20, 341–68.

Association Agreement (1991) 'Europe Agreement establishing an association between the European Communities and their Member States and the Republic of Poland', online at http://wits.worldbank.org/GPTAD/PDF/archive/EC-Poland.pdf, date accessed 1 March 2011.

Bair, J. (2010) 'On difference and capital: gender and the globalisation of production', *Signs* 36, 203–26.

Baldassar, L. and Merla, L. (eds) (2013) *Transnational Families, Migration, and Care Work*. New York: Routledge.

Barrett, M. and McIntosh, M. (1982) 'The "family wage"', in Whitelegg, E., Arnot, M., Bartels, E., Beechey, V., Birke, S., Himmelweit, S., Leonard, D., Ruehl, S. and Speakman, M. (eds), *The Changing Experience of Women.* Oxford: Martin Robertson.

Bartolomei, M. (2010) 'Migrant male domestic workers in comparative perspective: four case studies from Italy, India, Ivory Coast, and Congo', *Men and Masculinities* 13, 87–110.

Batalova, J. (2008) 'Mexican immigrants in the United States', Migration Policy Institute, http://www.migrationpolicy.org/, date accessed 25 May 2011.

Baumol, W. (1967) 'Macroeconomics of unbalanced growth: the anatomy of the urban crisis', *American Economic Review* 57, 415–26.

Baxter, J., Hewitt, B. and Western, M. (2009) 'Who uses paid domestic labor in Australia? Choice and constraint in hiring household help', *Feminist Economics* 15, 1–26.

Benería, L. (1999) 'Globalization, gender and the Davos man', *Feminist Economics* 5, 61–83.

Bettio, F. and Plantenga, J. (2004) 'Comparing care regimes in Europe', *Feminist Economics* 10, 85–113.

Bettio, F. Simonazzi, A. and Villa, P. (2006) 'Change in care regimes and female migration: the "care drain" in the Mediterranean', *Journal of European Social Policy* 16, 271–85.

Bianchi, S. M., Robinson, J. P. and Milkie, M. A. (2006) *Changing Rhythms of American Family Life.* New York: Russell Sage.

Bittman, M., Matheson, G. and Meagher, G. (1999) 'The changing boundary between home and market: Australian trends in outsourcing domestic labour', *Work, Employment and Society* 13, 249–73.

Bloom, L. and Riemer, R. (1949) *Removal and Return: The Socio-Economic Effects of the War on Japanese Americans.* Berkeley: University of California Press.

Bolderson, H. (2011) 'The ethics of welfare provision for migrants: a case for equal treatment and the repositioning of welfare', *Journal of Social Policy* 40, 219–36.

Bommes, M. and Geddes, A. (eds) (2000) *Immigration and Welfare: Challenging the Borders of the Welfare State.* London: Routledge.

Bonacich, E. and Modell, J. (1980) *The Economic Basis of Ethnic Solidarity: Small Business in the Japanese American Community.* Berkeley: University of California Press.

Bormann, F. H., Balmori, D. and Gebelle, G. T. (2001) *Redesigning the American Lawn: The Search for Environmental Harmony,* 2nd ed. New Haven, CT: Yale University Press.

Bourdieu, P. (2001) *Masculine Domination.* Stanford: Stanford University Press.

Bowman, J. R. and Cole, A. M. (2009) 'Do working mothers oppress other women? The Swedish "maid debate" and the welfare state politics of gender equality', *Signs* 35, 157–84.

Bradley H. (1989) *Men's Work, Women's Work.* Cambridge: Polity.

Brandth, B. and Kvande, E. (2009) 'Gendered or gender-neutral care politics for fathers?' *American Academy of Political and Social Science* 624, 177–89.

Brannen, J. (2012) 'Fatherhood in the context of migration: an intergenerational approach', *Zeitgrift Fur Biographieforsschung, Oral History und Lebenverlaufsanalyses BIOS* 24, 267–82.

Brannen, J. and Nielsen, A. (2006) 'From fatherhood to fathering: transmission and change among British fathers in four generation families', *Sociology* 40, 335–52.

Brenke, K., Yuksel, M. and Zimmermann, K. F. (2009) *'EU enlargement under continued mobility restrictions: consequences for the German labor market'*, IZA discussion papers, No. 4055.

Broom, A., Hand, K. and Tovey, P. (2009) 'The role of gender, environment and individual biography in shaping qualitative interview data', *International Journal of Social Research Methodology* 12, 51–65.

Burawoy, M. (1979) *Manufacturing Consent*. Chicago: University of Chicago Press.

Burawoy, M. (1998) 'The extended case method', *Sociological Theory* 16, 4–33.

Búriková, Z. and Miller, D. (2010) *Au Pair*. Cambridge: Polity Press (Foundation for the Improvement of Living and Working Conditions).

Burnett, S. B., Gatrell, C., Cooper, C. and Sparrow, P. (2010) 'Fatherhood and flexible working: a contradiction in terms?', in S. kaiser, M. Ringlstetter, D. R. Eikhof and M. P. Cunha (eds) *Creating Balance? International Perspectives on the Work-Life Integration of Professionals*, London: Springer.

Burrell, K. (2009) 'Introduction: migration to the UK from Poland: continuity and change in East-West European mobility', in Burrell, K. (ed.), *Polish Migration to the UK in the 'New' European Union After 2004*. Farnham: Ashgate.

Butler, J. (1990) *Gender Trouble. Feminism and the Subversion of Identity*. London: Routledge.

Cabrera, N. J., Tamis-LeMonda, C. S., Bradley, R. H., Hofferth, S. and Lamb, M. E. (2000) 'Fatherhood in the twenty-first century', *Child Development* 71, 127–36.

Cancedda, L. (2001) *Employment in Household Services*. Dublin: European Castles.

Cangiano, A., Shutes, I., Spencer, S. and Lesson, G. (2009) *Migrant Care Workers in Ageing Societies: Research Findings in the United Kingdom*. Oxford: COMPAS. http://www.compas.ox.ac.uk, date accessed 26 June 2012.

Castles, S. (2006) 'Guestworkers in Europe: a resurrection?', *International Migration Review* 40, 741–66.

Chant, S. with Craske, N. (2003) *Gender in Latin America*. New Brunswick, NJ: Rutgers University Press.

Chaplin, D. (1978) 'Domestic service and industrialization', *Comparative Studies in Sociology* 1, 97–127.

Clark, T. (2010) 'On being "researched": why do people engage with qualitative research?' *Qualitative Research* 19, 399–419.

Cohen, P. (2007) 'Confronting economic gender inequality', *Review of Radical Political Economics* 39, 132–7.

Collier, R. (2010) *Men, Law and Gender. Essays on the 'Man' of Law*. Oxon: Routledge.

Connell, R. (1987) *Gender and Power: Society, the Person and Sexual Politics*. Sydney: Allen and Unwin.

Connell, R. (1995) *Masculinities*. Sydney: Allen and Unwin.

Connell, R. (2011) *Confronting Equality. Gender Knowledge and Global Change*. Cambridge: Polity.

Connell, R. and Messerschmidt, J. W. (2005) 'Hegemonic masculinity: rethinking the concept', *Gender and Society* 19, 829–59.

Cox, R. (2006) *The Servant Problem: Domestic Employment in a Global Economy*. London: I B Tauris.

Cox, R. (2007) 'The au pair body. Sex object, sister or student?', *European Journal of Women's Studies* 14, 281–96.

Cox, R. (2010) 'Hired hubbies and mobile mums: gendered skills in domestic service', *Renewal* 18, 51–58.

Cox, R. (2012) 'The complications of "hiring a hubby": Gender relations and the commoditization of home maintenance in New Zealand, *Social and Cultural Geography*, http://dx.doi.org/10.1080/14649365.2012.704644, date accessed 01 August 2012.

Cox, R. and Watt, P. (2002) 'Globalization, polarization and the informal sector: the case of paid domestic workers in London', *Area* 34, 39–47.

Creighton, C. (1999) 'The rise and decline of the "male breadwinner family" in Britain', *Cambridge Journal of Economics* 23, 519–41.

Crompton, R. (2006) *Employment and the Family: The Reconfiguration of Work and Family Life in Contemporary Societies*. Cambridge: Cambridge University Press.

Crompton, R. and Lyonette, C. (2007) 'Are we all working too hard? Women, men and changing attitudes to paid employment', in Park, A., Curtice, J., Thomson, K., Phillips, M. and Johnson, M. (eds), *British Social Attitudes: The 23rd Report – Perspectives on a changing society*. London: Sage.

Crompton R. and Sanderson K. (1990) *Gendered Jobs and Social Change*. London: Unwin Hyman.

Daly, M. (2010) 'Shifts in family policy in the UK under New Labour', *Journal of European Social Policy* 20, 433–43.

Daly, D. (2011) 'What adult worker model? A critical look at recent social policy reform in Europe from a gender and family perspective', *Journal of European Social Policy* 18, 1–23.

Daniels, R. (1966) *The Politics of Prejudice*. Gloucester, MA: Peter Smith.

Datta, A. and Brickell, K. (2009) '"We have a little bit more finesse, as a nation": constructing the Polish Worker in London's Building Sites', *Antipode* 41, 439–64.

Davidoff, L. (1995) *Worlds Between: Historical Perspectives on Gender and Class*. Cambridge: Polity Press.

De Ruijter, E. and van der Lippe, T. (2009) 'Getting outside help. How trust problems explain household differences in domestic outsourcing in the Netherlands', *Journal of Family Issues* 30, 13–27.

Degiuli, F. (2007) 'A job with no boundaries. Home eldercare work in Italy', *European Journal of Women's Studies* 14, 193–207.

Demetriou, D. Z. (2001) 'Connell's concept of hegemonic masculinity: a critique', *Theory and Society* 30, 337–61.

Dermott, E. (2008) *Intimate Fatherhood*. London: Routledge.

Dex, S. and Ward, K. (2007) 'Parental care and employment in early childhood', Working Paper Series 75. Manchester: Equal Opportunities Commission.

Dial a Hubby. (2012) http://www.dialahubby.co.uk/, date accessed 20 July 2012.

Domenech-Rodríguez, M. D., Rodríguez, J. and Davis, M. (2006) 'Recruitment of first-generation Latinos in a rural community: the essential nature of personal contact,' *Family Process* 45, 87–100.

Doyle, N., Hughes, G. and Wadensjö, E. (2006) *Freedom of Movement for Workers from Central and Eastern Europe. Experiences in Ireland and Sweden*, Swedish Institute for European Policy Studies, Report No. 5.

Dreby, J. (2010) *Divided by Borders: Mexican Migrants and Their Children*. Berkeley: University of California Press.

Drinkwater, S., Eade, J. and Garapich, M. (2009) 'Poles apart? EU enlargement and the labour market outcomes of immigrants in the United Kingdom', *International Migration* 47, 161–90.

DTI (2000) *Work and Parents: Competitiveness and Choice*, Cm 5005. London: Stationery Office.

Dump a Hubby (2012) http://www.dialahubby.co.uk/dumpahubby.html, date accessed 20 July 2012.

Duncan, S. (2002) 'Policy discourses on "reconciling work and life" in the EU', *Social Policy and Society* 1, 305–14.

Düvell, F. (2004) 'Highly skilled, self-employed and illegal immigrants from Poland in the United Kingdom', Warsaw: Centre for Migration Studies Working Paper No 4.

Dyer, S., McDowell, L., Batnitzky, A. (2010) 'The impact of migration on the gendering of service work: the case of a West London hotel', *Gender, Work and Organization* 17, 635–57.

Dziennik Ustaw (1994) 'Układ Europejski ustanawiający stowarzyszenie między Rzeczpospolitą Polską, z jednej strony, a Wspólnotami Europejskimi i ich Państwami Członkowskimi, z drugiej strony', Brussels 16 December 1991, Dz. U. 1994, nr 11, poz. 39.

Ebery, M. and Preston, B. (1976) *Domestic Service in late Victorian and Edwardian England, 1871–1914*. Reading: University of Reading.

EC (2010) *Indicators for monitoring the Employment Guidelines including indicators for additional employment analysis*. 2010 Compendium, Brussels: European Commission. Version of: 20/07/2010, http://ec.europa.eu/social/main.jsp?catId= 101&langId=en&furtherPubs=yes, date accessed 4 May 2012.

EC (2011) *Gender Segregation in the Labour Market: Root Causes, Implications and Policy Responses in the EU*. Brussels: European Commission.

EHRC (2009) 'Working better: fathers, family and work – contemporary perspectives', Research Summary 43. London: Equalities and Human Rights Commission.

Ellis, M. and Wright, R. (1999) 'The industrial division of labor among immigrants and internal migrants to the Los Angeles economy', *The International Migration Review* 33, 1–26.

Epstein, C. F. (2006) 'Border crossings: the constraints of time norms in transgressions of gender and professional roles', in Epstein, C. F. and Kalleberg, A. L. (eds), *Fighting for Time*. New York: Russell Sage Foundation.

España-Maram, L. (2006) *Creating Masculinity in Los Angeles's Little Manila: Working-Class Filipinos, 1920s–1950s*. New York: Columbia University Press.

Esping-Andersen, G. (2002) 'Towards the good society, once again?' in Esping-Andersen, G., Gallie, D., Hemerijck, A. and Myles, J. (eds), *Why We Need a New Welfare State*. Oxford: Oxford University Press.

Esping-Andersen, G. (2009) *The Incomplete Revolution: Adapting to Women's New Roles*. Cambridge: Polity.

Evans, M. (1989) 'Immigrant entrepreneurship: effects of ethnic market size and isolated labor pool', *American Sociological Review* 54, 950–62.

Everingham, C. (2002) 'Engendering time, gender equity and discourses of workplace flexibility', *Time & Society* 11, 335–51.

Fagan, C. (2003) *Working-Time Preferences and Work-Life Balance in the EU: Some Policy Considerations for Enhancing the Quality of Life*. Dublin: European Foundation for the Improvement of Living and Working Conditions.

Farr, M. (2006) *Rancheros in Chicagoacan: Language and Identity in a Transnational Community.* Austin, TX: University of Texas Press.

Fihel, A. and Kaczmarczyk, P. (2009) 'Migration: a threat or a chance? Recent migration of Poles and its impact on the Polish labour market', in Burrell, K. (ed.), *Polish Migration to the UK in the 'New' European Union After 2004.* Farnham: Ashgate.

Flouri, E. (2005) *Fathering and Child Outcomes.* Chichester: John Wiley & Sons.

Folbre, N. and Nelson, J. (2000) 'For love or money – or both?' *Journal of Economic Perspectives* 14, 123–40.

Fomina, J. and Frelak, J. (2008) 'Next stopski London. Public perceptions of labour migration within the EU. The case of Polish labour migrants in the British Press', Research Report. Warsaw: Institute of Public Affairs.

Gaines, B. J. and Cho, W. K. T. (2004) 'On California's 1920 alien land law: the psychology and economics of racial discrimination', *State Politics and Policy Quarterly* 4, 271–93.

Garapich, M. (2008a) 'The migration industry and civil society: Polish immigrants in the United Kingdom before and after EU enlargement', *Journal of Ethnic and Migration Studies* 34, 735–52.

Garapich, M. (2008b) Odyssean refugees, migrants and power: construction of the 'other' and civic participation within the Polish community in the United Kingdom, in Reed-Danahay, D. and Brettell, C. (eds), *Citizenship, Political Engagement and Belonging.* Chapel Hill, NC: Rutgers University Press.

Garcia y Griego, M. (1983) 'The importation of Mexican contract laborers to the United States, 1942–1964', in Brown, P. and Shue, H. (eds), *The Border That Joins: Mexican Migrants and US Responsibility.* Totowa, NJ: Rowman and Littlefield.

Gardenseekers (2012) http://www.gardenseeker.com/landscape_gardeners_usa/index.htm, date accessed 20 July 2012.

Gelber, S. M. (1997) 'Do-it-yourself: constructing, repairing and maintaining domestic masculinity', *American Quarterly* 49, 66–112.

Gershuny, J. (1985) 'Economic development and change in the mode of provision of services', in Redclift, N. and Mingione, E. (eds), *Beyond Employment. Household, Gender and Subsistence.* Oxford: Basil Blackwell.

Glaser, B. G. and Strauss, A. L. (1967) *The Discovery of Grounded Theory: Strategies for Qualitative Research.* Chicago: Aldine.

Glendinning, C. (2008) 'Increasing choice and control for older and disabled people: a critical review of new developments in England', *Social Policy and Administration* 42, 451–69.

Glenn, E. N. (1986) *Issei, Nisei, War Bride: Three Generations of Japanese American Women in Domestic Service.* Philadelphia: Temple University Press.

Glenn, E. N. (1992) 'From servitude to service work: historical continuities in the racial division of paid reproductive labour', *Signs* 18, 1–43.

Główny Urząd Statystyczny (GUS) (2011) *Informacja o rozmiarach i kierunkach emigracji z Polski w latach 2004–2010.* Warszawa: GUS.

Glucksmann, M. (1989) '"What a difference a day makes": a theoretical and historical exploration of temporality and gender', *Sociology* 32, 239–58.

Glucksmann, M. (1990) *Women Assemble.* London: Routledge.

Goffman, E. (1968) *Stigma. Notes on the Management of Spoiled Identity.* London: Penguin.

Gonell, R. (director) (2011) *The Smurfs*. Los Angeles: Columbia Pictures.

Granovetter, M. (1973) 'The strength of weak ties', *American Journal of Sociology* 78, 1360–80.

Granovetter, M. (1985) 'Economic action and economic structure: the problem of embeddedness', *American Journal of Sociology* 9, 481–510.

Greater London Authority (GLA) (2009). *A Fairer London: The 2009 Living Wage in London*. London: Greater London Authority.

Gregson, N. and Lowe, M. (1994) *Servicing the Middle Classes*. London: Routledge.

Grenz, S. (2005) 'Intersections of sex and power in research on prostitution: a female researcher interviewing male heterosexual clients', *Signs* 30, 2091–113.

Grimshaw, D. and Rubery, J. (2012) 'The end of the UK's liberal collectivist social model? The implications of the coalition government's policy during the austerity crisis', *Cambridge Journal of Economics* 36, 105–26.

Groundworks Landscape. (2012) http://www.groundworksvip.com/services/, date accessed 20 July 2012.

Gumtree (2012) http://www.gumtree.com/london, date accessed 28 October 2012Gutiérrez-Rodríguez, E. (2010) *Migration, Domestic Work and Affect. A Decolonial Approach on Value and the Feminization of Labor*. London: Routledge.

Haeg, F. (2008) *Edible Estates: Attack on the Front Lawn*. New York: Metropolis Books.

Haile, A. G. and Siegmann, K. A. (2013) 'Masculinity at work? Identity constructions of undocumented migrant domestic workers in the Netherlands', in Trung, T. D., Berg, S. I., Gasper, D. and Handmaker, J. (eds), *Migration, Gender and Justice. Prospects for Human Security*. New York: Springer.

Halford, S. (2006) 'Collapsing the boundaries? Fatherhood, organization and home-working', *Gender, Work and Organization* 13, 383–402.

Hammer, L. B. and Neal, M. B. (2008) 'Working sandwiched-generation caregivers: prevalence, characteristics, and outcomes', *The Psychologist-Manager Journal* 11, 93–112.

Handy Squad (2012) http://www.handysquad.com/, date accessed 7 July 2012.

Harkness, S. (2008) 'The household division of labour: changes in families' allocation of paid and unpaid work', in Scott, J., Dex, D. and Joshi, H. (eds), *Women and Employment: Changing Lives and New Challenges*. Cheltenham: Edward Elgar.

Hays, S. (1996) *The Cultural Contradictions of Motherhood*. New Haven, CT: Yale University Press.

Haas, L. and Rostgaard, T. (2011) 'Fathers' rights to paid parental leave in the Nordic countries: consequences for the gendered division of leave', *Community, Work & Family* 14, 177–95.

Hatter, W., Vinter, L. and Williams, R. (2002) 'Dads on dad. Needs and expectations at home and at work', Research Discussion Series. Manchester: Equal Opportunities Commission.

Hearn, J. (2004) 'From hegemonic masculinity to the hegemony of men', *Feminist Theory* 5, 49–72.

Henry, M. G. (2003) '"Where are you really from?": representation, identity and power in the fieldwork experiences of a south Asian diasporic', *Qualitative Research* 3, 229–42.

Henry, S. E. (1978) *Cultural Persistence and Socio-Economic Mobility: A Comparative Study of Assimilation among Armenians and Japanese in Los Angeles.* San Francisco: R&E Research Associates, Inc.

Himmelweit, S. (2007) 'The prospects for caring: economic theory and policy analysis', *Cambridge Journal of Economics* 31, 581–99.

Hirahara, N. (ed.) (2000) *Green Makers: Japanese American Gardeners in Southern California.* Los Angeles: Southern California Gardeners' Federation.

Hire a Hubby (2012) http://www.hireahubbygroup.com/, date accessed 20 July 2012.

Hobson, B. and Fahlén, S. (2009) 'Competing scenarios for European fathers: applying Sen's capabilities and agency framework to work–family balance', *American Academy of Political and Social Science* 624, 214–33.

Hochschild, A. R. (1983) *The Managed Heart: The Commercialization of Human Feeling.* Berkeley: University of California Press.

Hochschild, A. R. (1997) *The Time Bind: When Work Becomes Home and Home Becomes Work.* New York: Metropolitan Books.

Hochschild, A. R. (2000) 'Global care chains and emotional surplus value', in Hutton, W. and Giddens, A. (eds), *On the Edge: Living with Global Capitalism.* London: Jonathan Cape.

Hochschild, A. R. (2003) 'Love and gold', in Ehrenreich, B. and Hochschild, A. R. (eds), *Global Woman. Nannies, Maids, and Sex Workers in the New Economy.* New York: Metropolitan Books.

Hochschild, A. R. (2012) *The Outsourced Self. Intimate Life in Market Times.* New York: Metropolitan Books.

Home Office (2003) 'Control of immigration: statistics United Kingdom 2003', http://www.archive2.official-documents.co.uk/document/cm63/6363/6363.pdf, date accessed 1 March 2011.

Hondagneu-Sotelo, P. (1994a) 'Regulating the unregulated: domestic workers' social networks', *Social Problems* 41, 201–15.

Hondagneu-Sotelo, P. (1994b) *Gendered Transitions: Mexican Experiences of Immigration.* Berkeley: University of California Press.

Hondagneu-Sotelo, P. (2001) *Doméstica. Immigrant Workers Cleaning and Caring in the Shadows of Affluence.* Berkley: University of California Press.

Hondagneu-Sotelo, P. and Avila, E. (1997) 'I'm here but I'm there": the meanings of Latina transnational motherhood', *Gender and Society* 11, 548–71.

Hondagneu-Sotelo, P. and Messner, N. (1997) 'Gender displays and men's power. The "new man" and the Mexican immigrant man', in Gergen, M. M. and Davis, S. N. (eds) *Towards a New Psychology of Gender.* New York: Routledge.

HPC (2011) 'Cheques with balances: why tackling high pay is in the national interest', High Pay Commission Final Report. http://highpaycommission.co.uk/wp-content/uploads/2011/11/HPC_final_report_WEB.pdf, date accessed 20 July 2012.

Huerta, A. (2007) 'Looking beyond "wow, blow and go": a case study of Mexican immigrant gardeners in Los Angeles', *Berkeley Planning Journal* 20, 1–23.

Hum, T. (2000) 'A protected niche? Immigrant ethnic economies and labor market segmentation', in Oliver, M. L., Johnson, Jr, J. H. and Valenzuela, Jr, A. (eds), *Prismatic Metropolis: Inequality in Los Angeles.* New York: Russell Sage Foundation.

ILO (2011) 'Text of the convention concerning decent work for domestic workers', http://www.ilo.org/ilc/ILCSessions/100thSession/reports/provisional-records/WCMS_157836/lang--en/index.htm, date accessed 20 July 2012.

Iphoen, R. (2011) 'Ethical decision making in qualitative research', *Qualitative Research* 11, 443–46.

Isaksen, L. W., Devi, S. U. and Hochschild, A. R. (2008) 'Global care crisis. A problem of capital, care chain, or commons? *American Behavioural Scientist* 52, 405–25.

Jacobs, J. and Gerson, K. (2004) *The Time Divide: Work, Family and Gender Inequality.* Cambridge, MA: Harvard University Press.

James, A. (2011) 'Work–life (im)'balance' and its consequences for everyday learning and innovation in the New Economy: evidence from the Irish IT sector', *Gender, Place & Culture: A Journal of Feminist Geography* 18, 655–84.

Japanese American National Museum (2007) 'Landscaping America beyond the Japanese Garden' (exhibit), June 17–October 21. Los Angeles, CA: Japanese American National Museum.

Jiobu, R. M. (1988) 'Ethnic hegemony and the Japanese of California', *American Sociological Review* 53, 353–67.

Jones, O. (2012) *Chavs: The Demonization of the Working Class.* London: Verso.

Jones, T. and Ram, M. (2007) 'Re-embedding the ethnic business agenda', *Work, Employment and Society* 21, 439–57.

Kaczmarczyk, P. and Okólski, M. (2008) 'Demographic and labour-market impacts of migration on Poland', *Oxford Review of Economic Policy* 24, 599–624.

Kaplan, D. H. and Li, W. (2006) 'Introduction: the places of ethnic economies', in Kaplan, D. H. and Li, W. (eds), *Landscapes of the Ethnic Economy.* Lanham, MD: Rowman & Littlefield.

Kaplanis, I. (2007) *The Geography of Employment Polarisation in Britain.* London: Institute for Public Policy Research.

Katz, C. (2008) 'Childhood as spectacle: relays of anxiety and the reconfiguration of the child', *Cultural Geographies* 15, 5–17.

Kay, T. (2009) 'The landscape of fathering', in Kay, T. (ed.), *Fathering Through Sport and Leisure.* Oxon: Routledge.

Kicinger, A. (2009) 'Beyond the focus on Europeanisation: Polish migration policy 1989–2004', *Journal of Ethnic and Migration Studies* 35, 79–95.

Kilkey, M. (2006) 'New labour and reconciling work and family life: making it fathers' business?', *Social Policy and Society* 5, 167–75.

Kilkey, M. (2008) 'Locating men in the relationship between globalization, migration and social reproduction: the case of migrant handymen', Paper presented at the Annual Social Policy Association Conference, 23rd–25th June 2008, Edinburgh.

Kilkey, M. (2010) 'Domestic-sector work in the UK: locating men in the configuration of gendered care and migration regimes', *Social Policy and Society* 9, 443–54.

Kilkey, M., Lutz, H. and Palenga-Möllenbeck, E. (2010) 'Introduction. Domestic and care work at the intersection of welfare, gender and migration regimes: some European experiences', *Social Policy and Society* 9, 379–84.

Kilkey, M. and Perrons, D. (2010) 'Gendered divisions in domestic-work time: the rise of the (migrant) handyman phenomenon', *Time and Society* 19, 239–64.

Kim, D. Y. (1996) 'The limits of ethnic solidarity: Mexican and Ecuadorian employment in Korean-owned businesses in New York city', Paper presented at the American Sociological Association Conference, 16–20 August, New York.

Kimmel, M. (2011) 'Global masculinities: restoration and resistance', *Gender Policy Review*, August Issue, http://gender-policy.tripod.com/journal/id1.html, date accessed 20 July 2012.

Klowden, K. and Wong, P. with Flaming, D. and Haydamack, B. (2005) 'Los Angeles economy project', Policy Report. Los Angeles, CA: Milken Institute.

Kraler, A. (2010) 'Civic stratification, gender and family migration policies in Europe', Final Report. Vienna, http://www.maiz.at/sites/default/files/files/final_report_family_migration_policies_online_final.pdf , date accessed 10 September 2011.

Krugman, P. (2002) 'For richer', *New York Times*, 20th October, http://www.pkarchive.org/economy/ForRicher.html, date accessed 20 July 2012.

Krugman, P. (2012) *End this Depression Now!* New York: Norton.

Kwong, P. (1996) *The New Chinatown*. New York: Hill and Wang.

Lamb, M. E. (1987) 'Introduction: the emergent American father', in Lamb, M. E. (ed.), *The Father Role: A Cross-Cultural Perspective*. Hillsdale, NJ: Lawrence Erlbaum.

Land, H. and Himmelweit, S. (2010) *Who Cares: Who Pays? A Report on the Personalisation in Social Care*. London: Unison.

Lareau, A. (2003) *Unequal Childhoods: Class, Race, and Family Life*. Berkeley: University of California Press.

Laslett, B. and Brenner, J. (1989) 'Gender and social reproduction: historical perspectives', *Annual Review of Sociology* 15, 381–404.

Lazaridis, G. (2007) 'Les infirmières exclusives and migrant quasi-nurses in Greece', *European Journal of Women's Studies* 14, 227–45.

Lee, D. (1997) 'Feminist research. Interviewing men: vulnerabilities and dilemmas', *Women's Studies International Forum* 20, 553–64.

Lee, J. (2002) *Civility in the City: Blacks, Jews and Koreans in Urban America*. Cambridge, MA: Harvard University Press.

Lewis, J. (2009) *Work-Family Balance, Gender and Policy*. Cheltenham: Edward Elgar.

Lewis, J. and Campbell, M. (2007) 'Work/family balance policies in the UK since 1997: a new departure?', *Journal of Social Policy* 36, 365–81.

Lewis, J. and Plomien, A. (2009) '"Flexicurity" as a policy strategy: the implications for gender equality', *Economy and Society* 38, 433–59.

Light, I. (1972) *Ethnic Enterprise in America*. Berkeley: University of California Press.

Light, I. and Bonacich, E. (1988) *Immigrant Entrepreneurs: Koreans in Los Angeles, 1965–1982*. Berkeley: University of California Press.

Light, I. and Gold, S. (2000) *Ethnic Economies*. San Diego, CA: Academic Press.

Lincoln, Y. S. and Tierney, W. G. (2004) 'Qualitative research and institutional review boards', *Qualitative Inquiry* 10, 219–34.

Lister, R. (2003) 'Investing in the citizen-workers of the future: transformations in citizenship and the state under New Labour', *Social Policy and Administration* 37, 427–43.

Lister, R., Williams, F., Anttonen, A., Bussemaker, J., Gerhard, U., Heinen, J., Johansson, S., Leira, A., Siim, B., Tobio, C. and Gavanas, A. (2007) *Gendering citizenship in Western Europe*. Bristol: Policy Press.

Lutz, H. (2008) 'Introduction: migrant domestic workers in Europe', in Lutz, H. (ed.), *Migration and Domestic Work. A European Perspective on a Global Theme*. Avebury: Ashgate.

Lutz, H. (2011) *The New Maids. Transnational Women and the Care Economy*. London: Zed Books.

Lutz, H. and Palenga-Möllenbeck, E. (2010) 'Care work migration in Germany: semi-compliance and complicity', *Social Policy and Society* 9, 419–30.

Madianou, M. and Miller, D. (2011) *Migration and New Media: Transnational Families and Polymedia*. London: Routledge.

Manalansan, M. F. (2006) 'Queer intersections. Sexuality and gender in migration studies', *International Migration Review* 40, 224–49.

Manning, A. and Petrongolo, B. (2008) 'The part time pay penalty for women in Britain', *The Economic Journal* 118, 28–51.

Matsuno, A. (2007) 'Nurse migration: the Asian perspective, the ILO/EU programme on the governance of labour migration publishes a series of working papers, technical note', http://pstalker.com/ilo/resources/Technical%20Note%20-%20Nurse%20Migration%20by%20A%20Matsuno.doc, date accessed 7 July 2012.

Mazzei, J. and O'Brien, E. E. (2009) 'You got it, so when do you flaunt it? Building rapport, intersectionality, and the strategic deployment of gender in the field', *Journal of Contemporary Ethnography* 38, 358–83.

McDowell, L. (2005) *Hard Labour. The Forgotten Voices of Latvian Migrant Volunteer Workers*. London: UCL Press.

McDowell, L. (2009a) 'Old and new European economic migrants: whiteness and managed migration policies', *Journal of Ethnic and Migration Studies* 35(1), 19–36.

McDowell, L. (2009b) *Working Bodies. Interactive Service employment and Workplace Identities*. Oxford: Wiley-Blackwell.

McDowell, L., Batnitzky, A. and Dyer, S. (2007) 'Division, segmentation, and interpellation: the embodied labors of migrant workers in a greater London hotel', *Economic Geography* 83, 1–25.

McDowell, L., Batnitzky, A. and Dyer, S. (2008) 'Internationalization and the spaces of temporary labour: the global assembly of a local workforce', *British Journal of Industrial Relations* 46, 750–70.

McDowell, L., Batnitzky, A. and Dyer, S. (2009) 'Precarious work and economic migration', *International Journal of Urban and Regional Research* 33, 3–25.

McDowell, L., Ray, K., Perrons, D., Fagan, C. and Ward, K. (2005) 'Women's paid work and moral economies of care', *Social and Cultural Geography* 6, 219–35.

McGregor, J. (2007) '"Joining the BBC (British bottom cleaners)": Zimbabwean migrants and the UK care industry', *Journal of Ethnic and Migration Studies* 33, 801–24.

Meldrum, T. (2000) *Domestic Service and Gender 1660–1750*. Harlow: Pearson Education Limited.

Menjívar, C. (2000) *Fragmented Ties: Salvadoran Immigrant Networks in America*. Berkeley: University of California Press.

Messner, M. (2009) *It's All For the Kids: Gender, Families and Youth Sports*. Berkeley: University of California Press.

Metcalf, H. (2009) 'Pay gaps across the equality strands: a review', Equality and Human Rights Commission, http://www.equalityhumanrights.com/uploaded_

files/research/14_pay_gaps_across_equalities_review.pdf, date accessed 20 July 2012.

Migration Observatory (2012) 'Migrants in the UK: an overview', http://migrationobservatory.ox.ac.uk/briefings/migrants-uk-overview, date accessed 5 July 2012.

Miller, R. (1991) 'Selling Mrs Consumer's advertising and the creation of suburban social spatial relations 1910–1930', *Antipode: A Radical Journal of Geography* 23, 263–301.

Milner, S. (2010) '"Choice" and "flexibility", in reconciling work and family: towards a convergence in policy discourse on work and family in France and the UK?' *Policy & Politics* 38, 3–21.

Miranda, V. (2011) 'Cooking, caring and volunteering: unpaid work around the world', OECD Social, Employment and Migration Working Papers No. 116, www.oecd.org/els/workingpapers, date accessed 29 May 2012.

Misra, J., Woodring, J. and Merz, S. (2006) 'The globalization of care work: neoliberal economic restructuring and migration policy', *Globalizations* 3, 317–32.

Moors, A. and de Regt, M. (2008) 'Gender and irregular migration: migrant domestic workers in the Middle East', in Schrover, M., van der Leun, J., Lucassen, L. and Quispel, C. (eds), *Gender and illegality*. Amsterdam: IMISCOE/AUPO.

Morris, L. (2002) *Managing Migration: Civic stratification and migrants' rights*. London: Routledge.

Moss, P. (2012) 'International review of leave policies and related research 2011', International Network on Leave Policies and Research, http://www.leavenetwork.org/fileadmin/Leavenetwork/Annual_reviews/Complete_review_2011.pdf, date accessed 1 June 2012.

Moya, J. C. (2007) 'Domestic service in a global perspective: gender, migration and ethnic niches', *Journal of Ethnic and Migration Studies* 33, 559–79.

Mutari, E. and Figart, D. M. (2001) 'Europe at a crossroads: harmonization, liberalization, and the gender of work time', *Social Politics* 8, 36–64.

Näre, L. (2010) 'Sri Lankan men working as cleaners and carers: negotiating masculinity in Naples', *Men and Masculinities* 13, 65–86.

Nyberg, A. (2006) 'Economic crisis and the sustainability of the dual-earner, dual carer model', in Perrons, D., Fagan, C., McDowell, L., Ray, K. and Ward, K. (eds), *Gender Divisions and Working Time in the New Economy*. Cheltenham: Edward Elgar.

O'Brien, M. (2005) 'Shared caring: bringing fathers into the frame', Working Paper 18. Manchester: Equal Opportunities Commission.

O'Brien, M. (2009) 'Fathers, parental leave policies, and infant quality of life: international perspectives and policy impact', *American Academy of Political and Social Science* 624, 190–213.

OECD (2011a) *International Migration Outlook 2011*. Paris: OECD.

OECD (2011b) *Divided We Stand. Why Inequality Keeps Rising*. Paris: OECD.

Ojeda, L., Flores, L. Y., Meza, R. R. and Morales, A. (2011) 'Culturally competent qualitative research with Latino immigrants', *Hispanic Journal of Behavioral Sciences* 33, 184–203.

Ong, P. (1984) 'Chinatown unemployment and ethnic labor markets', *Amerasia Journal* 11, 35–54.

ONS (2009) 'Annual survey of hours and earnings, 2009 results', http://www.ons.
gov.uk/ons/publications/re-reference-tables.html?edition=tcm%3A77-210656,
date accessed 29 May 2012.

ONS (2011a) 'More mothers working now than ever before', http://www.nomi-
sweb.co.uk/articles/ref/stories/3/Mother%20data.xls, date accessed 7 July 2012.

ONS (2011b) 'The effects of taxes and benefits on household income', 2009/201,
http://www.ons.gov.uk/ons/rel/household-income/the-effects-of-taxes-
and-benefits-on-household-income/2009-2010/index.html, date accessed
29 May 2012.

ONS (2012a) 'Provisional long term international migration (LTIM) estimates June 2011', http://www.ons.gov.uk/ons/publications/re-reference-tables.
html?edition=tcm%3A77-256033, date accessed 20 July 2012.

ONS (2012b) 'Families and households, 2001 to 2011', Statistical Bulletin,
http://www.ons.gov.uk/ons/dcp171778_251357.pdf, date accessed 11 April
2012.

ONS (2012c) *Labour Market Statistics April 2012*. London: ONS.

ONS (2012d) '2011 annual survey of hours and earnings', SOC 2000, http://www.
ons.gov.uk/ons/rel/ashe/annual-survey-of-hours-and-earnings/ashe-results-
2011/ashe-statistical-bulletin-2011.html, date accessed 20 July 2012.

Pahl, R. E. (1984) *Divisions of Labour*. Oxford: Basil Blackwell.

Pahl, R. E. and Wallace, C. (1985) 'Household work strategies in economic
recession', in Redclift, N. and Mingione, E. (eds), *Beyond Employment.
Household, Gender and Subsistence*. Oxford: Basil Blackwell.

Palenga-Möllenbeck, E. (2012) 'Polish "handymen" in Germany: an example of
the neglected "male" side of commodified reproductive work?', Paper presented
at International Workshop on Changing Patterns of Migration – Changing
Patterns of Social Inequalities? Borders and Boundaries in the Enlarged Europe,
Bielefeld University (Germany) 12–13 April 2012.

Parreñas, R. S. (2001) *Servants of Globalisation: Women, Migration and Domestic
Work*. Stanford, CA: Stanford University Press.

Parreñas, R. S. (2005) *Children of Global Migration: Transnational Families and
Gendered Woes*. Stanford: Stanford University.

Parreñas, R. S. (2012) 'The reproductive labour of migrant workers', *Global
Networks* 12, 269–75.

Passel, J., Cohn, D. and Gonzalez Barrera, A. (2012) 'Net migration from Mexico
falls to zero or perhaps less, Pew Hispanic center', http://www.documentcloud.
org/documents/346285-pew-report-on-the-decline-in-mexican-immigration.
html, date accessed 20 July 2012.

Perrons, D. and Plomien, A. (2010) 'Why socio-economic inequalities increase?:
facts and policy responses in Europe', EUR 24471 EN. Brussels, European
Commission.

Perrons, D., Plomien, A. and Kilkey, M. (2010) 'Migration and uneven development within an enlarged European Union: fathering, gender divisions and
male migrant domestic services', *European Urban and Regional Studies* 17,
197–215.

Pfau-Effinger, B. (2009) 'Varieties of undeclared work in European societies',
British Journal of Industrial Relations 47, 79–99.

Phillips, A. and Taylor, B. (1980) 'Sex and skill: notes towards a feminist
economics', *Feminist Review* 6, 79–88.

Pini, B. (2005) 'Interviewing men: gender and the collection and interpretation of qualitative data', *Journal of Sociology* 41, 201–16.

Pisani, M. J. and Yoskowitz, D. W. (2005) 'Grass, sweat, and sun: an exploratory study of the labor market for gardeners in south Texas', *Social Science Quarterly* 86, 229–51.

Pisani, M. J. and Yoskowitz, D. W. (2006) 'Opportunity knocks: entrepreneurship, informality, and home gardening in south Texas', *Journal of Borderland Studies* 21, 59–76.

Platzer, E. (2006) 'From private solutions to public responsibility and back again: the new domestic services in Sweden', *Gender and History* 18, 211–21.

Pleck, J. H. (1987) 'American fathering in a historical perspective', in Kimmel, M. S. (ed.), *Changing Men: New Directions in Research on Men and Masculinity.* Newbury Park, CA: Sage.

Pleck, J. H. (1997) 'American fathering in historical perspective', in Hansen, K. V. and Garey, A. I. (eds), *Families in the US: Kinship and Domestic Politics.* Philadelphia: Temple University Press.

Plomien, A. (2013) 'Becoming an academic: the role of gender, migration and work in qualitative research on gender, migration and work', Gender Institute Working Paper Series.

Pojmann, W. (2006) *Immigrant Women and Feminism in Italy.* Ashgate: Avebury.

Polish Builder (2011), http://www.polish-builder.com, date accessed 20 July 2011.

Polish Handymen (2012), http://www.polishhandyman.com/, date accessed July 2012.

Polish Plumbers (2012), http://www.polishplumbers.co.uk, date accessed 20 July 2012.

Portes, A. and Rumbaut, R. G. (2006) *Immigrant America: A Portrait*, 3rd ed. Berkeley: University of California Press.

Portes, A. and Stepick, A. (1985) 'Unwelcome immigrants: the labor market experiences of 1980 (Mariel) Cuban and Haitian refugees in south Florida', *American Sociological Review* 50, 493–514.

Qayum, S. and Ray, R. (2010) 'Male servants and the failure of patriarchy in Kolkata (Calcutta)', *Men and Masculinities* 13, 111–25.

Quiñones, S. (2002) 'Home, tense home: turbulent times in local Zacatecan clubs', *LA Weekly*, March 14, http://www.laweekly.com/content/printVersion/34676/, date accessed 15 January 2012.

Ramirez, H. (2011) 'Masculinity in the workplace: the case of Mexican immigrant gardeners', *Men and Masculinities* 14, 97–116.

Ramirez, H. and Hondagneu-Sotelo, P. (2009) 'Mexican immigrant gardeners: entrepreneurs or exploited workers?' *Social Problems* 56, 70–88.

Reindl, U., Kaiser, S. and Stolz, M. L. (2010) 'Integrating professional work and life: conditions, outcomes and resources', in Kaiser, S., Ringlstetter, M., Eikhof, D. R. and Cunha, M. P. E. (eds), *Creating Balance? International Perspectives on the Work-Life Integration of Professionals.* London: Springer.

Relationships Foundation (2011) *The Family Pressure Gauge. A measurement of progress towards the goal of making Britain the 'most family friendly' country in Europe.* Cambridge: Relationships Foundation.

Reeves, R. (2002) *Dad's Army: The Case for Father Friendly Workplaces.* London: The Work Foundation.

Reisch, L. (2001) 'Time and wealth. The role of time and temporalities for sustainable patterns of consumption', *Time & Society* 10, 367–85.

Rent a Hubby (2012) http://www.rentahubby.co.uk/, date accessed 7 July 2012.

Riessman, C. K. (1991) 'When gender is not enough: women interviewing women', in Lorber, J. and Farrel, S. (eds), *The Social Construction of Gender.* London: Sage.

Ruggles, S., Sobek, M., Alexander, T., Fitch, C. A., Goeken, R., Hall, P. K., King, M. and Ronnander, C. (2004) *Integrated Public Use Microdata Series: Version 3.0.*

Ruhs, M. (2012) *Briefing. The Labour Market Effects of Immigration.* Oxford: The Observatory at the University of Oxford.

Ryan, L. (2011) 'Transnational relations: family migration among recent Polish migrants in London', *International Migration* 49, 80–103.

Sales, R. (2007) *Understanding Immigration and Refugee Policy: Contradictions and Continuities.* Bristol: Policy Press.

Sarti, R. (2005) 'Conclusion. Domestic service and European identity', in Pasleau, S. and Schopp, I. (eds) with R. Sarti, *Proceedings of the Servant Project.* Liège: Éditions de l'Université de Liège.

Sarti, R. (2006) 'Domestic service: past and present in southern and northern Europe', *Gender and History* 18, 222–45.

Sarti, R. (2008) 'The globalisation of domestic service – an historical perspective', in Lutz, H. (ed.), *Migration and Domestic Work. A European Perspective on a Global Theme.* Avebury: Ashgate.

Sarti, R. (2010) 'Fighting for masculinity: male domestic workers, gender, and migration in Italy from the late nineteenth century to the present', *Men and Masculinities* 13, 16–43.

Sassen, S. (1984) 'Notes on the incorporation of Third World women into wage labor through immigration and offshore production', *International Migration Review* 18, 1144–67.

Sassen, S. (2001) *Global City: New York, London, Tokyo,* 2nd edn (Princeton: Princenton University Press).

Sassen, S. (2010a) 'Strategic gendering: one factor in the constituting of novel political economies', in Chant, S. (ed.), *International Handbook of Gender and Poverty: Concepts, Research, Policy.* Cheltenham: Edward Elgar.

Sassen, S. (2010b) 'A savage sorting of winners and losers: contemporary versions of primitive accumulation', *Globalizations* 7, 23–50.

Schrover, M., van der Leun, J. and Quispel, C. (2007) 'Niches, labour market segregation, ethnicity and gender', *Journal of Ethnic and Migration Studies* 33, 529–40.

Schwalbe, M. and Wolkomir, M. (2001) 'The masculine self as problem and resource in interview studies of men', *Men and Masculinities* 4, 90–103.

Scrinzi, F. (2010) 'Masculinities and the international division of care: migrant male domestic workers in Italy and France', *Men and Masculinities* 13, 44–64.

Seguino, S. (2010) 'The Global Economic Crisis, Its Gender and Ethnic Implications, and Policy Responses', *Gender and Development* 18, 179–99.

Shaw, S. M. and Dawson, D. (2001) 'Purposive leisure: examining parental discourses on family activities', *Leisure Sciences* 23, 217–31.

Skaff, M. M., Chesla, C. A., de los Mycue, V. and Fisher, L. (2002) 'Lessons in cultural competence: adapting research methodology for diverse ethnic groups', *Journal of Community Psychology* 30, 305–323.

Skeggs, B. (1997) *Formations of Class and Gender.* London: Sage.

Sklair, L. (2001) *The Transnational Capitalist Class.* Oxford: Blackwell.

Smith, A. (1976) *The Wealth of Nations.* Chicago: University Of Chicago Press.

Standing, G. (2011) *The Precariat: The New Dangerous Class.* London: Bloomsbury Academic.

Stiglitz, J. (2012) *The Price of Inequality.* London: Penguin Books.

Stola, D. (2010) *Kraj bez wyjścia? Migracje z Polski 1949–1989.* Warszawa: IPN and ISP PAN.

Strauss, A. and Corbin, J. (1994) 'Grounded theory methodology – an overview', in Denzin, N. K. and Lincoln, Y. S. (eds), *Handbook of Qualitative Research.* Thousand Oaks, CA: Sage Publications.

Such, L. (2009) 'Fatherhood, the morality of personal time and leisure-based parenting', in Kay, T. (ed.), *Fathering Through Sport and Leisure.* Oxon: Routledge.

Sullivan, O. (2004) 'Changing gender practices within the household: a theoretical perspective', *Gender and Society* 18, 207–22.

Tronto, J. (2002) 'The "nanny" question in feminism', *Hypatia* 17, 34–51.

Tsuchida, N. (1984) 'Japanese gardeners in southern California, 1900–1941', in Cheng, L. and Bonachich, E. (eds), *Labor Migration under Capitalism: Asian Workers in the United States Before World War II.* Berkeley: University of California Press.

Tsukashima, R. T. (1991) 'Cultural endowment, disadvantaged status, and economic niche: the development of an "ethnic trade"', *International Migration Review* 25, 333–54.

Tsukashima, R. T. (1995/1996) 'Continuity of ethnic participation in the economy: immigrants in contract gardening', *Amerasia Journal* 21, 53–76.

Tsukashima, R. T. (1998) 'Notes on emerging collective action: ethnic-trade guilds among Japanese Americans in the gardening industry', *International Migration Review* 32, 374–400.

UK Border Agency (2011) 'UK worker registration scheme to end 30 April 2011', News Release http://www.workpermit.com/news/2011-03-15/uk/worker-registration-scheme-to-end-30-april-2011.htm, date accessed 1 November 2011.

Ungerson, C. and Yeandle, S. (eds) (2007) *Cash for Care in Developed Welfare States.* Basingstoke: Palgrave Macmillan.

United States Census Bureau (2012) 'Quick facts', http://quickfacts.census.gov/qfd/states/06000.html, date accessed 23 March 2012.

Valdez, Z. (2008a) 'Mexican American entrepreneurship in the United States: a strategy of survival and economic mobility', in Rodriguez, H., Saenz, R. and Menjivar, C. (eds), *Latinas/os in the United States: Changing the Face of America.* New York: Springer.

Valdez, Z. (2008b) 'The effect of social capital on Korean, white, Mexican, and black business owners' earnings', *Journal of Ethnic and Migration Studies* 34, 955–74.

Vertovec, S. (2007) 'Super-diversity and its implications', *Ethnic and Racial Studies* 30, 1024–54.

Wajcman, J. (2008) 'Life in the fast lane? Towards a sociology of technology and time', *The British Journal of Sociology* 50, 59–77.

Walby, K. (2010) 'Interviews as encounters: issues of sexuality and reflexivity when men interview men about commercial same sex relations', *Qualitative Research* 10, 639–57.

Waldinger, R. and Lichter, M. I. (2003) *How the Other Half Works: Immigration and the Social Organization of Labor*. Berkeley: University of California Press.

Walker, R. (2010) *Focus on London 2010: Income and Spending at Home*. London: GLA.

Wall, K. and Nunes, C. (2010) 'Immigration, welfare and care in Portugal: mapping the new plurality of female migration trajectories', *Social Policy and Society* 9, 397–408.

Wallace, C. (2002) 'Household strategies: their conceptual relevance and analytical scope in social research', *Sociology* 36, 275–92.

Weeks, K. (2011) *The Problem With Work. Feminism, Marxism, Antiwork Politics and Postwork Imaginaries*. Durham and London: Duke University Press.

West, C. and Zimmerman, D. (1987) 'Doing gender', *Gender and Society* 1, 125–51.

White, A. (2011) *Polish Families and Migration Since EU Accession*. Bristol: The Policy Press.

Widding Isaksen, L. (ed.) (2010) *Global Care Work: Gender and Migration in Nordic Societies*. Lund: Nordic Academic Press.

Williams, F. (2005) 'Intersecting issues of gender, "race", and migration in the changing care regimes of UK, Sweden and Spain', paper presented at Annual Conference of International Sociological Conference Research Committee 19, 8th–10th September 2005. Chicago: Northwestern University.

Williams, S. (2008) 'What is fatherhood? Searching for the reflexive father', *Sociology* 42, 487–502.

Williams, F. (2010) 'Migration and care: themes, concepts and challenges', *Social Policy and Society* 9, 385–96.

Williams, F. and Gavanas, A. (2008) 'The intersection of child care regimes and migration regimes: a three-country study', in Lutz, H. (ed.), *Migration and Domestic Work. A European Perspective on a Global Theme*. Avebury: Ashgate.

Wills, J. (2008) 'Making class politics possible: organizing contract cleaners in London', *International Journal of Urban and Regional Research* 32, 305–23.

Wills, J., May, J., Datta, K., Evans, Y., Herbert, J. and McIlwaine, C. (2009) 'London's Migrant Division of Labour', *European Urban and Regional Studies* 16, 257–71.

Wills, J., Datta, K., Evans, Y., Herbert, J., May, J. and McIlwaine, C. (2010) *Global Cities at Work: New Migrant Divisions of Labour*. London: Pluto Press.

Windebank, J. (2007) 'Outsourcing women's domestic labour: the *Chèque Emploi-Service Universel* in France', *Journal of European Social Policy* 17, 257–70.

Wolkowitz, C. (2006) *Bodies at Work*. London: Sage.

Working Families (2011) *Working and Families. Combining Family Life and Work*. London: Working Families.

Wright Mills, C. (1953) *White Collar Work: The American Middle Classes*. Oxford: Oxford University Press.

Yeates, N. (2010) *Globalizing Care Economies and Migrant Workers. Explorations in Global Care Chains*. Basingstoke: Palgrave Macmillan.

Yeates, N. (2012) 'Global care chains: a state-of-the-art review and future directions in care transnationalization research', *Global Networks-A Journal of Transnational Affairs*. 12, 135–154.

Zhou, M. (1992) *Chinatown: The Socioeconomic Potential of an Urban Enclave.* Philadelphia: Temple University Press.

Zlolniski, C. (2006) *Janitors, Street Vendors, and Activists: The Lives of Mexican Immigrants in Silicon Valley.* Berkeley: University of California Press.

Zontini, E. (2004) 'Immigrant women in Barcelona: coping with the consequences of transnational lives', *Journal of Ethnic and Migration Studies* 30, 1113–144.

Index